Transcultural Poetics

This book examines many facets of transcultural poetics in the English translation of Chinese literature from 12 different expert contributors.

Translating Chinese literature into English is a special challenge. There is a pressing need to overcome a slew of obstacles to the understanding and appreciation of Chinese literary works by readers in the English-speaking world. Hitherto only intermittent attempts have been made to theorize and explore the exact role of the translator as a cultural and aesthetic mediator informed by cross-cultural knowledge, awareness, and sensitivity. Given the complexity of literary translation, sophisticated poetics of translation in terms of literary value and aesthetic taste needs to be developed and elaborated more fully from a cross-cultural perspective. It is, therefore, necessary to examine attempts to reconcile the desire for authentic transmission of Chinese culture with the need for cultural mediation and appropriation in terms of the production and reception of texts subject to the multiplicity of constraints in order to shed new light on the longstanding conundrum of Chinese-English literary translation by addressing Chinese literature in the multiple contexts of nationalism, cross-cultural hybridity, literary untranslatability, the reception of translation, and also world literature.

The book will be of great interest to students and scholars of translation studies, Chinese literature, and East Asian studies.

Yifeng Sun is Chair Professor of Translation Studies at the University of Macau and Editor-in-Chief of *Babel: International Journal of Translation*. His recent publications include *Translational Spaces* (2021) and *Translating Foreign Otherness* (2018).

Dechao Li is Associate Professor in the Department of Chinese and Bilingual Studies at the Hong Kong Polytechnic University. He is also Editor-in-Chief of *Translation Quarterly*, the official journal of the Hong Kong Translation Society.

Transcultural Poetics
Chinese Literature in
English Translation

**Edited by Yifeng Sun and
Dechao Li**

Routledge
Taylor & Francis Group
LONDON AND NEW YORK

First published 2023
by Routledge
4 Park Square, Milton Park, Abingdon, Oxon OX14 4RN

and by Routledge
605 Third Avenue, New York, NY 10158

Routledge is an imprint of the Taylor & Francis Group, an informa business

© 2023 selection and editorial matter, Yifeng Sun and Dechao Li; individual chapters, the contributors

The right of Yifeng Sun and Dechao Li to be identified as the authors of the editorial material, and of the authors for their individual chapters, has been asserted in accordance with sections 77 and 78 of the Copyright, Designs and Patents Act 1988.

All rights reserved. No part of this book may be reprinted or reproduced or utilised in any form or by any electronic, mechanical, or other means, now known or hereafter invented, including photocopying and recording, or in any information storage or retrieval system, without permission in writing from the publishers.

Trademark notice: Product or corporate names may be trademarks or registered trademarks, and are used only for identification and explanation without intent to infringe.

British Library Cataloguing-in-Publication Data
A catalogue record for this book is available from the British Library

ISBN: 978-1-032-43622-7 (hbk)
ISBN: 978-1-032-43629-6 (pbk)
ISBN: 978-1-003-36816-8 (ebk)

DOI: 10.4324/9781003368168

Typeset in Times New Roman
by Apex CoVantage, LLC

Contents

	List of Contributors	vii
	Introduction YIFENG SUN AND DECHAO LI	1
1	Chinese Text and World Literature YIFENG SUN	7
2	Chinese Literature in Translation, World Literature as Genre TODD FOLEY	33
3	The Translator's Individual Approach: English Translation of Chinese Poetry AUDREY HEIJNS	52
4	On the "Clamour of Voices" in Translation Anthologies of Contemporary Chinese Literature XIULU WANG	66
5	Repositioning *The Injustice to Dou E* in a Global Generic Context ERSU DING	83
6	Translating Traditional Chinese Opera for the Stage: The Cult of *Qing* and the English Script of *The Peony Pavilion* (*The Young Lovers' Edition*) WENJING LI	95

Contents

7 The Silence of Anxiety and Trauma in the English
   Translation of *Selected Stories of Xi Ni Er* 113
   YI-CHIAO CHEN

8 Silenced Interstitiality: Translated Hong Kong Literature in
   English and French Anthologies 132
   MAIALEN MARIN-LACARTA

9 Cultural Untranslatability of Heteroglossia: Hong Kong
   Poetry in Colonial Time 152
   CHRIS SONG

10 Translating Hybrid Texts in Hong Kong: A Case Study
   of the English Translation of Chan Koon Chung's
   Kamdu cha canting 169
   DECHAO LI

11 "Big Translation" and Cultural Memory: The Construction
   and Transmission of National Images 188
   XUANMIN LUO

12 The Function of Literary and Cultural Communication
   of English 201
   NING WANG

   Index 216

Contributors

1. **Yi-Chiao Chen,** National University of Singapore, Singapore
2. **Ersu Ding,** Shanghai International Studies University, China
3. **Todd Foley,** New York University, U. S. A.
4. **Audrey Heijns,** Chinese University of Hong Kong, China
5. **Dechao Li,** Hong Kong Polytechnic University, China
6. **Wenjing Li,** Hong Kong Polytechnic University, China
7. **Xuanmin Luo,** Guangxi/Tsinghua University, China
8. **Maialen Marin-Lacarta,** Universitat Oberta de Catalunya, Spain
9. **Chris Song,** University of Toronto, Canada
10. **Yifeng Sun,** University of Macau, China
11. **Ning Wang,** Shanghai Jiaotong University, China
12. **Xiulu Wang,** Sun Yat-sen University, China

Introduction

Yifeng Sun and Dechao Li

Translating Chinese literature into English is a special challenge. There is a pressing need to overcome a slew of obstacles to the understanding and appreciation of Chinese literary works by readers in the English-speaking world. Hitherto only intermittent attempts have been made to theorize and explore the exact role of the translator as a cultural and aesthetic mediator informed by cross-cultural knowledge, awareness, and sensitivity. Given the complexity of literary translation, sophisticated poetics of translation with regard to literary value and aesthetic taste needs to be developed and elaborated more fully from a cross-cultural perspective. It is, therefore, necessary to examine attempts to reconcile the desire for authentic transmission of Chinese culture with the need for cultural mediation and appropriation in terms of the production and reception of texts subject to the multiplicity of constraints in order to shed new light on the longstanding conundrum of Chinese-English literary translation by addressing Chinese literature in the multiple contexts of nationalism, cross-cultural hybridity, literary untranslatability, the reception of translation, and also world literature.

Whether or not the target language is their native tongue, translating from Chinese in to English has always been a challenging undertaking for translators. In the early days after the founding of the People's Republic of China in 1949, the country experienced manifold hardships in recuperating from a war that had torn it apart. The international environment was not without animosity against China's global status. Yet despite all this, in 1951, this "young" country launched an English magazine titled *Chinese Literature*. It is the first and only official publication dedicated to translating Chinese literature and artworks for foreign countries in a timely and systematic manner. The publication of the magazine is an emblematic milestone in building a cultural bridge to the rest of the world. Since then, sustained efforts have been made to translate Chinese literature into English. This is due in part to the rising need to redress the cross-cultural imbalance in translations into and out of Chinese, which is mirrored in an unequal interaction between China and the West. Apart from the fact that the number of English translations of Chinese literature is disappointingly modest in relative terms, most of these translations need to be greatly enhanced in terms of effectiveness. Asymmetrical transcultural contact is implied by literary translation. All translations, according to André Lefevere, are rewriting practices with two components: ideology and poetics (Lefevere, 1992, p. vi). While the ideological dimension of rewriting has received much critical attention, the evident but neglected fact that not enough attention has been paid to the poetics of translation is a weak link in research on literary translation in relation to world literature.

This volume examines many facets of transcultural poetics in Chinese literature in English translation. Its scope is by no means confined to modern or contemporary Chinese literature: translations of classical Chinese texts, including poetry, are also covered. Given the variable and intricate nature of literary translation, complex poetics of translation concerning literary value and aesthetic taste is required from a cross-cultural perspective. Although it is desirable to convey authentic Chinese culture through translation, transcultural mediation and reflective appropriation in a variety of contexts are crucial. The central question is how to better deal with this. While this may seem unfashionably prescriptive in modern translation studies, it is at least necessary to look for ways to improve the reading experience of the target text by analyzing published translations to explore the mechanisms and interactions that underlie translation. The extent to which interventions are justified also needs to be closely examined. Displacement and reconstruction complicate transcultural poetics, which are interwoven with dynamics, performance, and transformation, all of which boil down to the conditions and outcomes of reception. Among other things, stylistic features, denotations, connotations, and intertextual collages are seen as insufficiently reproducible, calling into question the aesthetic norms of the target culture and thus the effectiveness of cross-cultural communication. Translation entails a process of poetically reconfiguring the multiple elements of the original to help the target reader experience a different world in a different but comparable way. The task of transferring and reshaping a cultural context for a translated text has never been easy. Cultural untranslatability or limited cultural translatability requires the translator to search for a corresponding set of aesthetic norms in the target system.

Almost without exception, any translation is likely to cause or provoke disagreement or controversy. Translation shifts meaning from one text to another, not only from one linguistic context to another but also, and perhaps more importantly, from one cultural context to another. To translate something is to rewrite it in another language. The process of rewriting is fraught with tensions and conflicts, as it always involves intervention and manipulation of some kind. The pivotal role that translation plays in modern Chinese history cannot be overstated. The cultural, political, and social landscape of the country has been shaped and greatly influenced by translation into Chinese. China, on the other hand, has made efforts to share its culture with the world. Translating Chinese literature into English has increasingly become a cross-cultural task that requires a high degree of literary acumen and consummate skill. Mainly due to the multiple linguistic and cultural incompatibilities or incommensurabilities between Chinese and English, translators are regularly confronted with translation problems. In keeping with translational poetics, it is also important to understand and conceptualize the inevitable manipulation in translation that occurs when trying to resolve various translation problems. Manipulation can be driven by the contextualized intention to recreate accessibility, communicate better, and help the target reader respond to a different world and time of experience as a result of translation. Primarily for this reason, transcultural poetics is central to the translation of Chinese literature into English.

The chapters in this volume analyze from different perspectives, offering the reader an understanding of and explanation for the labyrinth of literary translation in the context of China and the West. Cultural untranslatability or limited cultural translatability requires the translator to identify and search for a corresponding set of aesthetic norms in the target system. Offering answers to the questions raised from a variety of perspectives, this book brings together a series of interrelated chapters by translation and literary scholars who examine and analyze the multi-faceted forms of translation by identifying pitfalls that threaten and compromise the quality of translation. In addition to addressing specific case studies of the translation of drama, fiction, and poetry, the 12 contributors offer general theoretical reflections that actively challenge traditional concepts and paradigms of literary translation.

A word of explanation seems in order with respect to the definition of Chinese literature discussed in the context of this edited volume. It is broadened to refer to literature written in Chinese, including Chinese texts written in Hong Kong and Singapore, as represented in this collection, as well as in other parts of the world. Chinese-language literature from Hong Kong and Singapore is not adequately represented in anthologies and edited volumes related to the translation into Chinese. Yet they are, of course, part of the Chinese cultural heritage and share the same literary tradition and continuum. Admittedly, due to different historical circumstances and developments, different translation problems are to be expected. Chinese literature in Hong Kong, like its counterpart in Singapore, is a minority literature and also deserves global visibility through English translations. This "Sinophone sphere," defined as such (Chen, 2015, p. 52), has yet to be adequately explored in terms of English translation. Although both Hong Kong and Singapore are supposedly bilingual, many local writers prefer to write in Chinese or are only competent in it. English translation plays an irreplaceable role in introducing this Sinophone literature to the rest of the world.

In his chapter, "Chinese Text and World Literature," Yifeng Sun elaborates on the need for careful handling of cross-cultural untranslatability in order to promote the internationalization of Chinese literature. Sun first introduces some crucial concepts of literary translation, namely, poetics, literariness, and aesthetic quality. He then analyzes and discusses the translation practices of famous translators such as Howard Goldblatt and Anna Holmwood to show how to translate Chinese literature into English based on their exemplary translation practices. Despite the elusiveness of the concept of translational poetics, it is explored with a contextualized focus by discussing aesthetic or literary untranslatability, which is coupled with the intricate linkage between Chinese literature and world literature. By acknowledging the importance of translation in the canonization of Chinese literature, the chapter has laid the groundwork for this edited volume. Also, in the context of world literature, Todd Foley begins his chapter, "Chinese Literature in Translation, World Literature as Genre," by first reporting on the controversy surrounding the literary works of Mo Yan, winner of the Nobel Prize in Literature. Foley explores the relationships between translatability and universality through a close reading of Mo Yan's *Sandalwood Death*. By attempting to examine the translatability of Mo Yan's works and their status in world literature, Foley challenges the traditional conceptualization of world literature and proposes to reconceptualize it as a genre with only a limited degree of universality inherent in it. This chapter dethrones the traditional universal paradigm and argues for a reconceptualization of world literature.

The discussion on the promotion of Chinese literature and the dissemination of the Chinese culture in a globalized world cannot avoid dealing with the translation of poetry, one of China's most classical and prestigious literary genres. In her chapter titled "The Translator's Individual Approach: English Translation of Chinese Poetry," Audrey Hejins attempts to trace the unique fingerprint of translators. She has delineated the translator's individual approach to translating Chinese poetry into English through a close reading of the English translations of the poems of Jidi Majia and Jiang Hao, Yang Mu and Ye Mimi, Xi Xi and Liu Waitong, as well as through an analysis of other textual materials about the translation process or the translator's experience. It is expected that this research will expand our understanding of translation and transcultural value transmission through the lens of translators.

Xiulu Wang has focused on translation anthologies of contemporary Chinese literature. In her chapter, "On the 'Clamour of Voices' in Translation Anthologies of Contemporary Chinese Literature," she highlights some existing problems related to translation anthologies of Chinese literature with a detailed overview of their current path in the English-speaking world. Drawing on the notion of "clamour of voices," Wang emphasizes the need to take cultural diversity and literary heterogeneity into account when compiling translation anthologies, as demonstrated by a case study of a typical translation anthology called *By the River: Seven Contemporary Chinese Novellas*. This chapter has provided some refreshing insights and practical editorial suggestions on how to effectively create a polyphonic literary space through translation anthologies of Chinese literature.

Ersu Ding's chapter titled "Repositioning the Injustice to Dou E in a Global Generic Context" focuses on drama translation as its primary topic of discussion. Despite the fact that it is one of China's best-known tragedies, *The Injustice to Dou E* has not been presented as a piece of tragic drama literature when it was translated to the Western world. Ding's chapter addresses this issue of generic identity. It examines the reasons why *The Injustice to Dou E* was not presented as a tragedy to Western readers, and then provides cogent evidence to support these explanations. This informative chapter clarifies several common misconceptions about Oriental drama in the Western world, as well as the many similarities that the literature of tragic drama shares in both Eastern and Western contexts.

"Translating Traditional Chinese Opera for the Stage: The Cult of Qing and the English Script of *The Peony Pavilion* (The Young Lover's Edition)," the chapter by Wenjing Li, is another interesting case study on drama translation. More specifically, this chapter examines the translation of Tang Xianzu's most famous drama, *The Peony Pavilion*. It uncovers the translation strategies adopted in the English script of an edition of *The Peony Pavilion* tailored to a modern audience and takes a closer look at the representation of the concept of "qing" in the English script. Though a household name as a playwright in China, he is not as world-famous as his Western counterpart, Willian Shakespeare, which may be partly due to the unsatisfactory reception of Tang Xianzu's works in the global market. This study of a successful adaptation of his play could be instructive for the future rewriting of Chinese literature, especially theatrical production.

The chapter by Yi-Chiao Chen, "The Silence of Anxiety and Trauma in the English Translation of *Selected Stories of Xi Ni Er*," stands out as a unique research contribution in this volume because it is a case study of the translation of Chinese literature from Singapore into English. Based on an in-depth study *Xi Ni Er Selected Stories* and their translation, Chen has pinpointed the two prominent themes that pose challenges to translators: anxiety over losing one's mother tongue and culture, and the trauma caused by the Japanese invasion. Meanwhile, Chen refers to previous literature and provides viable strategies for solving the translation problems he has identified. This contribution is a practical guide for translators and translation scholars interested in translating or researching Singaporean Chinese literature.

This volume contains three studies of Hong Kong literature that focus on the translation of literary genres, including anthologies, poetry, and fiction. Maialen Marin-Lacarta's chapter, "Silenced Interstitiality: English and French Anthologies of Translated Hong Kong Literature," addresses the peripheral status of Hong Kong literature and its representation for international readers. It systematically examines 30 translation anthologies of Hong Kong literature. This research displays a general picture of how well these anthologies have challenged stereotypical images of Hong Kong and disseminated local voices. The results are rather disappointing: Hong Kong literature is still stuck in interstitiality, as their translations fail to capture the uniqueness of Hong Kong literature due to omissions. The way to refute the marginalization of Chinese literature requires learning from the past, in this case, from the inadequacy of the anthologies studied.

Chris Song has pointed out the hybrid linguistic features in Hong Kong poetry. His chapter, "The Untranslatability of Heteroglossia in Hong Kong Poetry," presents a history of heteroglossic poetry in Hong Kong that spans several critical periods and describes the influence of hybridity on modern Chinese poetry. It also discusses the untranslatability of the heteroglossic elements in Hong Kong poetry, analyzing various factors involved in translating poetry in Hong Kong's complex context.

Dechao Li's chapter, "Translating Hybrid Texts in Hong Kong: A Case Study of the English Translation of Chan Koon Chung's Fiction Kamdu cha canting," also focuses on Hong Kong literature. It mainly analyzes how a hybrid literary text, that is, of Chan Koon Chung's fiction *Jindu cha canting* (Can-do Tea Restaurant), is treated in the English translation. A close reading of the text reveals that the new language deliberately created by Chan Koon Chung is less salient in the translated version because it does not reflect the unique cultural context of the "in-between" in Hong Kong. Li contends that a translator may opt for a scenes-and-frames model to better translate hybrid literature. This volume also contains contributions that address the translation of Chinese literature from a more macro perspective and suggest possible methods to tackle problems with the unsatisfactory reception of Chinese literature by international readers. The chapter "Cultural Memory and the Translation of Chinese Literature in a Global Context," by Xuanmin Luo, stresses the paramount role of major translation in promoting Chinese literature in a global context. Big translation contributes to the construction of collective cultural memory, promoted by various forms of lingual-semiotic translation such as words, texts, images, paintings, music, dances, and even inscriptions. This study argues that the cultural awareness of translators and target readers can be greatly enhanced through big translation, giving marginal literature a permanent place in world literature. This study provides valuable guidance to translators and other stakeholders to pave the way for Chinese literature to enter the world. Acknowledging the status of English as a lingua franca in a globalized world, Ning Wang emphasizes the role of English as an effective tool for promoting Chinese literature and humanities. In his chapter titled "The Function of Literary and Cultural Communication of English," he analyzes both successful and unsuccessful examples of translating literary and humanities works. He concludes that instead of translating from Chinese into English, a more active form of cross-cultural translation should be chosen, namely, writing directly in English.

References

Chen, L. (2015). When Does 'Diaspora' End and 'Sinophone' Begin? *Postcolonial Studies*, 18 (1), 52–66.

Lefevere, A. (1992). *Translation, Rewriting, and the Manipulation of Literary Fame*. London: Routledge.

1 Chinese Text and World Literature

Yifeng Sun

Introduction

In the modern Chinese history of literary translation, translating for international distribution is a seemingly insurmountable task for Chinese literature. Much has been written about this subject, and much regret has been felt about the general lack of success in producing high-quality translations. The fact that Mo Yan was awarded the Nobel Prize for Literature in 2012 has rekindled interest in the effectiveness of translating Chinese literature into English to gain international recognition. The result is a great yearning for more outstanding Chinese literary texts to be translated and made available to the rest of the world. For quite some time, translating Chinese texts into English has become a national obsession. In a related vein, how to translate Chinese largely centers on what translation can do to promote cosmopolitanism, which is the foundation upon which Chinese literature has a chance to make its way onto the world stage. Undeniably, in this regard, there is still a long way to go. Given the general futility of attempting to translate Chinese literary texts well enough to be received and recognized internationally, increasing attention has been paid to the success of Howard Goldblatt's translations of modern and contemporary Chinese literature. Much food for thought has come out of his translation practice. Indeed, many translation scholars have studied his translation work in an effort to unravel the secret to successful translation from Chinese into English.

Translation is a linguistically and culturally fettered activity, persistently subject to socio-historical-cultural-political-ideological conditions: not only in the selection of texts, but also in how these texts are or can be translated into another language. With the uncovering of the multilayered complexities surrounding selection, editing, translation, production, and dissemination, it comes as little surprise to deduce the unpredictability of the haphazard nature of translation. Translation, especially literary translation, is a nonlinear transcultural journey across time, space, and borders. The quality of the translated language is a major concern in the first instance. Since well-qualified Sinologists whose native language is English are in short supply, Chinese translators have been entrusted with this task. But in most cases, the result is not entirely satisfactory. Literary translation entails much more than semantic transmission and must also be at the same time poetically competent. Mere linguistic virtuosity bereft of aesthetic appeal means that a literary translation is deprived of readability by the absence of poetic proficiency. In the related realm of rhetoricity, the issue of what is literarily translatable or untranslatable is an unavoidable consideration. Indeed, when it comes to literary translation, the literary quality of the original text is of critical consideration, and it must be adequately and/or often creatively rendered in order to cope with the precarious instability of signification and performativity. Ultimately, one cannot ignore whether and to what extent the translated text resonates with the target reader. After all, a literary text is supposed to function cross-culturally, transnationally, and above all, translationally. Moreover, ideologies and cross-cultural aesthetic taste also contribute to the poorly understood complexity of recognition, reception, and circulation regarding literary translation.

1. Translational Poetics

It can be said that literary translation, generally concerned with literary language, is the focus of translational poetics. It is also necessary to point out that no clear boundary exists between literary and nonliterary languages, which makes the definition and discussion of what makes up a literary language difficult and contentious. Unlike nonliterary texts, literary texts are viewed from either an essentialist or a relativist perspective. Literary translation refers to the translation of literary or aesthetic features and values. At the operational level, literary translation fundamentally challenges the assumption that the literary features of the source text can be transferred to the target language, especially in a pair of languages as dissimilar as Chinese and English, whose linguistic and cultural systems are not always comparable. Albaladejo and Chico-Rico's statement supports this problematic assumption:

> The transfer of such literary features becomes essential for the translation of a literary text to remain a literary text, one showing the features, characteristics or peculiarities thanks to which it will be received and valued as having that status.
> (Albaladejo & Chico-Rico, 2018, p. 115)

The implication of this message quoted above, representative of popular opinion, raises the question of how this is possible without mediation or negotiation or, simply put, without appropriation. The assumed transferability of cultural or aesthetic features of the original text may not be attainable, as numerous translation cases have shown.

More specifically, any discussion of literary translation is inextricably linked to literariness, which in turn is much concerned with the concept of aesthetic value, and this concept has been elusive in the West for several centuries (Walton, 1993, p. 500). This situation is exacerbated by the fact that "even if we set aside cross-cultural communication, aesthetic value as a single concept may be questionable" (Walton, 1993, p. 499). Moreover, Albaladejo and Chico-Rico write as follows:

> Literariness, which is the quality as literary that some texts have in their corresponding communication contexts, must be owned by the source text and

the target text alike, which entails a requirement that needs to be fulfilled during the translation process: the person who carries out this task must maintain it beyond the source language and its communicative context in the target language and its corresponding communication context.

(Albaladejo & Chico-Rico, 2018, p. 116)

Sure enough, there is good reason to expect literariness, which is an abstraction from literary features, to be maintained or reproduced in the target text. However, it makes more sense to speak of maintaining literariness rather than transferring it, as stated by Albaladejo and Chico-Rico (2018, p. 117). They use the two verbs "maintain" and "transfer" interchangeably (Albaladejo & Chico-Rico, 2018, p. 118). This also seems problematic since literariness often cannot be passively maintained.

In their argument, the phrase "creative space" is correlated to "interpretation" (Albaladejo & Chico-Rico, 2018, p. 118). This could be taken as a sign that interpretation generates this creative space rather than merely maintaining or even transferring the literariness of the original. Moreover, literary translation, which is clearly distinguishable from other forms of translation in this respect, exhibits attributes or vestiges of literariness that are irreducible to the result of rhetorical devices to achieve distinctiveness. The poetics of translation is grounded in an investigation of literariness and its production. Despite the shift away from traditional literary approaches such as Russian Formalism, New Criticism, Structuralism, and others that emphasize the inherent "literariness" of texts toward a greater emphasis on other forces in literary works, such as sociological, political, philosophical, economic, and cultural forces, the question of literariness remains a general concern that leaves the question of it unresolved. While there is no denying that essentialist claims about literariness are untenable, there is nonetheless a propensity to grapple with them when it comes to literary translation. It is argued that

> [l]iterariness is the quality of linguistic objects considered as literary texts. It manifests itself through a use of language or a referential constitution or a communication that are [sic.] distinguished from the usual ones, which occur in non-literary texts.
>
> (Albaladejo & Chico-Rico, 2018, p. 117)

But the usefulness of this definitional description is severely limited, not to mention problematic. As stated earlier, there is so-called literariness in nonliterary works as well. The line between literary and nonliterary traits is permeable and flexible in postmodern thought. Albaladejo and Chico-Rico advise that the translator should "keep the literary features of the original work" (2018, p. 117). The problem is, after identifying these literary features, to find a way to convey them effectively in translation.

In reality, however, a literary translation is about more than just retaining the stylistic features of the original. It goes without saying that the distinctive identity of the literary source text must be protected so that it can be properly represented in the translated text. Again, according to Albaladejo and Chico-Rico,

> to achieve this, the mediation of translation must maintain the literary status – i.e. the literariness – that is characteristic of the source text in such a way so that the latter can properly function as a literary text in its corresponding communication context and suitably represent the text in the original language.
> (Albaladejo & Chico-Rico, 2018, p. 117)

Domesticating poetics allows for a crude or violent form of mediation, or rather the lack thereof, for it is rather an interference for the sake of a better reception. Most likely, it cannot fulfill the task of adequately rendering the source text. It is common knowledge today that translation, especially literary translation, presupposes mediation and appropriation but within a certain range.

Miall and Kuiken contend, "Briefly, literariness is constituted when stylistic or narrative variations defamiliarize conventionally understood referents and prompt reinterpretive transformations of a conventional feeling or concept" (Miall & Kuiken, 1999, p. 123). As a result, the perception of defamiliarization becomes problematized. If, as posited by Russian formalists, literary language is a defamiliarized language, translation may entail double defamiliarization, especially in the case of foreignization. But the result of double defamiliarization may not necessarily be literary translation from the perspective of the target language. Moreover, literary translation presents a special kind of translation problem: aesthetic untranslatability. There are possible degrees of literariness, just as there are degrees of translatability or untranslatability in any text. For the most part, this has to do with the degree of cultural referentiality. Walton reminds us that "[w]e must not assume that all cultures in which people produce and enjoy or find satisfaction in what we call works of art even recognize anything much like our notion of aesthetic value" (Walton, 1993, p. 499). In this light, simply replicating defamiliarization of the source text in the target text risks depriving the target reader of the opportunity to find pleasure in reading translation by subverting the aesthetic integrity of the source text because the same integrity cannot be assumed in the target text. As a defining feature of literary language, defamiliarization is cross-culturally sensitive, and the assumption that defamiliarization can be transmitted without mediation is open to debate.

The combination of linguistic, cultural, and aesthetic untranslatability makes literary translation a particularly difficult task. Additionally, lexical transfer may lead to aesthetic untranslatability. Or to put it another way, if something cannot be translated well in a poetic sense, it may be due to aesthetic untranslatability. It can also be said that, in practice, anything that can be translated competently should also be translated poetically. This is what is referred to by Barbara Folkart as "poetically competent translation" (Folkart, 2007, p. xiii), which comes about through "the poetically viable translation" (Folkart, 2007, p. xiv). She presses the point further by stating that "the poetically competent translator succeeds in appropriating a poem in language A and metabolizing it, via the raw material of language B, into a poem that really *is* a poem" (Folkart, 2007, p. xv). To appropriate the source text poetically in a poetically different context is the task of the literary translator. The otherwise utter banality of the language of translation detracts from the original text's vividness, and it is precisely against this background that poetic appropriation is needed. Despite this, a text that has a poetic value attached to it is better and more enduringly appreciated. Although it is difficult to pin down exactly what constitutes poetic value, and there is rarely a cross-cultural consensus, it would be a mistake to believe that all cultures in which people produce and enjoy literary texts have the same aesthetic worth.

Translational poetics is intimately linked with transcultural poetics. A literary text is culturally and aesthetically different when it is perceived by the source and target readers from related yet dissimilar perspectives based on different cultural systems and traditions. Various other varieties of appreciation are part of a dialogic situation in which literariness is performative. Given that aesthetic and functional features are often interrelated and intertwined in literary translation, the pragmatic dimension of translation is of equal significance along with the perception of beauty. Lefevere notes "the incompatibility of poetics" of various cultural systems (Lefevere, 1992, p. 74). This incompatibility is intrinsically linked to the irreducibility that literary translation entails. As Venuti emphatically states, translation is "mediated by values, beliefs, and representations in the receiving situation" (Venuti, 2012, p. 180). Neglecting the complexity of the original tends to result in a less satisfactory translated version. On the other hand, whether it is possible to capture and reproduce multiplicity is a critical concern. There are equally encouraging and frustrating instances of how differently translators approach transcultural poetics that is essential to illuminating literary translation. Leo Lee's critique of Yang Xianyi's translation style is that "In short, the Yangs' style is eminently pleasing, suitable to some works but not to others. Perhaps this is a problem for all translators" (Lee, 1985, p. 566). Depending on the type of incompatibility, translational poetics is tenuous and always uncertain.

The Chinese and Western cultural systems are vastly different, and English is linguistically and culturally distant from Chinese. In the long run, the only hope is a growing cosmopolitanism that can bridge or reduce these differences. But before cosmopolitanism takes hold, the literary features of the original are not easy to replicate in translation. As noted earlier, Albaladejo and Chico-Rico have mentioned the transfer of "literary features," although there is no verifiable basis for assuming that "literary features" are transferable, and later in the same article they refer to the possibility that "the representation" of the source text can be "expressed differently" (Albaladejo & Chico-Rico, 2018, p. 118). However, when it is "expressed differently," these features inevitably are no longer maintained or transferred. Moreover, Albaladejo and Chico-Rico define "creativity" very narrowly in the context of translation (Albaladejo & Chico-Rico, 2018, p. 118).

Some other similarly simplistic pronouncements of theirs are similarly unhelpful as they claim that "The text resulting from literary translation is a literary one, the same as the source text" (Albaladejo & Chico-Rico, 2018, p. 118). This is not a thoughtful remark. They even claim that the translated text "has literariness at the same linguistic levels and semiotic contexts as the original one" (Albaladejo & Chico-Rico, 2018, p. 118). But it cannot be presupposed that there is ever a built-in sameness, certainly not at the same levels and in the same contexts as in the source text. If we accept that literary features are not readily transferable, it is at least possible to capture and reproduce their traces, based on which to reconstruct them. Even if a translated text is faithfully reproduced and all literary features are scrupulously maintained or transferred, it may nonetheless be devoid of literary merit. Literal literariness rarely works in translation because invariably rhetorical figures are processed differently in different linguistic and cultural systems.

What is indisputably irreducible is perhaps the poetic function of language and related matters. As one of the six aspects or functions of language developed by Jakobson (1960/1990), its relevance to literary translation is significant (p. 69). Concentrating on rhetorical devices is necessary, if not always attainable. The real problem, however, is that translation, especially literary translation, tends to focus on one and neglect the other. The translator is "like a painter doesn't faithfully represent a building with three or four facades by giving it just one" (de Barcos, 1956, p. 291). To be fair, sometimes the other three or four facades are not necessarily presented in the original, but only hinted at, and the source text reader would have no problem figuring out or imagining them. The target reader, however, may not be able to imagine them because their intertextual knowledge and experience can be insufficient. Without a cross-cultural imagination on the part of the target reader, the effectiveness of literary translation is weakened. Meanwhile, we must not lose sight of the signified as represented by the subtext. According to Da'an Pan, "The subtext and the surface text form the semiotic relationship between the signified and the signifier. Such a relationship is essentially intertextual, resulting in the intertextuality of the text" (Pan, 2000, p. 58). Hugh Kenner points out that "Pound's reiterated advice to translators" is "to convey the energized pattern and let go the words" (Kenner, 1971, p. 150). All this suggests that translation must penetrate literariness residing at the surface level and bring out the inherent vitality rooted in the signified.

2. Rewriting and Manipulation

Translation is rewriting, as André Lefevere repeatedly claims. The theory of rewriting that Lefevere sets forth in his book *Translation, Rewriting and the Manipulation of Literary Fame*, first published in 1992, is deeply tied to ideology and translational poetics and has been published for 30 years. It is influential in its discussion of patronage and ideology. The book has been cited numerous times, including in languages other than English. One of the most salient facets of Lefevere's argument is that he unremittingly ties poetics to ideology. He believes that rewriting is heavily influenced by ideology, though not exclusively. Inexplicably, however, hitherto insufficient attention has been paid to the factor of poetics. Translation necessitates rewriting, which simultaneously energizes and frustrates translation while creating an environment conducive to manipulation. Rewriting is subject to a multiplicity of factors that are an integral part of the dialogic process. Although it may appear to be distortion, it almost always involves the introduction of an ontological difference in the sense that the translated text differs from its source or is even intentionally made different. In the context of literary translation, the terms "rewriting" and "manipulation" are almost synonymous, but they are in fact different in terms of motivation and attitudes. The study of poetics may be more important than the consideration of ideology, depending on the circumstances of literary translation. Over the years, Leferever's work has sparked a tremendous amount of interest in the ideological component, while poetics has been relegated to the background.

However, in a book chapter by Leferever published in 1985, poetics is accorded a higher level of prominence. It is important to note his phrasing: "poetics or ideology" and "the ideology and/or the poetics" (Lefevere, 1985, pp. 225, 239). It is suggested that ideology and poetics can be treated separately or independently, although ideology and poetics are discussed together. As he puts it, "[t]he functional component of a poetics is obviously closely tied to ideological influences from outside the sphere of the poetics proper, generated by ideological forces in the environment of the literary system" (Lefevere, 1985, p. 229). Certainly, ideological forces are at work, and it became evident that in his later work he shifted to the apparent inseparability between ideology and poetics. In his 1992 book, poetics is constantly and tenaciously linked to ideology. This inseparability should not be taken for granted, however, unless ideology is very precisely defined in a particular context. As his earlier view suggests, "in the source text, among other things, ideology and poetics mingle and clash" (Lefevere, 1985, p. 233). Moreover, of course, the target text may well represent rival poetics, and two different poetics can also "mingle and clash."

It is palpable that Lefevere's earlier investigation of the concept of poetics in literary translation, freed from an unyielding preoccupation with ideology, is notably more meaningful and relatable. Literary translation necessitates a poetic rewriting that accordingly focuses on the poetic value of the original. By drawing attention to the poetic dimension of literary translation, Levinson privileges the artistic form as a multivocal artifact that urges the target reader to reflect on the literariness manifested in "forms, qualities, and meanings" and also their "interrelations" (Levinson, 1996, p. 6). Perhaps it can be said that when it comes to literary translations, it is more likely that poetic rather than ideological manipulations are the order of the day. It remains to be seen whether the stylistic variations in the source text are captured and reproduced in the translated text. The literary translator is thus required to act as a frontal intermediary between two linguistic and cultural systems. This does not imply, however, that the ideological dimension should be neglected. Rather, it suggests that an overemphasis on the ideological dimension detracts and distracts from the task of rearticulating the literary quality of the original.

According to Lefevere, a literary system functions through the use of a code that enables communication (at least potentially) between author and reader. This code is referred to as poetics,

> and it can be said to consist of two components: one is an inventory of literary devices, genres, motifs, symbols, prototypical characters and situations,

the other a concept of what the role of literature is, or should be, in society at large.

(Lefevere, 1985, p. 229)

In addition, normative expectations of poetics suggest competition between the original poetics and the dominant poetics in the target system. In certain cases, this can generate tension and the need for conscious poetic manipulation. One should be aware that more than one set of aesthetic principles involved in translation is appropriate for different cultural traditions and practices.

Manipulation, ideological, stylistic, or otherwise, is usually associated with literary translation. Whatever form it takes, it is innately transcultural in the sense that it must address cross-cultural challenges. Christian Refsum speaks of "the creative tensions between authorship and translatorship" (Refsum, 2019, p. 1). Inevitably, manipulation is quintessentially involved in rewriting, which implies an implicit change of textual ownership. The authorial role played by the translator in rewriting the source text has been explored by a number of scholars. Anthony Pym cautions against overstating the claim that authorship replaces translatorship (Pym, 2011, p. 32). It is undeniable that the nature of translation imposes constraints on translational creativity. In light of this fact, while the transformative power of translation is unleashed, it is also met with varying degrees of resistance. Nonetheless, the "counterfeit" offered by the translator, as argued by Arrojo, blurs the difference between writing and rewriting, which becomes indistinct (Arrojo, 2018, p. 147).

Translation is not possible without rewriting the original and also interpreting it, for rewriting refuses simple transfer and inevitably feeds on interpretation. Pound's version, according to Hsieh, is "at once good poetry and faithful translation" (Hsieh, 1938, p. 422). There is little doubt that Pound's translation is "good poetry." But the claim that his translation is also a faithful translation is hard to believe. Wen Tung Hsieh argues further:

> For what he lacked in lingual access, however, Mr. Pound almost made up in an astonishing interpretative acumen, by which he often penetrated through the veil of an alien text to the significant features of the original: tone, poetic intention and verbal felicity.
>
> (Hsieh, 1938, p. 423)

This is nothing short of amazing. How Pound managed to do this has always puzzled and fascinated translation scholars and translation practitioners alike. The intrinsic literariness was successfully recreated. If for no other reason than this, this success was owing to his "interpretative acumen," and the literariness contained in the original was not taken at face value by the translator. The original "poetic intention," though elusive and not always knowable, was recognized by Pound despite not knowing Chinese and simply relying on the unreliable notes of Ernest Fenollosa to assign meaning to an alien form (Hsieh, 1938, p. 423). This is a rare case of ingenuity.

In China, the concept of elegance in relation to translation, especially in literary translation, can be seen as a conscious effort to create an aesthetic effect for the target reader. The famous three-part dictum of *xin, da*, and *ya* (faithfulness, expressiveness, and elegance) was formulated by Yan Fu in the preface to his translation of Thomas Huxley's *Evolution and Ethics*. Since then, the dictum has evolved into three principles, with "elegance" being particularly important for literary translation, especially poetry translation. It is, however, the most controversial concept because it has been imprecisely and amorphously formulated and defined in a variety of cross-cultural situations. With no definitive definition of what constitutes elegance, it is often difficult to determine exactly what is meant by elegance when it is used so loosely and in such a wide variety of contexts. In literary translation, there seems to be a heightened awareness of the need to invoke an aesthetic appeal for the target reader in order to provide a reading experience comparable, if not equivalent, to that of the source reader.

Characteristically, and close to a truism, literary translation must exhibit recognizable features of literariness, the reproduction of which is crucial and indispensable to qualify a translation as literary. Almost unwittingly, an aesthetic value is ingrained in the way a translation is perceived and received. If a translation is described as elegant, it has certain aesthetic value. The epitome of successful translation is known to be "elegance" or "sublimity." In order for a literary work to be well received in a different cultural context where the aesthetic experience of the reader of the source text may not be successfully reproduced, it is essential that the aesthetic appreciation of a literary translation be fostered. Things can get out of hand, however, if taken too far. Rewriting takes various forms, some more radical than others. In broad terms, there can be creative rewriting as opposed to noncreative rewriting. Translation leads to various forms of rewriting, and beyond that, there is a spectrum of rewriting, transcreation, and adaptation, depending on the degree of deviation from the original. It should be noted that transcreation is much more than dynamic equivalence. It comprises derivativeness and creativeness, which in their combination are subsumed under the rubric of translation. However, when the part of creativeness predominates, it comes close to adaptation.

It is often assumed that transcreation is used primarily for advertising and marketing rather than literary texts. Although it is generally assumed that adaptation differs substantially from translation at the textual level, transcreation borders on or strays into a retelling of the story, characterized by "a large dose of creativity" pertaining to the "conceptual design" of the worlds that emerge out of the retelling (Dybiec-Gajer & Oittinen, 2020, p. 3). The awareness of the "needs and expectations" of the target reader "makes transcreation not at all far removed from the tenets of the Skopos theory" (Dybiec-Gajer & Oittinen, 2020, p. 4). But transcreation, for obvious reasons, is considerably less restrained. This is said to be out of consideration "for the benefit" of the target reader (Oittinen, 2020, p. 16). Yet it is difficult to rule out the possibility that there are other reasons or motives for transcreation. Even intertextual rewriting is not the same as transcreation, which can, however, be a convenient and dangerous excuse to avoid, among other things, untranslatability. Moreover, there might also be an ethical issue at play.

3. World Literature Through Translation

Despite Susan Bassnett's observation of "the "abyss between the study of world literature and the study of translation" (Bassnett, 2019, p. 1), world literature and translation studies are jostled together to share something in common: communication across languages, cultures, and poetic traditions and, more fundamentally, difference, be it historical, cultural, political, ideological, and aesthetic. A shared tangible interface between these two academic fields is untranslatability. A central argument in Emily Apter's polemical work *Against World Literature* is that the validity of world literature is brought into question because it is predicated on "a translatability assumption" (Apter, 2013, p. 3). Bassnett's response is as follows:

> On the surface, this looks like an important point, but as anyone who has ever engaged in translating anything knows, the primary task for any translator is to engage with untranslatability which is an inevitable aspect of all translating.
>
> (Bassnett, 2019, p. 5)

In other words, untranslatability is nothing new. Translators, especially literary translators, have been wrestling with it all along. There seems to be no need to be reminded of seemingly insurmountable translation problems embodied in the form of untranslatability.

The "translatability assumption" formulated by Apter is correct in that it turns out to be false. It is an ostensibly naive and utopian assumption; probably no literary translator would make such an assumption. Another point is Apter's conflation of incommensurability and untranslatability. Behind the issue of untranslatability are a series of assumptions. The "translatability assumption," as stated by Apter, refers to an overarching optimistic assumption regarding the dubious prospect of universal translatability. Its underlying premise is that it is disagreeable or unacceptable to domesticate a foreign text in the target language. In the quest for inclusiveness or completeness, as well as the representation of all formal features and stylistic traces of the original, translatability is overemphasized. Apter is in favor of Derrida's tenor of irreducibility in translation while disapproving of simplification. She approvingly cites Barbara Johnson's summary of Derrida's "ingenious translations" of foreign texts, which are said to "render all the often contradictory meanings of a term in such a way that crucial logical complexities are not oversimplified" (Apter, 2013, p. 250). Apter hits on an important point here: even at the risk of confounding or antagonizing the target reader, the complexity of meaning is irreducible. For Apter, irreducible representations of the literary attributes of the original are essential. This amply demonstrates that translatability is always more limited and contingent than is usually assumed. Optimism about translatability is indubitably unwarranted. A key point in this connection is that Apter is implicitly but specifically concerned with literary untranslatability. It encompasses both linguistic and cultural untranslatability but also denotes the near impossibility of reproducing the inherent literariness or aesthetic quality of the original.

Modern translation studies has shifted from prescriptive to descriptive approaches. To some extent, this has freed translation studies from the accusation of doing little or nothing about untranslatability. Still, what is at stake is the lack of sufficient translatability pertaining to the perennial concern with the loss of meaning. The central argument of *Against World Literature* is straightforward: if untranslatability is not eliminated, there can be no world literature, assuming that its existence depends on adequate translation. Apter seems to indirectly blame translation studies for not coming to grips with untranslatability. Yet it is commonplace in translation studies that compensation and thick translation are considered important means to bring out the full meaning in its original context. Curiously, however, there is no mention of these two translation strategies in *Against World Literature*. Meanwhile, it cannot be denied that inadequate translation is less of a concern for modern translation scholars like Gideon Toury than acceptability. Adequacy and acceptability are unfortunately seen as antithetical and irreconcilable. Acceptability would be compromised if an excessive emphasis were placed on inclusiveness, which is not only impractical but can also be counterproductive. However, this does not mean that the lack of adequacy is acceptable, hence the persistent efforts to compensate for it. It is commonly understood that translation is constrained by a multitude of factors. Compensation is a prevalent way of offsetting losses, and thick translation has become the last resort for dealing with untranslatability.

Untranslatability, at its most fundamental level, signifies inaccessibility or very limited accessibility. Apter raises concerns about the ecumenical applicability of world literature because of the "incommensurability" and "untranslatability" of source texts of different linguistic and cultural origins. But forcing the target reader to learn the original is not feasible. It is in this sense, incommensurability is referred to by Apter as untranslatability (Apter, 2013, p. 3). Although incommensurability is largely responsible for untranslatability, it should not be equated and confused with the latter. Translation, despite its shortcomings and imperfections, is indispensable in contributing to the creation and growth of world literature. But in practical terms, Apter's concern is not unwarranted. The question is whether translation is sufficiently enabling. Apter believes that both world literature and translation studies have a propensity to treat translatability as a given. If untranslatability is an insurmountable obstacle for world literature, it is also a sign of the failure of translation studies. Literary translation is often done inadequately, or at least anything but satisfactorily. It can be argued that the crisis of world literature is embedded in the crisis of translation studies. The focus is on the inadequacy of translation, which ultimately has a negative impact on its acceptability in a global context. Untranslatability is of course not absolute. There are varying degrees of untranslatability that create a space for manipulation (variously motivated) and transformation (intended or unintended) as the translated text, whether consciously or unconsciously, can repurpose the meaning inherent in the original.

The resurgence of world literature in the first decade of the twenty-first century coincided with the creative energy of Chinese literature. The cross-cultural desire to export Chinese culture to the rest of the world has never diminished. It has been pointed out that

> China has many excellent writers and works, but they have not been disseminated internationally due to lack of translations, and good works have not had the opportunity to be shown to the world to be understood and recognized by Western readers.
>
> (Zhang, 2018, p. 114)

This is a widely held belief among Chinese scholars and contains much truth. This deplorable situation is due not only to the lack of translations but, more importantly, to the lack of good translations. Another widely held view is that "we should take the initiative to bring Chinese culture and literature to the outside world, rather than passively waiting for Western scholars to discover it" (Zhang, 2018, p. 114). This is tantamount to saying that when Chinese literature needs to be translated into other languages, we can hardly rely on native speakers of those languages, who are unlikely to help change the situation dramatically. Chinese translators would most likely be needed to translate Chinese texts into various target languages. Zhang continues:

> China is known as an important translation country. In recent years, nearly 10,000 new books have been published and translated every year, and there are more than 60,000 professional translators. However, there are very few excellent translators in China. There is a serious shortage of excellent translators.
>
> (Zhang, 2018, p. 115)

The demand for well-trained translators who can competently translate Chinese literary texts into English is overwhelming. But the stark reality is that even Sinologists and native English speakers do not necessarily have the expertise to produce high-quality translations. Even Gladys Yang, a respected translator of Chinese literature, acknowledges this in the preface to her translation of Gu Hua's work:

> Owing to the limitations of my English, now out of date after over forty years in China, I have failed to convey the raciness and earthiness of Gu Hua's language, which heavily draws on Chenzhou colloquialisms. I hope some younger sinologists will before long make new translations to do justice to his graphic, pungent style.
>
> (Lee, 1985, p. 11)

"The raciness and earthiness" of the source language are part of the so-called literary language. When these features or properties are lost in translation, much of the vitality and verve of the source text is lost, to the detriment of the literary value or aura that is to be restored in the target culture.

It is generally assumed that cross-cultural negotiations are needed to cope with untranslatability. As maintained by Damrosch, "even a single work of world literature is the locus of a negotiation between two different cultures" (Damrosch, 2003, p. 514). This negotiation seeks to attend to both adequacy and acceptability, both of which constrain translation from different directions. Adequacy implies a level of inclusiveness, while acceptability stems from the preference for target-orientedness of modern translation theory as posited by Toury. However, inclusiveness is not a realistic option in literary translation because source-orientedness typically risks unintelligibility and incoherence. A plethora of variables influences the translator's decision or preference. And the act of rewriting is replete with a variety of concerns and motives. There is extensive rewriting or circumscribed rewriting, as well as radical rewriting or moderate rewriting. Literary translation is expected to bring the source text to life in another language, while paradoxically often failing to do it sufficient justice, or even damaging it. In the case of the Australian poet John Kinsella, Apter cites the reason why he was not included in the "global canon":

> Naturalized in the British and American literary market, his writing is not exotic enough, while a poet like Lionel Fogarty – whose dense, compelling verse incorporates Aboriginal language – fails to cross over because his writing remains too exotic for mainstream taste.
>
> (Apter, 2001, p. 2)

What matters most is not inclusiveness but the target readership's expectation of acceptability. At stake here is not even untranslatability but rather how the source text is manipulated or negotiated, as well as what form of rewriting translation takes. With this in mind, Apter raises the question: "How do some works gain international visibility, while others do not?" (Apter, 2001, p. 2) It is possible that sometimes extra-textual rather than textual factors are the determining factors, for instance, social-political, economic, and others.

4. Translation and Nobel Prize

The Nobel Prize for Literature in 2012 was awarded to Mo Yan, bringing unprecedented attention to the significance of literary translation (Liu & Xu, 2014, p. 7). Howard Goldblatt garnered a large share of the credit for the successful international reception of Mo Yan's works because he "has masterfully translated many of his works into English" (Braester, 2016, p. 307). There is no doubt that Goldblatt's translation strategy succeeded, but it is not without controversy. First of all, his radical rewriting of the original in the form of abridgments has met with disapprobation from some Chinese critics. Apter would also disfavor this practice. In an interview, Wolfgang Kubin, the German Sinologist known for his outspoken views on modern Chinese literature, contends that Mo Yan's books, as translated by Goldblatt, should have two authors (Zhao, 2013). The translation of the last chapter of Mo Yan's work *The Garlic Ballads* is considered the watershed moment in modern Chinese translation history. This was the moment "when Goldblatt abandoned a more scholarly attitude of fidelity and requested that the author rewrite the final chapter of his novel" (Stalling & Schleifer, 2021, p. 33). But Goldblatt has not abandoned fidelity altogether: at least he did not rewrite in the sense that he changed the last chapter itself. This does not amount to co-authorship. One can say that the translator intervened but did not interfere.

Since Mo Yan received the Nobel Prize, there have been numerous critiques and debates about Goldblatt's translations, especially among Chinese scholars. Those who applaud him act as if he has added a magical touch to Mo Yan's novels through his meritorious translations. Goldblatt himself is effusive in his admiration for Mo Yan: "His imagery is striking, his tales often bewitching, and his characters richly appealing. He is, quite simply, one of a kind" (Goldblatt, 2009, p. 28).

What has the translator done to bring forth all the admirable attributes of the original? Goldblatt, almost without fail, took the task of translation very seriously. As recorded by Mo Yan, "Howard and I began our collaboration in 1988. We've exchanged more than a hundred letters and spoken innumerable times over the telephone" (Mo, 2000, p. 473). Together they circumnavigated the thorny problems of translation in a good working relationship. Such correspondence between the two entails in-depth discussion. According to Mo Yan, "Often, we confer over a phrase or an object with which he's unfamiliar. Sometimes, I have to call upon my primitive drawing skills to sketch something for him" (Mo, 2000, p. 473). The nature of this collaboration shows that what seemed untranslatable can be overcome. Given that Goldblatt asked Mo Yan to change the ending of *The Garlic Ballads*, some critics felt that the translator took liberties with the original by deleting certain parts without serious hindrance. However, the translator was given some leeway by the author to treat certain content, such as sex scenes, in a way that would appeal to the target reader. Mo Yan explains that this is "why the English and Chinese versions may seem different" (Mo, 2000, p. 473). This inevitably raises the question of the legitimacy of the parts of a translation that markedly deviate from the original. Indeed, it is possible that a translation in the conventional sense has been replaced by the product of co-authorship within a given range of parameters.

As a translator, Goldblatt is mindful of the target reader's expectations, knowing full well that the author is writing for his Chinese readers, and it is his job to make his translated texts "palatable" to the target reader (Stalling, 2014, p. 9). Goldblatt has heard "talk," which has also been called a "rumor," that he is the true author of these highly acclaimed novels published under the name Mo Yan, but the translator has "categorically" denied the veracity (Goldblatt, 2014, p. 23). At the same time, the identity of the author, whose works have been translated into several languages by various translators, has become somewhat nebulous. Multiple linguistic and cultural identities attached to the author in different ways are fluid and malleable, as can be claimed by his Swedish translator Anna Gustafsson Chen, Japanese translator Tomio Yoshida, French translators Noël Dutrait and Chantal Chen-Adndro, Norwegian translator Brith Sæthre and Italian translator

Patrizia Liberati. And of course, Howard Goldblatt is also on the list (Goldblatt, 2014, p. 23). All these translators were invited by Mo Yan to attend the Nobel Prize ceremony in Stockholm. The author Mo Yan seemed to be a collective gathering of his translators and himself. This was essentially a symbolic gesture to honor the various afterlives made possible by these translators. The dynamic interaction and interplay between author and translator continued on this occasion as Mo and Goldblatt discussed issues of translation and distribution. Mo Yan once said to Goldblatt, "Do what you want. I can't read what you've written. It's your book" (Goldblatt, 2014, p. 24). It may come as a shock to hear an author say this to a translator. The unqualified willingness to disown the source text shows that its fate is placed in the hands of the translator. Does this mean that the translator is given carte blanche to be unfaithful to the original?

Not really. The translator cannot be exempt from textual accountability, for they must keep all the constraints in mind. Goldblatt is scrupulous in translating the difficult passages in the original, which shows that he is a careful negotiator rather than an author in his own right. Wherever possible, the original syntactical structure is retained: 花生花生花生花花生, 有男有女阴阳平 (Mo, 2012, p. 8). This is rendered as "Peanuts peanuts peanuts, boys and girls, the balance of yin and yang" (Goldblatt, 2012, p. 7). This registers a perfect match with the original version without causing problems in understanding the meaning. About his experience in translating Mo Yan's *Sandalwood Death*, Goldblatt says the following:

> Mo Yan was writing for a literate Chinese audience who would understand the various levels of the articulation among the characters and the datedness of the early twentieth-century Chinese to a twenty-first-century reader, but I was writing for an American publisher and for an American reader.
> (Goldblatt, 2014, p. 7)

Here Goldblatt renounces his assumed role: instead of a translator, he assumes the role of an author whose audience is clearly different from Mo Yan's. His argument is compelling: to simply translate, the characters are made to speak English, which no one understands. At this point, the translator must write the story in a way that makes the characters' English intelligible to the target audience. Mo Yan recalled their collaboration in translating *The Republic of Wine*. The novel, as he points out, was "created together" by him and Goldblatt (Mo, 2000, p. 473). Certainly, the translator can assume multiple identities, considering that they assume multiple roles at the same time – for example, author, reader, and of course, translator – and all these different roles are performed by one and the same person who is simultaneously involved in all these different tasks.

In a 2013 interview with Stephen Sparks for the *Los Angeles Review of Books*, Howard Goldblatt outlines his strategies for dealing with historical and literary references in the source text. While they are not innately untranslatable in principle, they can indeed pose problems for the translator. There is one telling example. If rendered literally as "driven to Mount Liang," the meaning would be lost if the "historical and literary references" are not included. The original meaning of the phrase is that people are compelled to rebel.[1] It derives from the famous Chinese novel *Water Margin* (translated by Pearl Buck and Sapore Li). However, if this reference is missing, the expressive power is significantly reduced. If it is turned into "a Robin Hood-ish reference," the reader cannot fully understand it "without a brief tutorial on the significance and origins of the phrase."[2] On the other hand, such a tutorial, however brief, might just be distracting. Goldblatt does not countenance footnotes, although endnotes are sometimes used. He makes an interesting point here. Expressions such as "driven to despair" are usually preferred without the need to make "quaint references" to historical and cultural sources. The reason is that many historical or cultural expressions, even if Goldblatt does not say so explicitly, are used as everyday expressions depending on the context. That being the case, relying too heavily on clichéd proverbs or common phrases is not only unnecessary but also detrimental to a stylistically appealing and substantively effective text. To avoid overwhelming or overburdening the target reader by "making every alien reference or concept clear" to them, Goldblatt deliberately leaves it "unexplained, welcoming the reader to skip it, figure it out, or curse the translator."[3]

This has brought to light the critical dimension of literary translation, namely, cross-cultural intertextuality. It is important to establish resonance between the two groups of readers, the source and the target, when there is clearly no formal equivalence between the two languages. This may be due to the target reader's lack of intertextual knowledge, without which it would be difficult to establish resonance. If the "significance of the intertextual relation," as Venuti puts it, is not recognized by the target reader, there is little likelihood that translation will be accepted (Venuti, 2009, pp. 158–159). The translator is clearly in a dilemma here. Venuti notes that

> to compensate for the loss of intertextuality, the translator might rely on paratextual devices, such as an introductory essay or annotations, which can be useful in restoring the foreign cultural context and in articulating the cultural significance of an intertextual relation as well as its linguistic basis. Yet in making such additions the translator's work ceases to be translating and becomes commentary. Moreover, not only does the translation acquire a typically academic form, potentially restricting its audience, but it fails to have the immediate impact on its reader that the foreign text produced on the foreign reader. An equivalent effect is again pre-empted.
> (Venuti, 2009, p. 159)

Paratextual information supplements translation, and rather than replacing it, as Venuti fears, its provision is nonetheless essential. Moreover, if paratextual information is simplified and confused with commentary, the identity of translation is called into question. As for "immediate impact," its loss is admittedly inevitable. But there are other means than just "an introductory essay or annotations," such as paraphrasing and substitution.

5. *Martial Arts Fiction*

Schleiermacher's famous either/or method is often rigidly applied as if there are only two options in translation: either to bring the reader to the author or the author to the reader (Starr, 2012, p. 116). In fact, however, there are a variety of options on the spectrum between these two extremes. There can be ramifications that are motivated differently. Douglas Robinson makes the following point:

> One simplistic binary schema that is often imposed on this collection of approaches is foreignization/domestication, where (a) source-orientation is reductively (and typically rather vaguely) called foreignizing and (b) target-orientation is equally reductively and vaguely called domesticating.
> (Robinson, 2017, p. 452)

In general, Chinese and English have few lexical and syntactic similarities, and borrowing in a peripheral locus is usually one-sided. The general public's knowledge of Chinese culture in the West is limited. Various configurations of literary space in a cross-cultural context need to be explored to find ways to translate competently while maintaining cultural identity.

For a long time, martial arts novels were derided in China as a subgenre of popular literature, but with the advent of the novels of Jin Yong, the pen name of Louis Cha Leung-yung, all that changed. The publication of *Legends of the Condor Heroes I: A Hero Born* in English translation in 2018 was a great success and attracted international attention. Translating martial arts fiction is a cross-cultural challenge. Cultural untranslatability is a central concern in the translation of martial arts novels. Aside from the usual intertextual references in poems and songs, martial arts movements and ethereal and spiritual connotations are notoriously difficult, if not impossible, to render in translation. In light of this, paratextuality is a crucial link between the source text and its cultural and historical aspects that add to contextual complexity and is provided by the translator, Anna Holmwood. The provision of paratextual utterances and supplements, reminiscent of thick translation, useful as it is, is particularly complex and risky. While this helps the target reader understand the cultural significance of the original, it can compromise the readability and literary quality of the translated text. To the translator's credit, she has taken precautions to avoid or reduce the possibility of paratextual interference by including essential information about the historical background and cultural specificities in the prologue and three appendices. Also supplied is a glossary that serves as an aid to comprehension as the reader navigates the maze of culturally alien reading.

In the case of translating *Legends of the Condor Heroes I: A Hero Born*, Holmwood has displayed ingenuity in coping with cross-cultural untranslatability, demonstrating that the fragility of translatability is underscored when responding to the absence of intertextuality. In this instance, "paratextual devices" are required for "restoring the foreign cultural context and in articulating the cultural significance of an intertextual relation as well as its linguistic basis" (Venuti, 2009,

p. 159). As noted previously, despite Venuti's apprehension that the translation would become a "commentary," which is far from the truth, the intertextual information is provided separately from the translated text itself. The claim that there is a better solution than deleting from the translated text the parts or elements that overwhelm the target reader makes no sense. The result is that the irreducibility of the original is destroyed, and the problem of untranslatability remains. This is precisely what Apter finds unsettling from her perspective. World literature cannot possibly be based on severely abridged, mutilated, or disfigured translations.

The fear of inaccuracy and inadequacy is compounded by the consideration of readability in terms of retaining the aesthetic appeal of the original. The fact that translation is susceptible to a plethora of constraints makes the task of translating Chinese martial arts fiction particularly difficult. Reshaping lexical items is required, and since lexical items represent linguistic and cultural features, any deviation from them in translation is not bereft of risk. However, any attempt to strive for an exact match between the lexical items of the source language and those of the target language can only make translation impossible. In short, literal translation kills literary translation. But a moderate amount of literalness such as "the 18 palm attacks to defeat dragons," which is a literal translation of a kung fu move, can be relished by the target reader in Holmwood's view. This is "derived from a Taoist classic ascribed to Lao Tzu, dating from 2,500 years ago, and containing a strong philosophical element in addition to movement" (Quoted by Thorpe, 2017). The richness of cultural meaning is not exactly irreducible in this context. Her strategy is that "I don't explain everything, although I have written a very short prologue to introduce some of the elements of the story" (Thorpe, 2017). Unlike academic translation, the target reader does not have to grasp every detail. According to Nick Frisch, who reviewed Holmwood's translation favorably in *The New Yorker*, the translator takes into account the priority of narrative energy, which must not be obscured by "the novel's thicket of historical names, florid kung-fu moves, and branching narratives" (Frisch, 2018).

For literary translation, it is undoubtedly essential to reproduce the representative and significant lexical and syntactic features of the original, but some form of intervention is also required to maintain a congruent and reconciling balance. Frisch approvingly comments on Holmwood's approach to some of the most prevalent translation challenges that emerge when translating martial arts fiction, such as the following:

> Proper names, which read smoothly in snappy Chinese syllables but become cumbersome in English, must sometimes be diluted, sacrificing strict fidelity to keep the text breathing. (Without these adjustments, a kung-fu maneuver like *luo ying shen jian zhang*, a fleeting five syllables in Chinese, becomes the clunkier "Wilting Blossom Sacred Sword Fist.")
>
> (Frisch, 2018)

It is undeniable that "strict fidelity," which is not to be confused with thoughtful foreignization, rarely works in literary translation. The presence of a high density of linguistic and cultural references and allusions can stifle translation. Adaptive adjustments and modifications to what is perceived as obstructive in translation are aimed toward acceptability that results from negotiation and mediation so that Jin Yong's literary heritage can be recovered after translation.

The swashbuckling translation of this novel is epitomized by the fact that it has been hailed a Chinese *Lord of the Rings* (Steger & Huang, 2017). It succeeds in resonating with an English-speaking audience, and the translator "has made the impossible possible" (Mei, 2018, p. 22). Thanks to her deft maneuvering in different linguistic and cultural contexts, the original richness and appeal to the target readership remain functionally intact. However, the three earlier translations of Jin Yong's novels were not well received and sold only mediocrely in the market. They are *Fox Volant of the Snowy Mountain* in Olivia Mok's translation, first published in 1993 (the second edition appeared in 1996, followed by another printing in 2004). John Minford translated and published the three-volume novel *The Deer and the Cauldron* in 2002, and *The Book and the Sword*, translated by Graham Earnshaw, came out in 2004. Among other complicating factors, which include the quality of translation, the condition of reception is undoubtedly crucial. The internationally successful film *Crouching Tiger, Hidden Dragon* directed by Ang Lee was released in 2000, and made Chinese *kung fu* attractive to an international audience, as did the film *Red Sorghum*, which cleared the path for Mo Yan's novels in English translation. Along with cultural exchange between China and other parts of the world increases, cultural untranslatability decreases, and the translator is hampered by fewer constraints. Cross-cultural incommensurability, then, is a dynamic rather than static characterization of the act of translation, both constrained and liberated by larger cultural contexts. Despite the long-term specter of untranslatability, there is less reason to be pessimistic about creating global cultural products that indicate a tendency toward less alienation and better integration of the foreign. It is a matter of balancing protean variables in the process of translation so that translation can function properly in the target system.

6. Cross-cultural Experience

Strongly aligned to this is the problem of reading literary translations, which is experienced in the context of cross-cultural communication and dialogue. The interplay between the translated text and the experience of reading it necessitates an attempt to decipher how literary translations work. A variety of factors can influence the reading experience of literary texts in translation. In general, translations that are tailored to the target culture are more likely to be received positively without disregarding adequacy. But even if linguistic awkwardness is reified in foreignization, the longing for the experience of foreign otherness is one of the main reasons to read translations. Thus, when a rich intertextual web of literary references and associations is rendered, the degree of foreignization increases accordingly, affecting the reading experience, for it is not always the best strategy to facilitate the reading experience by resorting to domestication that amounts to abundant tampering with the original text. The translator's decision to reinterpret or faithfully reproduce the source text functions at various levels of the reading experience. In a transcultural context, different kinds of difference and different levels of difference between the source and target texts are registered. Furthermore, varied forms of readerly engagement generate different reading experiences. The translation of literary texts is underpinned by a poetic strategy that may encompass the conscious manipulation of a wide range of literary devices contained in the source text. The effectiveness of literary translation abides in whether and how well the corresponding literary attributes are reproduced in the target text.

As is well-known, translation is subject to social, historical, cultural, political, and ideological conditions and constraints: not only in the selection of texts for translation, but also in the way these texts are or can be translated into English. In translating Chinese literature into English, one of the most difficult tasks is to reconcile the different cultural and literary traditions and values inherent in the two languages. Sometimes cultural and literary meaning can be made directly or immediately accessible to the target reader, while at other times it is made indirectly or not so immediately accessible to them. Literary features can be striking and evocative and as such form an essential part of the reading experience, which is also the reason for recovering or reproducing them in translation. In many instances, however, literary features are barely transferrable, especially with regard to textual minutiae. The translator must work with partial or limited transferability. Cross-cultural untranslatability can lead to awkward translations that undermine the aesthetic appeal of the original and detract from the reading experience. For example, Qian Zhongshu's *Fortress Besieged*, hailed by many as a modern Chinese classic and translated into English by Jeanne Kelly and Nathan K. Mao, is an "uninspired translation" because it "hardly reproduces the dazzling, spiked wit for which the original is renowned" (Lovell, 2005). Although it is largely competently translated and retains much basic information, it suffers from "aesthetic poverty" (Lovell, 2005). As a result, it gives the Anglophone reader the impression of low literary value. A salient weakness resides in the "literally translated Chinese proverbs with explanatory footnotes bolted on" (Lovell, 2005). This is a poignant illustration of how a faithful or accurate translation may, ironically, gravely damage the source text.

At the other extreme is the radical adaptive translation that wants to please the target reader all too much. *Luotuo xiangzi* (Rickshaw Boy) by Lao She, also known as Lau Shaw, was first translated into English by Evan King. The publication of the translation in 1945 by Reynal & Hitchcock in New York was a phenomenal success. But the translation retold the story in a very different way. Jean M. James brought out another translation version in 1979, prompted largely by her dissatisfaction with King's lack of fidelity. In "A Note on the Text and the Translation," she protests,

> Those who have read Evan King's translation published in 1945 as *Rickshaw Boy* will wonder if *Rickshaw* is the same novel. It is. King cut, rearranged, rewrote, invented characters, and changed the ending. The girl student and

One Pock Li are King's, not Lao She's. King also added considerable embellishment to the two seduction scenes.

(James, 1979, p. vi)

In contrast to the earlier translation, James claims that her translation version "omits nothing and alters nothing." But she hastens to add that she has made "some small additions" to "clarify terms and allusions that the non-Chinese reader will not understand" (James, 1979, p. vi). Nevertheless, her additions are clearly within the reasonable parameters of a faithful translation, while King has added characters and details that cannot be traced back to the source text. The juxtaposition of the source and target texts reveals that in some places they are not even two parallel texts. King's rewriting and manipulation of the original text have far exceeded the basic boundaries of translation and were not authorized by the author, clearly violating the ethics of translation.

But James's translation is not an exemplar for it does not do aesthetic justice to the source text. Despite repeated efforts in modern times to free translation from the vexatious restrictions imposed by traditional notions of fidelity and equivalence, these remain powerful constraining forces responsible for maintaining the identity of translation. This explains why untranslatability poses such a threat to literary translation and the formation of world literature. As the previous two translation versions of *Rickshaw Boy* demonstrate, fidelity and equivalence are better viewed from a dynamic perspective. Clive Scott maintains: "Fidelity and equivalence are not, of course, simple terms, and have become increasingly relativised" (Scott, 2012, p. 13). One of the ramifications of the latter is Eugene Nida's dynamic equivalence. When a text is translated with a dynamic vigor similar to that of the original, a wooden effect can be avoided to breathe life and multidimensional character into the translated text. The Chinese notion of "shensi" (spiritual resemblance), which is similar to but different from dynamic equivalence, goes beyond "xingsi" (formal resemblance). Because of the indefinable nature of spirit, it has never really caught on. However, because of its proclivity for aesthetic interpretation and function, it has implications for the reading experience of translation.

Without a question, unrestrained transcreation remains highly controversial. As the term implies, transcreation is more than translation, and a poorly mutilated translation amounts to a form of cultural castration, denying the target reader access to the original. Do authorial creations go hand in hand with translatorial recreations? Yes, but not to the same extent and not in the same way. Transcontextual transferability is challenged by the constraints with regard to translation, which sometimes manifest themselves in the extreme form of untranslatability. Such constraints suggest the need for transcreation. To be clear, engaging creatively with literary texts is not the same as transcreation or transediting (especially with regard to journalistic translation in the latter case). The vital linkages between source and target texts must be maintained preferably without noticeable deviation, and textual indebtedness to the source text cannot be denied. Thus, to achieve an optimal balance between deprivation and overburdening, careful reframing and reconfiguration are necessary. To bring out all these attributes is an inevitable part of literary translation. Scott argues that

> translation is a recipe in which the source text is the main ingredient, the meat. Other ingredients, the translator's way of reading and hearing the source text, are designed to infuse the meat with particular flavours and provide accompanying sauces.
>
> (Scott, 2012, p. 156)

However, this is only partially true. Translation is not just the meat; it comes with its own other ingredients and sauces, but these sometimes need to be substituted with local ones. Still, the metaphor is interesting. It often turns out that the other original ingredients and sauces are not reusable in translation.

Empirically, the translated text may be aesthetically worse or better than its original, and there may be aesthetic objections to a certain way of approaching a translation task. Without a doubt, certain arbitrary assumptions can be identified in different linguistic and cultural contexts, owing mostly to different artistic traditions. Translation entails shifted perspectives and changed contexts. Two parallel, though admittedly distinct, reading experiences may be seen, with one being more compelling or captivating than the other at different points in the reading experience. This is a fascinating phenomenon, but also a potentially frustrating endeavor for the literary translator. According to Chloë Starr, "to read *The Story of the Stone* in English was an entirely different experience to reading *Hongloumeng* in Chinese, and that to read the two texts in parallel creates a third, different reading experience" (Starr, 2012, p. 116). Parallel to these two reading experiences, one can add that reading *The Dream of the Red Chamber* in English, another translated version, would create yet another reading experience that is different from the previous two. Different translators present or represent the author in different ways. Translation creates or opens new spaces for imagination and interpretation, that is, a different reading experience. To reproduce the same reading experience by the source text reader is conceivable but by no means feasible. For a bilingual reader like Starr, reading *Hongloumeng* in the original and its English translation *The Story of the Stone* are two different experiences. Naturally, reading different translated versions yields different experiences. Having an aesthetic experience is related to the poetic value that such an experience is meant to convey. In a cross-cultural context, poetic value is perceived differently in many cases, which makes the whole discussion of aesthetic experience confusing and insufficiently grounded. Nevertheless, it is still possible to develop some form of dialogic communication, arising out of the dynamic interaction between adequacy and acceptability.

In any event, reading literary translations is an experience of encountering foreign otherness, and an overemphasis on accessibility or readability is not conducive to this goal. Ideally, the reading experience of the target reader should be comparable to that of the source reader. However, enabling the transfer of experience and making that experience shareable speak to the quest for a universal commonality that ultimately accedes to world literature. In terms of reading experience, readability is often underscored, suggesting a sense of enjoyment with an eye toward the components of experiential pleasure. In his rebuttal to Scuton's definition of aesthetic experience as enjoyment, Robert Stecker contends that "it is not clear that enjoyment is always required for positive aesthetic experience. We may value the experience offered by shocking or grotesque works of art without necessarily enjoying it" (Stecker, 2006, p. 2). This can be further complicated by how enjoyment is defined. Is it possible that such an experience is desired and appreciated but not experienced outwardly? In this regard, enjoyment is an intricate matter, which is perhaps not always substitutable with pleasure. Even if the text is shocking or grotesque, it can still yield implicit pleasure, though not explicit enjoyment. It is possible that many a sensual pleasure can be given up in order to experience a higher realm of enjoyment. Additionally, pleasure can be multilayered and operate on multiple levels. Despite all this, reading is a personal and indescribable experience marked by mixed emotions. There are also grounds for saying that cultural traditions may shape perceptions of aesthetic pleasure.

Conclusion

While there is a gradual but sure process of internationalization of Chinese literature with a growing number of Chinese literary texts being translated into English, it must be recognized that some basic theoretical and practical issues need to be further explored. A hodgepodge of references, including recondite allusions, does not allow for a simplistic or reductionist treatment in translation. The problem of untranslatability, whether linguistic or cultural, has been chronically scrutinized in view of a lack of cross-cultural knowledge and an intertextual perspective. This is precisely why doubts are raised about the validity of world literature. The popular assumption of transferability is potentially misleading and must be reconsidered with caution since it deductively implies the absence of appropriation, mediation, and negotiation, which refutes the core of translation as an act of rewriting and manipulation. That is to say, rewriting cannot be avoided, but retelling can, and the latter, which falls under the category of transcreation, can impair the identity of translation. Moreover, concern for accuracy may lead to linguistic equivalence taking precedence over aesthetic equivalence, while concern for reception may lead to the opposite. But overall, it is objectionable to allow linguistic equivalence to prevail over aesthetic equivalence in literary translation. Translation is essentially about dependence and derivation and also about proximation and improvisation. The interplay of literal and metaphorical meanings gives rise to both tensions and dynamics. Situated at the intersection between the representation of cultural information in the source text and its effective rendering in the target text, the task of literary translation is to reconcile the incongruence between Chinese and English cultural traditions and literary practices in the context of introducing Chinese literature to a global readership.

This is a reason for sophisticated and resourceful translation to competently deal with untranslatability of various types and degrees and to achieve cross-cultural resonance with the target reader. It must be said that there is no overarching framework for understanding translational poetics that can triumphantly overcome literary untranslatability. Given the dearth of discussions on transcultural poetics in the Chinese context, there is a compelling and urgent need to address the issues involved and their implications. By drawing on and analyzing the successful practices of literary translators such as Goldblatt and Holmwood, their exemplary virtuosity in solving myriad challenging translation problems can be demonstrated to shed light on how literary untranslatability can be circumvented, if not overcome altogether. Their demonstrable strength influenced the canonization of Chinese works as part of world literature. Moreover, the poetic competence and creative imagination expressed in their translated texts serve as an indexical reference to translational poetics. This also convincingly shows that the search for ingenious ways to deal with literary untranslatability through resourceful mediation and negotiation is not devoid of empirical proof. The cultural labyrinth of the translator's imagination is in many respects tantamount to that of the original author in the process of recontextualizing and reproducing poetically viable translation. Literary rewriting is a byzantine undertaking governed or determined by umpteen intricate factors. The translator is challenged to be linguistically and cross-culturally adventurous and innovative, without needlessly losing the richness and nuance of the original, in order to realign the target reader's reading experience and reshape their perspective and mode of thought, even if perhaps only fleetingly. Caught between creativity and constraints, literary translation is fraught with tensions and compromises. A heightened awareness of creativity enforced by constraints and occurring within constraints reveals the nature of literary translation.

Notes

1 https://lareviewofbooks.org/article/translating-mo-yan-an-interview-with-howard-goldblatt/
2 Ibid.
3 Ibid.

References

Albaladejo, T., & Chico-Rico, F. (2018). Translation, style and poetics. In S. Harding & O. C. Cortés (Eds.), *The Routledge handbook of translation and culture* (pp. 115–133). London and New York: Routledge.
Apter, E. (2001). On translation in a global market. *Public Culture, 13*(1), 1–12.
Apter, E. (2013). *Against world literature: On the politics of untranslatability*. London and New York: Verso.
Arrojo, R. (2018). *Fictional translators: Rethinking translation through literature*. London and New York: Routledge.
Bassnett, S. (2019). Introduction: The rocky relationship between translation studies and world literature. In S. Bassnett (Ed.), *Translation and world literature* (pp. 1–14). London: Routledge.
Braester, Y. (2016). Mo Yan. In K. A. Denton (Ed.), *The Columbia companion to modern Chinese literature* (pp. 307–312). New York: Columbia University Press.

Damrosch, D. (2003). World literature, national contexts. *Modern Philology*, *100*(4), 512–531.

De Barcos, M. (1956). *Correspondance de Martin de Barcos* (Ed. L. Goldmann). Paris: PUF. Quoted and Trans. by Elisabeth M. Loevlie (2009). God's invisible traces: The sacred in fallen language. *Literature and Theology*, *23*(4), 442–458.

Dybiec-Gajer, J., & Oittinen, R. (2020). Introduction: Travelling beyond translation – Transcreating for young audiences. In J. Dybiec-Gajer, R. Oittinen, & M. Kodura (Eds.), *Negotiating translation and transcreation of children's literature: From Alice to the Moomins* (pp. 1–9). Singapore: Springer.

Folkart, B. (2007). *Second finding: A poetics of translation*. Ottawa: The University of Ottawa Press.

Frisch, N. (2018, April 13). The gripping stories, and political allegories, of China's best-selling author. *The New Yorker*. www.newyorker.com/books/page-turner/the-gripping-stories-and-political-allegories-of-chinas-best-selling-author

Goldblatt, H. (2009). Mo Yan's novels are wearing me out: Nominating statement for the 2009 Newman Prize. *World Literature Today*, *83*(4), 28–29.

Goldblatt, H. (2012). *Big breasts and wide hips*. London: Methuen Publishing.

Goldblatt, H. (2014). A mutually rewarding yet uneasy and sometimes fragile relationship between author and translator. In A. Duran & Y. Huang (Eds.), *Mo Yan in context: Nobel Laureate and global storyteller* (pp. 23–36). West Lafayette: Purdue University Press.

Hsieh, W. T. (1938). English translation of Chinese poetry. *Criterion*, *17*(68), 403–424.

Jakobson, R. (1990). The speech event and the functions of language. In L. R. Waugh & M. Monville-Burston (Eds.), *On language* (pp. 69–79). Cambridge, MA: Harvard University Press. (Original work published 1960)

James, J. M. (Trans.). (1979). Note on the text and the translation. In L. She (Ed.), *Rickshaw: The novel of Lo-t'o Hsiang Tzu*. Honolulu, HI: University of Hawaii Press.

Kenner, H. (1971). *The pound era*. Berkeley, CA: University of California Press.

Lee, L. O. (1985). Contemporary Chinese literature in translation – A review article. *The Journal of Asian Studies*, *44*(3), 561–567.

Lefevere, A. (1985). Why waste our time on rewrites? The trouble with interpretation and the role of rewriting in an alternative paradigm. In T. Hermans (Ed.), *The manipulation of literature: Studies in literary translation* (pp. 215–243). New York: St. Martin's Press.

Lefevere, A. (1992). *Translation, rewriting, and the manipulation of literary fame*. London: Routledge.

Levinson, J. (1996). *The Pleasures of Aesthetics*. New York: Cornell University Press.

Liu, Y., & Xu, J. 刘云虹、许钧. (2014). The modes of literary translation and the translation of Chinese literature into foreign languages – On Howard Goldblatt's translation 文学翻译模式与中国文学对外译介 – – 关于葛浩文的翻译. *Journal of Foreign Languages* 外国语, *37*(3), 6–17.

Lovell, J. (2005, June 11). Great leap forward. *Guardian*. www.theguardian.com/books/2005/jun/11/featuresreviews.guardianreview29

Mei, J. (2018, June 22). Triumph of translation. *China Daily*. http://europe.chinadaily.com.cn/epaper/2018-06/22/content_36432649.htm

Miall, D. S., & Kuiken, D. (1999). What is literariness? Three components of literary reading. *Discourse Processes*, *28*(2), 113–121.

Mo, Y. (2000). My 3 American books. *World Literature Today*, *74*(3), 473–476.

Mo, Y. (2012). *Big breasts and wide hips* 丰乳肥臀. Shanghai: Shanghai Literature and Art Publishing Group 上海：上海文艺出版社.

Oittinen, R. (2020). From translation to transcreation to translation: Excerpts from a translator's and illustrator's notebooks. In J. Dybiec-Gajer, R. Oittinen, & M. Kodura (Eds.),

Negotiating translation and transcreation of children's literature: From Alice to the Moomins (pp. 13–37). Singapore: Springer.

Pan, D. (2000). De-otherizing the textual other: Intertextual semiotics and the translation of Chinese poetry. *Comparative Literature: East & West, 2*(1), 57–77.

Pym, A. (2011). The translator as non-author, and I am sorry about that. In C. Buffagni, B. Garzelli, & S. Zanotti (Eds.), *The translator as author. Perspectives on literary translation* (pp. 31–43). Berlin: LIT Verlag.

Refsum, C. (2019). When poets translate poetry. Authorship, ownership, and translatorship. In C. A. Annjo, K. Greenall, H. Jansen, & K. Taivalkoski-Shilov (Eds.), *Textual and contextual voices of translation* (pp. 101–117). Amsterdam: John Benjamins.

Robinson, D. (2017). What kind of literature is a literary translation? *Target, 29*(3), 440–463.

Scott, C. (2012). *Literary translation and the rediscovery of reading*. Cambridge: CUP.

Stalling, J. (2014). The voice of the translator: An interview with Howard Goldblatt. *Translation Review, 88*(1), 1–12.

Stalling, J., & Schleifer, R. (2021). Unpacking the Mo Yan archive: Actor-network translation studies and the Chinese literature translation archive. In L. Gerber & L. Qi (Eds.), *A century of Chinese literature in translation (1919–2019)* (pp. 20–38). London and New York: Routledge.

Starr, C. (2012). Mind the gap: The Hawkes-Minford transition in the story of the stone. In T. Liu, K. P. Wong, & S. Chan (Eds.), *Style, wit and word-play: Essays in translation studies in memory of David Hawkes* (pp. 115–138). Newcastle: Cambridge Scholars.

Stecker, R. (2006). Aesthetic experience and aesthetic value. *Philosophy Compass, 1*(1), 1–10.

Steger, I., & Huang, E. (2017, November 17). The "lord of the rings" of Chinese literature is finally being translated into English. *Quartz*. https://qz.com/quartzy/1125004/jin-yongs-epic-condor-trilogy-the-lord-of-the-rings-of-chinese-literature-is-finally-being-translated-into-english/

Thorpe, V. (2017, November 26). A hero reborn: 'China's Tolkien' aims to conquer western readers. *The Guardian*. www.theguardian.com/books/2017/nov/26/chinese-fantasy-kung-fu-legend-of-the-condor-jin-yong

Venuti, L. (2009). Translation, intertextuality, interpretation. *Romance Studies, 27*(3), 157–173.

Venuti, L. (2012). World literature and translation studies. In T. D'haen, D. Damrosch, & D. Kadir (Eds.), *The Routledge companion to world literature* (pp. 180–193). London and New York: Routledge.

Walton, K. L. (1993). How marvelous! Toward a theory of aesthetic value. *The Journal of Aesthetics and Art Criticism, 51*(3), 499–510.

Zhang, W. 张文娟. (2018). The dilemma and strategies of Chinese literature going out from the perspective of cosmopolitanism 世界主义视域下我国文学走出去的困境与解决策略. *Journal of Inner Mongolia University of Finance and Economics* 内蒙古财经大学学报, *16*(4), 114–117.

Zhao, D. 赵笛. (2013, March 19). German scholar Kubin: The English version of Mo Yan's Novel should be Bylined by two authors 德国学者顾彬：莫言的英文版小说应该有两个作者. *China News* 中新网. www.chinanews.com.cn/cul/2013/03-19/4657239.shtml

2 Chinese Literature in Translation, World Literature as Genre

Todd Foley

The aim of this essay is to demonstrate that world literature is a genre and that certain problems may be solved by clearly recognizing it as one. Efforts to recast world literature as a "mode" have done little to mitigate the conflict between a more common and practical understanding of world literature, which seems to persist in its robust existence as a genre, and the particular anxiety in the realm of Chinese literature, writers and scholars of which continue to yearn for universal recognition while bemoaning the unequal standards of literary valuation. Persistent attempts to cast Chinese literature as world literature[1] belie an enduring and anxious presumption that this sort of visibility through categorization – often arrived at by deploying world literature as a mode – can bestow a certain legitimacy. Furthermore, while these efforts often recognize the situatedness of literary evaluation, be it historical, cultural, political, ideological, etc., they still seem to accept a certain universality presumed to be translatable and accessible in what is ultimately a single register: the amorphous but undying, zombie realm of "world literature."

I would first of all like to be clear that I am suggesting a certain deflation rather than a *devaluing* of world literature, recognizing it as contingent rather than singularly authoritative – to reference Owen's (2014) metaphor, world literature is not so much a food court, offering a generic, over-salted, fast-food version of national cuisines, as it is a selection of dishes from around the world that actually happen to turn out well when reproduced in, for example, a standard American kitchen. As an English cookbook for Continental cuisine notes, "The natural qualities which give [a foreign] dish its flavor are with us partially absent; besides, the air we eat it in, the stove we cook it on, and the pot we cook it in are different" (Gray & Boyd, 1957, p. 1). Maybe some dishes will be exquisite, while others simply won't turn out as well in the absence of certain conditions. It should go without saying that the many "dishes" of Chinese literature don't turn out the same in English, and that even if they did, tongues may be culturally conditioned to perceive them differently. This is a general point that most discussions of world literature in English translation acknowledge; I bring it up here, however, to emphasize that a wide range of outcomes result when Chinese works of a similar caliber (i.e., held in equally high esteem in their original contexts) are translated into English. Some simply work better than others, and this, I think, often has little to do with the translator and everything to do with the nature of the work itself. The greatness of some great Chinese works shines through greatly in English; for others, not so much. This is why world literature can only be conceived of as a genre. Instead of a presumed collection of the "best" literary productions in the world – an infinitely problematic notion that, if we actually thought it were possible, would be inescapably based on a number of cultural chauvinisms – it can only ever consist of whatever happens to work in English.

While this might seem like a rather ham-handed way of putting things, I want to be clear that formulating world literature as a genre is not a dismissal of the presumption of a universal in favor of certain essentialist claims of the particular, nor does it mean to lessen or even necessarily question the perceived literary merit of the works that "make it." Rather than an authoritative arbiter of literary value, it is a category of literature characterized by its translatability, one that is a practical result of mediating between the contradictory and inescapable coexistence of Apter's (2006) first and last theses on translation: that "nothing is translatable" and that "everything is translatable" (pp. xi–xii). It also offers an alternate response to her hypothesis in *Against World Literature* (2013) that "translation and untranslatability are constitutive of world forms of literature" (p. 16). I am not suggesting what I think "should" or "could" be part of this genre, or whether it is even a good or bad thing. Nor am I offering a moral judgment on the extent to which Chinese literature is or isn't, or should or shouldn't, be part of this genre. I am merely proposing a descriptive paradigm for what I've observed to be the dominant state of affairs. In general, I adopt Sontag's (2002) attitude toward translation as an ethical task: "to extend our sympathies; to educate the heart and mind; to create inwardness; to secure and deepen the awareness (with all its consequences) that other people, people different from us, really do exist." More translation is always better. But whether or not a translated work "works" as world literature, understood as a genre, is a different matter.

The most recent evidence of the continued tension between Chinese literature and the conventional notion of world literature (à la Goethe) may be found in the edited volume, *The Making of Chinese-Sinophone Literatures as World Literature* (Chiu & Zhang, 2022). In his review for *Modern Chinese Literature and Culture* (MCLC), Suher (2022) praises the high quality of the volume's insightful contributions while ultimately arriving at the crucial question: "Why do we want to make Chinese-Sinophone literature into world literature, anyway? To be honest, this volume feels a little belated. David Damrosch's *What is World Literature*, cited in nearly every chapter, was published almost twenty years ago in 2003." This observation about the publication date of Damrosch's book raises another important question: Why did that not solve the problem of this continued anxiety of Chinese literature *as* world literature?

Damrosch's landmark publication has offered a helpful and influential response to many of the problems of world literature, reformulating it as a "mode": "My claim," he writes, "is that world literature is not an infinite, ungraspable canon of works but rather a mode of circulation and of reading" (p. 5). More specifically, his conclusion offers a "threefold definition":

1. World literature is an elliptical refraction of national literature.
2. World literature is writing that gains in translation.
3. World literature is not a set canon of texts but a mode of reading: a form of detached engagement with worlds beyond our own place and time.

(p. 281)

As a category, Damrosch describes world literature as "encompass[ing] all literary works that circulate beyond their culture of origin, either in translation or in their original language" (p. 4). This notion is refreshingly expansive and hard to find fault with as it's based on fact rather than a measure of value. Yet it is so broad and ecumenical that it seems to have been not very effective in dislodging the more traditional, operational notion of world literature: the Nobel Prize is still awarded, universities still promote undergraduate survey courses, anthologies are still published, and serious people still take great pains to cast Chinese literature as "world literature."

As a mode, Damrosch's proposal is echoed differently in the realm of Chinese literary studies by Klein (2016), who draws upon Roland Barthes' notion of the "sideways glance" to suggest overcoming the problem of ideological predetermination and situatedness with a "translational reading," which allows one to

> approach a text – both before and after it has been translated – as a kind of translation, through which not only can the reader access its source and target cultures, but through which source and target cultures can access each other, as well.
>
> (p. 191)

This is an intriguing proposal in its own right. But what I would like to point out is that both Klein and Damrosch approach the "world literature" problem (either explicitly or implicitly) by shifting from a noun – the category of "world literature" – to a verb-oriented understanding – a "mode of reading." In the real world, though, and in a practical sense, we still seem to be stuck with a dominant and seemingly intransigent category of literature – "world literature" – that can't be fully grappled with by redefining it as a mode. Even when we attempt to "world literature" Chinese literature, the problems remain, which is why I propose taking world literature as a genre.

In recognizing world literature as a genre, I would like to avoid offering a fixed definition of what "world literature" is (beyond the fact that it is a genre), and the same goes for the term "Chinese." My discussion will retain the frustratingly open ambiguity these categories necessarily involve, meaning different things at different times, according to their operation in various discourses. What is world literature generally presumed to be? Maire and Edward Said, in the introduction to their translation of Auerbach's "Philology and *Weltliteratur*" (they keep the term in its original to maintain focus on "the rather unique traditions behind the German word"), felt the need to state that world literature "is not to be understood as a selective collection of world classics or great books – although Goethe often seemed to be implying this – but rather as a concert among all the literature produced by man about man" (1969, p. 1). Here we can find the same sort of issue Damrosch's work encounters over 30 years later: in the first part of the Saids' statement, we are presented with what is commonly taken as world literature, while simultaneously being implicitly reminded there are obvious problems with such a notion (which is why it must be stated that world literature cannot be what it is commonly taken to be). In the second part of the statement – passing over the fact that Goethe himself seemed to regard world literature so simplistically – we are met with a conception that is both incredibly broad and also more verb-oriented (in the sense of an active "concert"), making it seem less problematic and more palatable through its ostensible departure from a hegemonic and hierarchical sense of literary valuation. Nevertheless, it is similarly based on presumptions of universality (literature "by man about man") and does little to practically dislodge the initial mistaken assumption.

In what follows, I will briefly trace some of the major debates in the field of Chinese literary studies in English in order to show how they all – in one way or another, and right up to the present moment – revolve around the same problem of "world literature." This will unfortunately afford only limited opportunity to engage with the many relevant theoretical discussions of world literature, but since the reasoning behind the recognition of world literature as genre is a practical one, based on the actual state of literature in the world rather than a negotiation of theoretical conceptualizations of world literature, I have chosen to rely on these case studies to illustrate the point. By outlining three of the most famous debates, I hope to demonstrate that while the content and tenor of these discussions has differed, they all in one way or another begin with an authoritative negative assessment of certain works or writers of Chinese literature, and are then met with responses that demonstrate the cultural, political, historical, or ideological presumptions of the original criticisms. In short, they all pivot around the unsolvable problems implicit in the notion of world literature.

*****

In 1961, C. T. Hsia, a professor at Columbia who completed his undergraduate education in China and a PhD in English at Yale, published *A History of Modern Chinese Fiction*. The work offered the first comprehensive treatment in English of an array of modern Chinese writers, complete with biographical information, summaries and descriptions of their works, and Hsia's critical assessments. As insightful, useful, and enduring as his *History* has proven to be, it was clearly written from a certain ideological standpoint, as we might glean from his commentary on Lu Xun, whose "adulation" he dismisses as a "communist enterprise" (1999, p. 28). "[B]ecause his basic ideas are few even if they are often trenchantly applied," Hsia writes, "the overall impression of his fifteen volumes of *tsa-wen* is that of a quarrelsome garrulity. A more fundamental criticism will be that, as a satiric commentator on passing events, Lu Hsün is not free from the sentimental bias of his age" (p. 52). In a nearly 50-page review, Prusek (1962) immediately points out that "the criteria according to which Hsia evaluates and classifies authors, are first and foremost of a political nature and not based on artistic considerations" (p. 358).

From here, Prusek's approach is to show how Hsia has inadequately addressed the historical circumstances in which the literature he evaluates was produced: "Instead of blaming Chinese writers for subordinating their literary work to social needs," writes Prusek, "it would have been more appropriate to show what the necessities were which induced them to take such a course, to give a picture of the historical situation which determined the character of modern Chinese literature" (p. 362). While he points out that no writers had "either the time or the peace of mind to be able 'to engage in disinterested moral exploration,' as recommended by C. T. Hsia" (p. 363), Prusek goes further to render his own value judgment: "we see that the radical Chinese thinkers, such as Ch'ien Hsüan-t'ung, Lu Hsün, Li Ta-Chao and others were entirely in the right" (p. 365). From here, Prusek goes on to offer his own assessments of Lu Xun's work, providing literary analyses that have an almost exact inverse relation to those provided by Hsia.

While Prusek quite clearly demonstrates Hsia's particular political and ideological situatedness – criticisms that seem both warranted and legitimate – he also aspires to refute Hsia's overall assessment with an approach underwritten by the presumption of universal standards of literary evaluation. "A closer look at C. T. Hsia's picture of the development of Chinese literature," he writes, "reveals that the author is not capable of [bringing] the literary phenomena of which he treats... into relation with world literature" (p. 367). Along these lines, Prusek chides Hsia for a "lack of a systematic and scientific approach" (p. 368) and the inability "to approach his work with a proper measure of objectivity" (p. 372).

Hsia seizes on this criticism in his equally long response, "On the 'Scientific' Study of Modern Chinese Literature: A Reply to Professor Prusek" (1963). He begins by announcing that "I am principally moved to protest the advisability of a rigid and indeed dogmatic scientific approach to literary problems" (p. 429). He continues:

> [F]or a pioneer survey of modern Chinese fiction, the primary task is, I repeat, discrimination and evaluation: ... until we have distinguished the possibly great from the good writers, and the good from the poor, we cannot begin the study of influence and technique, however temptingly scientific the latter kinds of study might be.... In dealing with the modern period in China, because so many of the native critics, aside from their dubious training in their craft, were too much involved in the making of this modern literature to be unpartisan, the need to start from scratch appeared especially imperative.
> (p. 430)

In terms of the problems of world literature, the interesting thing about this debate is the assumption by both Hsia and Prusek that the debate can somehow be won on universal grounds, though each adheres to a different universality (which are both part and parcel of modernity): for Prusek, it is the "scientific method" (p. 367); for Hsia, it is the standards of literary evaluation according to the New Criticism. Prusek makes strides in his argument against Hsia by demonstrating the historical conditions that Hsia downplays because of his ideological commitments; it is impossible to have a full appreciation of Lu Xun without giving full attention to the specific historical and social circumstances of his writing and thought, and failing to do so will obviously produce a superficial and lackluster image of the writer. But he also seems to feel there is a universally objective[2] way of "bringing writers into relation with world literature" through a "literary scientific method," which he then attempts to demonstrate through a more rigorously historicized analysis of Lu Xun's work. Hsia, on the other hand, rejects the idea that literature should be subjected to the rigidity of a scientific approach, while paradoxically noting his own objectivity over and above the partisan nature of "native critics," which seems to be invoking scientific authority in a different way. The implication is that "native" producers and critics of their own literature are unable to see it objectively and are therefore unable to assess its presumably universal truth – is it good or bad? In other words, is it good or bad according to Hsia's skilled practice of New Critical formalism?[3] Finally, what reveals that both Prusek and Hsia presume the possibility of a definitively universal assessment of modern Chinese literature is the fact that they engage in a discussion of this literature without ever mentioning the dynamics of translation. They assume the true literary merit of Chinese literature can be arrived at through a discussion in English conducted across the Atlantic. Even if both are analyzing and assessing the original Chinese texts, they are still translating the texts into very different contexts and environments with very different standards of literary evaluation. Aside from their differing political views, they are also examining Chinese literature through the different lenses of Ivy League literary studies and European Sinology.

In the second edition of Hsia's *History*, published in 1971, he included a now infamous appendix called "Obsession with China: The Moral Burden of Modern Chinese Literature," which states that "the price [the Chinese writer] pays for his obsession with China is . . . a certain patriotic provinciality" (1999, p. 536). If only Chinese writers "had the courage or insight," Hsia laments, "to equate the Chinese scene with the condition of modern man, he would have been in the mainstream of modern literature" (p. 536). As I mentioned before, in arguing for world literature as genre, I am not trying to deny or downplay the expression of universal humanity in literature. But Hsia's comments here imply that Chinese literature is kept apart from world literature because of the commonly held presumption that in world literature, expressions of universal humanity are immediately identifiable as universal and not so concerned with the particular that the universal is not readily visible (when read by, for example, a New Critic). Here we see another commonality that the following two debates will share, which is an initial negative assessment based on the failure or unwillingness to seriously engage with the literature on its own terms.

Nearly 30 years after the Hsia and Prusek exchange, Stephen Owen made waves with a complaint that was nearly the opposite of Hsia's "obsession with

China": that Bei Dao, one of the most highly regarded poets in post-Mao China, represents "the strange phenomenon of a poet who became the leading poet in his own country because he translated well" (Owen, 1990, p. 32). In his review of Bonnie McDougall's translation of *The August Sleepwalker*, Owen suggests that Bei Dao's poems have "become publishable only because the publisher and the readership have been assured that the poetry was lost in translation. But what if the poetry wasn't lost in translation? What if this is it? This is it" (p. 31). Huang (2002) plainly observes that "such a shocking statement is of course scandalous," and many other scholars (perhaps most famously Chow (1993)) have effectively addressed the wide array of problematic issues that the review manages to contain, including Owen's seeming desire for a privileged classical poetic form, his presumption and prescription of what "Chinese" poetry should be, and his complete lack of attention to the specific context of Bei Dao's poetry. Klein (2018), however, in what is perhaps the most up-to-date and complete catalogue of the debate, notes that not all responses to Owen's review have been negative, indicating "that the criticisms have not won the debate" (p. 11).

Edmund (2012) devotes a chapter of his book *A Common Strangeness* to examining the issues at play in this debate, and his thoughtful and nuanced treatment leaves little to add. Foregrounding the strangely paradoxical nature of Owen's criticism, Edmund notes that "a poem describing the isolation and erasure of tradition in the Cultural Revolution comes to be read as an allegory of an international literature without connection to a place, time, people, or language." He then makes the crucial point that

> instead of fixing literature and history within a single story – a single world or world literature – or set of binaries (local/global or individual/collective), Bei Dao's use of allegory emphasizes the historical flux and contested readings that gave birth to our current era.
>
> (p. 96)

This is the element of Edmund's analysis that has the most bearing on my argument for world literature as genre: while the initial criticism of the literary work, and much of the response to this criticism, attempts to "fix literature and history within a single story," that is, "world literature," the work itself shows that this is not possible.[4] "In abjuring any single context or box," Edmund writes, "Bei Dao's poetry emphasizes the impossibility of a single national or world literature and produces an allegory of that impossibility" (p. 101). Edmund then embarks on a compelling analysis of Bei Dao's poetry in the original Chinese, while also situating it in the very specific historical contexts of its production, publication, and reception. He also reveals the situatedness and differing motivations behind the poetry's translation and its English reception:

> In the Cold War context, McDougall emphasized the translatability and universal images of Bei Dao's poetry. By appealing to the notion of a world

literature based on universal literary values, she sought greater scholarly recognition for contemporary Chinese literature in the West. . . . In the post-Cold War world, Owen connected translatability to globalization and [Fukuyama's] end of history. In this new era of globalization, Owen read Bei Dao's work not as national but as global allegory, marking the shift to a postnational condition that he wished to suggest.

(p. 113)

This discussion is helpful and revealing, but at the end of the day, we are left with the same question Owen posed at the very beginning: "What is world poetry?" Edmund traces how "national and world literature are mutually constituted and contested by acts of translation," and that "these acts relate language to the world, but reach no dialectical resolution in the end of history, nor in a truly global literature" (p. 124). This is absolutely the case. His illuminating interpretations necessarily require recourse to the original language and historical context. But then what, to repose the annoying question buzzing around like a mosquito, is world poetry? I suppose Stephen Owen actually ends up giving the best answer here: poetry that is taken at face value in translation, which can provide enough material for artistic and poetic contemplation that someone like Owen will not label it "embarrassing" and akin to something he wrote at age 13 (p. 30). Why Owen is so ignorant (or at least pretends to be) of the specific context and situatedness of Bei Dao's poetry is hard to say, and his insistence that the original is so generic and vapid that nothing has been lost in translation is baffling, to say the least. Yet it forces us to face an unsettling, practical point: basically, that what you see is what you get. Jacob Edmund is not going to meticulously annotate for us every Bei Dao poem translated into English, and the necessity for an extensive exegetical supplement doesn't exactly aid in a work's self-evident greatness or its recognition and currency in translation (especially as explanatory notes are often strongly discouraged by publishers of translations).[5]

When Damrosch weighs in on the episode, he states that

> our reading of Bei Dao, or Dante, will benefit from a leavening of local knowledge, an amount that may vary from work to work and from reader to reader but that will remain less than is needed for a full contextual understanding of a work within its home tradition.
>
> (p. 22)

While this is certainly true, his following examination of two translations of an excerpt from Bei Dao's "The Answer" (回答) seems to demonstrate the rather hopeless situation Bei Dao faces in this regard. To be sure, Damrosch is not attempting to demonstrate the "worth" or "literary merit" of Bei Dao's poetry here. Yet nothing about his comparative analysis of the translations, which focuses on English word choices that he finds to be either "stilted and unpoetic," or which "assort well with the debt to American modernism," suggests an enhanced appreciation through a "leavening of local knowledge." He writes that his brief look at Bei Dao can suggest ... [that] works of world literature take on a new life as they move into the world at large, and to understand this new life we need to look closely at the ways the work becomes reframed in its translations and its new cultural contexts.

(p. 24)

While there is, once again, little to find fault with in this statement, the "new life" in English that Damrosch has demonstrated for Bei Dao's poetry actually comes off as quite limited to a superficial aesthetic reception entirely in the context of the target language – does it sound clunky, or recall Eliot's "Waste Land"? Without much "leavening of local knowledge" – that is, without mentioning some very basic contextual information that makes Bei Dao's poetry meaningful in its original context, such as Mao's 1942 talks at Yan'an, the Cultural Revolution, the humanism debates of the immediate post-Mao years, etc. – it may admittedly seem difficult to see Bei Dao's poetry as anything better than Owen's pubescent jottings. So it turns out that Owen seems implicitly vindicated, at least partially – not in his inaccurate supposition that Bei Dao became the leading poet in China because he translated well, but, to quote Jones (1994), "in the way . . . he situates 'world poetry' within the larger problem of Western cultural hegemony" (p. 176). By assessing Bei Dao's poetry with only the most superficial engagement, both Owen and Damrosch performatively demonstrate the realpolitik of world literature – if some kind of significance (if not *the* significance) is not immediately visible when the work is out of context and in translation, then too bad.

The drawn-out nature of the Bei Dao affair should leave little room for surprise that the issues at the heart of the debate are also present in the more recent Nobel prize controversies. Here I will focus on Mo Yan's win in 2012, as the controversy surrounding Gao Xingjian's win was largely centered in the Chinese-speaking world and is thus not the most immediately relevant to my situated (but extendable) discussion of world literature in English. Before turning to the controversy surrounding Mo Yan's win, however, it is worth noting the particularly revealing role the Nobel Prize plays in the issues at hand. In her book examining Gao Xingjian's win and the entire "Nobel complex" in China, Lovell (2006) effectively "demonstrate[s] the fallacy" of "a faith in a universal standard of evaluation in world literature" (p. 30), noting, among many other conflicting dynamics, "the two-tier system of criteria used by the Nobel Committee," by which "writers in the Western tradition are judged on their intrinsic artistic qualities, while non-Western writers are commended as representatives of their respective nation-states" (p. 39). Of course, as a crystallization of the amorphous ideal of world literature, the Nobel Prize shows just how impossible the ideal is to realize: its judgments will always be culturally and historically situated, and have the effect of centering an authoritative standard of literary evaluation (often facilitated through the mediation of translation). Like translators, the Nobel Committee (sex scandals aside) is doomed to perpetual criticism. The Committee's choice of Mo Yan seemed to in some ways challenge its limits, and the effect of selecting a writer whose life and works did not perfectly align with Western political and literary values unsurprisingly caused some discontent.

Two of Mo Yan's major detractors, Link (2012a, 2012b) and Sun (2012), bemoaned his Nobel win with a number of criticisms: he's a member of the government-supported Writers Association and thereby supported by a repressive authoritarian regime; he hasn't adequately condemned censorship or championed freedom and democracy; his works dismiss historical trauma through "daft hilarity"; his writing lacks "aesthetic conviction," is detached from the classical tradition, and written in a "diseased" language. The obvious problems with these criticisms have been effectively addressed by Laughlin (2012) and Klein (2016), and I will not catalogue them all here but will address certain aspects that I think have the most bearing on my discussion.

In a follow-up to his initial criticism, in an essay titled "Politics and the Chinese Language: What Mo Yan's Defenders Get Wrong," Link (2012b) doubles down and paradoxically levels the charge of "West-centrism" at Mo Yan's "defenders," seemingly based on his irritation with Mishra's (2012) essay in *The Guardian* that suggests Link and other Mo Yan critics "pause" to reflect on

> an unexamined assumption lurking in the Western scorn for Mo Yan's proximity to the Chinese regime: that Anglo-American writers, naturally possessed of loftier virtue, stand along with their governments on the right side of history.

For Link, this amounts to a moral infraction, which he illustrates by imagining the following example:

> How do you think a Chinese liberal, sitting on a bench in a drab prison, would feel to hear an American liberal, sitting on a couch with the *Guardian*, say "you and I both live under oppressive governments, my friend; I must pause before criticizing yours"?

The first observation we might make here is that Link has boiled down the debate to be *only* a matter of politics and ideology. In order for this scenario to make a relevant point, the person on the couch would probably have to say something like, "I must pause before uncritically adopting my own government's ideals to evaluate your literature and your literature's relationship to your government's hypocrisy." This sounds more reasonable, albeit more awkwardly phrased.

But Link's charge of "West-centrism" is especially strange because it is hard to imagine a more "West-centric" evaluation of Mo Yan than Link's. One of Link's major grumbles is what he calls Mo Yan's "daft hilarity," which he claims makes "no mention of starvation that cost 30 million or more lives." On a basic level, this complaint seems to willfully ignore the extensive description of starvation in *Big Breasts and Wide Hips* (one of the many books his initial essay was supposedly meant to review). For example, in Howard Goldblatt's translation (Mo, 2011), the sixth section of Chapter 6 begins as follows:

> In the spring of 1960, when the countryside was littered with the corpses of famine victims, members of the Flood Dragon River Farm rightist unit were transformed into a herd of ruminants, scouring the earth to quell their hunger.

Aside from Link's charge being untrue, his notion of "daft hilarity" is an entirely political judgment based on how he feels Mo Yan should narrate history (he applies it to some of Yu Hua's works as well). This is likely why the term, thankfully, has not gained any traction in the study of Chinese literature. But more significantly, we might turn to Link's deep dissatisfaction with Mo Yan's language. He begins his essay by quoting Sun's assessment of Mo Yan's language:

> Sun finds Mo Yan's language, on virtually "any page," to be "a jumble of words that juxtaposes rural vernacular, clichéd socialist rhetoric, and literary affectation." Sun attributes much of the problem to Mo Yan's schooling in Communist jargon and in *Mao-ti* (Maoist literary form), which Laughlin also refers to, calling it MaoSpeak. . . . I agree with Sun.[6]

Again, obviously, the problem is political. Link mentions Mo Yan's *Sandalwood Death*, which I will turn again to shortly, to note that it is

> set during the Boxer Rebellion of 1900, well before the advent of socialist jargon, and yet the characters in the story spout socialist jargon. A young woman refers to her *lingdaozhe*, or "leader" – a word no one used in 1900. Is this satire? Of what? I think it is more likely that Mo Yan was writing too quickly.

As in the previous debates, the problem, once again, is refusing to take the literature seriously on its own terms, while simultaneously assuming the vantagepoint of universal assessment (in this case, a particularly righteous one). Part of Rey Chow's critique of Stephen Owen comes to mind here, as one of Link's problems seems to be the existence of the "living members" (Chow, 1993, p. 4) of the PRC, who have grown up and lived with the influence of "MaoSpeak" on everyday language. Should they not use or address this in their literature? But the real question here is, why must Mo Yan adhere to certain standards of historical realism, especially when one of his signature literary characteristics, at least according to most critics in China, is that he "exceeds realism" (超越现实主义)? Is it permissible for an author to create a historical narrative in a blatantly anachronistic language? Is it permissible for an author to have a complicated, not entirely denunciatory attitude toward communism? Western defenders of freedom would, of course, permit it but not prefer it, given their own commitment to certain moral, political, and ideological standards. At any rate, it would at the very least be irresponsible for a literary scholar to so easily dismiss the unique and remarkable hodgepodge of language in which Mo Yan writes. In his discussion of *Republic of Wine*, Zhang (2008) explains how Mo Yan's language invites the examination of

> the interconnection between the linguistic level and the semantic level; between verbal constructions and social experiences; between discursive sedimentations and the multiplicity of historical memories – all of which correspond to the interconnection between the allegory of the breaking of the Subject and the breakdown of its sociomoral as well as cultural-intellectual form.
>
> (p. 248)

It would seem, then, that other narrative possibilities exist outside the spectrum of realism or satire.

To connect this debate to the previous two, Mo Yan's critics, like C. T. Hsia, assess Chinese literature from a clear political and ideological standpoint. Opposite to Hsia, however, Link sees the social impact of literature as a major ethical concern ("My own worry is about the actual readers [in China]. How does 'daft hilarity' affect them?"), demonstrating the different standards of literary evaluation even among professors of Chinese literature at prestigious American universities, separated by a few decades. Both Link and Sun refer to Mo Yan's use of the Chinese language to then comment on the value of Mo Yan's work in general, presuming, as with the other two debates, the possibility of a definitively universal assessment of modern Chinese literature – in other words, the author's work in Chinese is seemingly coterminous with its English translation in terms of its literary merit. Furthermore, Link and Sun assume a standpoint that is very similar to Hsia's authoritative claim of objectivity, purporting to see the dangers of Mao-Speak more clearly from positions at American universities than Chinese writers and readers themselves and, in Sun's case, taking a longer (and very selective) view[7] of the history of Chinese literature to demonstrate what a sorry outlier Mo Yan is.

But does Mo Yan write world literature? If we view world literature as a genre, the answer is probably not. This is where the Mo Yan controversy meets the Bei Dao debate. Sun makes the interesting observation that most contemporary Chinese literature "is not widely known in the West."

> It is worth noting that many superb Chinese writers' work does not read well in translation. . . . Take the example of Eileen Chang. . . . [N]o matter how good the translator might be, since much of Chang's power resides in her subtle and masterly use of the Chinese language, it is very difficult to convey it through translation. Indeed, the most popular work by Chinese writers in English translation today is often the kind of work that has broad strokes, vivid characters, and dramatic plots, such as Mo Yan's novels.

Sun even goes on to bring up Stephen Owen's suggestions that works with certain clear political messages are more readily accepted in the West and that some modern Chinese poetry is written in an easily translatable language without achieving mastery in Chinese.

The important suggestion here is that the Chinese works that end up "making it" in English translation are not necessarily "the best" works. Sun's example of Eileen Chang might be debatable, as many English translations of Chang's works have been issued by prestigious publishers like Penguin and the New York Review Books Classics series, but the general point about the problems Chinese literature faces in English translation is real. Sun is so desperate to assure the English-language reading public that Mo Yan's prose is terrible that she goes so far as to suggest that "the English translations of Mo Yan's novels, especially by the excellent Howard Goldblatt, are in fact superior to the original in their aesthetic unity and sureness." She supports this with a blurb from the *Washington Post* on the back cover of *The Republic of Wine* that praises Goldblatt's translation for relaying Mo Yan's "shimmering poetry." She says that Goldblatt is the one responsible for the poetry.

Goldblatt's "Translator's Note" before the novel, however, shows that the "aesthetic unity" Sun feels he achieves is most likely a result of the impossibility of capturing the original's creatively disjointed linguistic style:

> Mo Yan has filled his novel with puns, a variety of stylistic prose, allusions – classical and modern, political and literary, elegant and scatological – and many Shandong localisms. It would serve little purpose to explicate them here, particularly since a non-Chinese reader could not conceivably "get" them all.
>
> (Mo, 2012, p. v)

In Chinese, whether Link and Sun like it or not, this is a major aspect of his work that is clearly inextricable from his unique approach to narrating history. *Sandalwood Death* is probably the most extreme example of this style, powerfully subverting any notion of an orthodox narrative, which simply can't be captured in English. Despite what the reader of the English translation might know of the Boxer Rebellion, the work's underlying philosophical structure hinges upon Mo Yan's complicated spoof on a local form of Shandong opera called "maoqiang," which ultimately interrogates the borders between history, fiction, reality, performance, and experience. It is not impossible for this to come through in translation, but it requires significant guidance, specialist knowledge from consulting the original, and an intense commitment on the part of the reader. Even Howard Goldblatt's rendering of the opening lines of the novel clearly shows the difficulty of translating Mo Yan's uniquely incongruous style, especially when it involves a number of titles and objects from the Chinese-speaking world that are not readily expressible in English:

> That morning, my gongdieh, Zhao Jia, could never, even in his wildest dreams, have imagined that in seven days he would die at my hands, his death more momentous than that of a loyal old dog. And never could I have imagined that I, a mere woman, would take knife in hand and with it kill my own husband's father. Even harder to believe was that this old man, who had seemingly fallen from the sky half a year earlier, was an executioner, someone who could kill without blinking. In his red-tasseled skullcap and long robe, topped by a short jacket with buttons down the front, he paced the courtyard, counting the beads on his Buddhist rosary like a retired yuanwailang, or better yet, I think, a laotaiye, with a houseful of sons and grandsons.
>
> (2013, p. 3)

By the detached sort of Anglophone aesthetic standards we've seen wielded so far by Hsia, Owen, Damrosch, Sun, and Link, does this really sound that great? It's hardly "shimmering poetry." Howard Goldblatt's translation is, I think, the best we could possibly hope for. He presents a reasonable and refreshing example of "foreignization," which stretches the English language and pushes readers out of their domestic comfort zone toward the original text,[8] but practically speaking, that, combined with the fact that the translation is over 400 pages of tightly crammed text and is published by the University of Oklahoma Press, with its limited distribution, has hardly caused it to fly off the shelves like a Murakami novel.

There is one more point worth emphasizing, which is that literary demands of ideological purity – such as those made by Sun and Link, and to a lesser extent Hsia – are anti-literary and offer no way to truly negotiate present (and future) experience with the past. This matters for the idea of world literature, and a good illustration of this is *The Columbia Anthology of Modern Chinese Literature*.[9] Anthologies, often maligned in discussions of world literature as exclusionary visions of a privileged canon, are, as any undergraduate instructor knows, incredibly useful in a practical sense. Yes, choices have to be made. The Columbia anthology chooses to omit examples of socialist realism from the Mao period, and offers only a brief paragraph in the introduction mentioning Mao's 1942 talks on literature and art at Yan'an. The editors give the following reasoning:

> Burdened with such ideological expectations, the literature of the Maoist era, particularly during the catastrophic years of the Cultural Revolution (1966–1976), cannot be expected to impress as a self-sufficient aesthetic entity, since its primary function was to celebrate the accomplishments of the new society.
> (Lau & Goldblatt, 2007, p. xxiv)

This statement reveals the way world literature really works: literature in translation aims to "impress as a self-sufficient aesthetic entity." Aside from important questions like, "By whose standards?" and "In what language?", we see here why many advocates of Chinese literature feel it has not gotten its fair shake "as world literature." The post-Mao literary selections in the anthology are all very capable translations of works by major writers, but they are presented in a way that papers over any possible dialogue with the aesthetic and ideological formations of the preceding historical period, as if they just dropped in out of nowhere. How can we begin to understand stories from the 1980s PRC, with all their gory violence, misogyny, disaffected attitudes, didactic speeches, and naive pronouncements of love, without any attention to literary representations of the incredibly anomalous political, ideological, social, and aesthetic formations that preceded and gave rise to them?[10] Of course, we can still read and in many ways appreciate these stories in the anthology. But we should also not be surprised that they are not automatically catapulted into the canon of world literature in English on their immediately apparent literary merit, simply as "self-sufficient aesthetic entities."

"To read Bei Dao's poems in English," writes Damrosch, "we should be alive to the relevant aspects of the context of their production, but we don't finally need the Chinese context in all its particularity" (p. 22). It's true and inevitable that full-throttle specialist knowledge need not be required for reading something as world literature because, otherwise, how could we presume to read anything from places and times we don't know much about? Hence Damrosch's "detached engagement." But the presumption seems to be that some sort of universal core of the work will shine through regardless, which will make a great work worth reading even if we don't fully understand the cultural, historical, political, and linguistic context of the original. This is roughly Benjamin's (1968) idea – that the inherent truth within a literary work of art, while captured in a particular way by the original, *and yet still not exactly*, becomes articulated in different ways by the translation, thus allowing the translation to express it anew (in the work's "afterlife"). Just how directly, compellingly, and artistically this universal can be accessed and articulated by the translation, though, remains in question. "God's remembrance" is not equally accessible. As Schleiermacher (1992) notes,

> Every language ... contains within itself a system of concepts which, because they touch, connect with, and complement each other in the same language, are one whole whose individual parts, however, do not correspond to any of the systems of other languages, perhaps not even with the exception of God and Being, the primal noun and the primal verb. For even that which is universal, although situated outside the sphere of specific characteristic traits, is still illuminated and colored by language.
>
> (p. 50)

Cuiyuan, the young woman protagonist in Eileen Chang's "Sealed Off" (封锁), realizes this too. Although she has been a model daughter and achieved impressive success as a university English professor in the bourgeois society of wartime Shanghai, "Cuiyuan wasn't very happy."

> Life was like the Bible, translated from Hebrew into Greek, from Greek into Latin, from Latin into English, from English into Chinese. When Cuiyuan read it, she translated the standard Chinese into Shanghainese. Gaps were unavoidable.
>
> (Zhang, 2007, p. 177)

It's no wonder, then, that Can Xue's novels, which she explicitly produces as universal works of high modernism without much attention to language (2003, p. 29)[11] and which she says could be set anywhere in the world and at any time (2011, p. 2), have found significant success in English translation disproportionate to their status in China, and that Wang Anyi's subtle depictions of the afterlives and permutations of competing socialist and pre-socialist value systems and subjectivities in contemporary China have not.

*****

After moving through all these contentious debates, I would like to try to end on a more conciliatory note. At the end of his chapter in *The Making of*

Chinese-Sinophone Literatures as World Literature, the recent volume mentioned at the beginning of this essay, Zhang (2022) issues a plea:

> If we would like to have great Chinese poets and writers and their canonical works become part of world literature, a great deal of hard work still needs to be done in literary translation and literary criticism, and that is a task for all those scholars who have the linguistic skills as well as the dedication to, and love of, Chinese literature and world literature.
>
> (p. 74)

I completely agree with Zhang that a great deal of hard work needs to be done in literary translation and criticism. If I could offer my version of Zhang's sentiment, in line with the idea of world literature as genre, it would be this: great Chinese literary works should be translated, *regardless of whether or not* they become part of the genre of world literature in English. As I stated earlier, I agree with Sontag's notion of translation as an ethical task – the more of it, the better. However, I think that tying this simple, ethical notion of translation to the aspirations of world literature is never going to yield satisfactory results – in fact, I think it's a "golden millet dream." Whatever works of Chinese literature manage to enter into some canon of world literature, great; if some (or most) works don't, that's okay too, because world literature is not an authoritative marker of legitimacy or greatness, it's just a genre of great works that are more translatable than others.

Notes

1 As the nature of this discussion and the title of the volume should make clear, I will be discussing world literature in its Anglophone form and commenting on its dynamics from this perspective. While the Chinese-reading world is generally more receptive of literature in translation than the English-reading world, I think the idea of "world literature as genre" should be applicable everywhere, as no realization of "world literature" in any context can ever be truly free of its situatedness.

2 Commenting on the general notion of "objectivity" in literary translation, Wai-lim Yip notes that "such a position necessarily erases the differences between the author and his (many) readers, and appeals to a common humanity . . . in order to achieve 'objectivity,' but such objectivity must necessarily be predicated on the unchangeability of meaning, its reproducibility and definability, all of which are problematic and delusive" (2004, p. 81).

3 Peter Button (2009) uses the example of Mao Dun to demonstrate how far C. T. Hsia's literary philosophy was from that of May Fourth writers, noting that "Hsia's New Critical convictions meant that he would necessarily abhor any instrumentalist literary practice as much as he would disdain all those other activities into which Mao Dun's conception of art and the role of the artist would lead him" (p. 4).

4 Furthermore, noting "Owen's notion of a hegemonic, unidirectional system of world literature" (p. 97), Edmund also observes that "most respondents to Owen reproduce [a] binary mode of literary analysis in cultural terms, so that the 'world' designates that which is either extrinsic or intrinsic: Bei Dao's poetry is either inside a heterogeneous world literature separated from homogenous national and global literatures by its hybrid multiplicity, or it is inside a heterogeneous Chinese literature separated from a homogenous global literature by its Chineseness" (p. 100).

5 While I agree with Andre Lefevere (1999) that adding supplemental explanatory materials would help us "learn to skip the leap we often call 'of the imagination' but which could be much more aptly called 'of imperialism,'" this can only help bring us closer to, but never fully realize, a true universality of literature through "understanding other cultures 'on their own terms'" (p. 78).
6 Sun comes out even stronger, calling Mo Yan's language "diseased" by "the conscious renunciation of China's cultural past at the founding of the People's Republic of China in 1949. Mo Yan's writing is in fact a product of the aesthetic ideologies of Socialist China." For an effective response on this idea of "disease," see Klein (2016).
7 Sun laments Mo Yan's stylistic departure from great writers in history like Li Bai, Cao Xueqin, and Tang Xianzu; Laughlin points out her selective privileging of the lyric tradition.
8 This is "foreignization" in the standard sense promoted by translation theorists from Schleiermacher to Venuti (2008), not Zhang's (2022) equation of the practice with exotification meant to intrigue or titillate (pp. 72–73).
9 To be crystal clear, this is different from *The Columbia Companion to Modern Chinese Literature,* Ed. Kirk Denton, which presents an efficient, thorough, and nuanced view of modern Chinese literature through a collection of critical essays and overviews.
10 Yip (2004) offers a much more expansive view of this point, commenting on the implicit intertextuality of every literary work: "When we open a book and read its words, phrases, and sentences, other books – from antiquity, from the recent past, or even in foreign languages – will be opened simultaneously, and words, phrases, or sentences from these will at once appear in our consciousness along with those in front of our eyes, trembling, ready to speak to us" (p. 81). Yip continues: "even if we are able to recover most of these echoes, we will probably find that they can work *only* in the source text; they cannot be resurrected intact in a target language that does not share the same or a similar signifying system or mechanism" (p. 85).
11 "I don't care about wording," says Can Xue. "If someone wants to take out a few characters or sentences, it won't cover over the individuality and distinguishing characteristics of my language" (my translation).

References

Apter, E. (2006). *The translation zone: A new comparative literature.* Princeton, NJ: Princeton University Press.
Apter, E. (2013). *Against world literature: On the politics of untranslatability.* New York: Verso.
Auerbach, E. (1969). Philology and *Weltliteratur* (M. & E. Said, Trans.). *The Centennial Review, 13*(1), 1–17.
Benjamin, W. (1968). *Illuminations: Essays and reflections* (H. Arendt, Ed.; H. Zohn, Trans.). New York: Schocken Books.
Button, P. (2009). *Configurations of the real in Chinese literary and aesthetic modernity.* Leiden: Brill.
Can, X. 残雪. (2003). *Weile baochou xie xiaoshuo* 为了报仇写小说. Changsha: Hu'nan wenyi chubanshe.
Can, X. 残雪. (2011). *Wuxiangjie* 五香街. Beijing: Zuojia chubanshe.
Chiu, K., & Zhang, Y. (Eds.). (2022). *The making of Chinese-Sinophone literatures as world literature.* Hong Kong: Hong Kong University Press.
Chow, R. (1993). *Writing diaspora: Tactics of intervention in contemporary cultural studies.* Bloomington, IN: Indiana University Press.
Damrosch, D. (2003). *What is world literature?* Princeton, NJ: Princeton University Press.

Edmund, J. (2012). *A common strangeness*. New York: Fordham University Press.
Gray, P., & Boyd, P. (1957). *Plats du Jour*. Harmondsworth: Penguin.
Hsia, C. T. (1963). On the 'scientific' study of modern Chinese literature: A reply to professor Prusek. *T'oung Pao, 50*(4), 428–474.
Hsia, C. T. (1999). *A history of modern Chinese fiction*. Bloomington, IN: Indiana University Press.
Huang, Y. (2002). *Transpacific displacement: Ethnography, translation, and intertextual travel in twentieth-century American literature*. Berkeley, CA: University of California Press.
Jones, A. (1994). Chinese literature in the world literary economy. *Modern Chinese Literature, 8*, 171–190.
Klein, L. (2016). A dissonance of discourses: Literary theory, ideology, and translation in Mo Yan and Chinese literary studies. *Comparative Literature Studies, 53*(1), 170–197.
Klein, L. (2018). *The organization of distance: Poetry, translation, Chineseness*. Leiden: Brill.
Lau, J. S., & Goldblatt, H. (Eds.). (2007). *The Columbia anthology of modern Chinese literature* (2nd ed.). New York: Columbia University Press.
Laughlin, C. (2012). *Why critics of Chinese Nobel Prize-Winner Mo Yan are just plain wrong*. Asia Society: Asia Blog. https://asiasociety.org/blog/asia/why-critics-chinese-nobel-prize-winner-mo-yan-are-just-plain-wrong
Lefevere, A. (1999). Composing the other. In S. Bassnett & H. Trivedi (Eds.), *Post-colonial translation: Theory and practice* (pp. 75–94). New York: Routledge.
Link, P. (2012a, December 24). Politics and the Chinese language: What Mo Yan's defenders get wrong. *ChinaFile*. www.chinafile.com/politics-and-chinese-language
Link, P. (2012b, December 6). Does this writer deserve the prize? *The New York Review of Books*. www.nybooks.com/articles/2012/12/06/mo-yan-nobel-prize/
Lovell, J. (2006). *The politics of cultural capital: China's quest for a Nobel Prize in literature*. Honolulu, HI: Hawai'i University Press.
Mishra, P. (2012, December 13). Why Salman rushdie should pause before condemning Mo Yan on censorship. *The Guardian*. www.theguardian.com/books/2012/dec/13/mo-yan-salman-rushdie-censorship
Mo, Y. (2011). *Big breasts and wide hips* (H. Goldblatt, Trans.). New York: Arcade.
Mo, Y. (2012). *The republic of wine* (H. Goldblatt, Trans.). New York: Arcade.
Mo, Y. (2013). *Sandalwood death* (H. Goldblatt, Trans.). Norman, OK: University of Oklahoma Press.
Owen, S. (1990). What is world poetry? *The New Republic, 19*, 28–32.
Owen, S. (2014). Stepping forward and back: Issues and possibilities for 'World' Poetry.' In D. Damrosch (Ed.), *World literature in theory*. Malden, MA: Wiley Blackwell.
Prusek, J. (1962). Basic problems of the history of modern Chinese literature and C. T. Hsia, a history of modern Chinese fiction. *T'oung Pao, 49*(1), 357–404.
Schleiermacher, F. (1992). From 'on the different methods of translating' (B. Waltraud, Trans.). In R. Schulte & J. Biguenet (Eds.), *Theories of translation: An anthology of essays from Dryden to Derrida* (pp. 36–54). Chicago, IL: The University of Chicago Press.
Sontag, S. (2002). *The world as India*. www.susansontag.com/prize/onTranslation.shtml
Suher, D. (2022, June). Review: The making of Chinese-Sinophone literatures as world literature. *MCLC Resource Center Publication*. https://u.osu.edu/mclc/book-reviews/suher/
Sun, A. (2012). The diseased language of Mo Yan. *The Kenyon Review*. https://kenyonreview.org/kr-online-issue/2012-fall/selections/anna-sun-656342/

Venuti, L. (2008). *The translator's invisibility: A history of translation*. New York: Routledge.
Yip, W. (2004). Debunking claims of *Xin, Da* and *Ya:* The afterlife of translations. In L. T. Chan (Ed.), *Twentieth-century Chinese translation theory: Modes, issues and debates*. Amsterdam: John Benjamins Publishing Company.
Zhang, A. (2007). Sealed off (K. S. Kingsbury, Trans.). In *The Columbia anthology of modern Chinese literature* (pp. 174–184). New York: Columbia University Press.
Zhang, L. (2022). Chinese literature, translation, and world literature. In *The making of Chinese-Sinophone literatures as world literature* (pp. 25–39). Hong Kong: Hong Kong University Press.
Zhang, X. (2008). *Postsocialism and cultural politics: China in the last decade of the twentieth century*. Durham, NC: Duke University Press.

3 The Translator's Individual Approach
English Translation of Chinese Poetry

Audrey Heijns

Introduction

While poets have their own unique style, intention, and inspiration, so do translators have their own individual approach. During the translation process, translators constantly make choices and decisions. As Lingenfelter (2017) writes, "Translation is dialogue, interactive criticism, analysis by analogue. It is also highly individual" (p. 73). In Klein's (2017) words, translators have their own "translatorial style" (p. 16), although he does add that literary translators "tend to be interested in reproducing and representing their translated poets' styles more than insisting on their own" (p. 16). Nevertheless, the choices and decisions that translators make influence the effect of the translation. Hence, as Feeley (2017) notes, "There is no sole, absolute version of the literary work in translation, there is no fixed equivalence between languages and cultures" (p. 70). Although there may be various factors that influence the translator's choice, in this study I argue that it is the translator's perception of the special feature or "the central quality of the source text" (Feeley, 2017, p. 70), in the words of Feeley, that determines the translator's approach to translation of a poet's work.

This special feature or central quality of the source text is often the decisive factor for the translator to select the poems because the source text has a special quality that is appealing and worth introducing to the target reader. At the same time though, often the translation problems they encounter are related to this central quality, that is, words or phrases that are difficult to translate, so-called "untranslatables." There may be a variety of equivalents in the target language, but none of them fully capture the original intent, or there are near-equivalents that may have different connotations or associations. Recent debate about the notion of "untranslatability" was caused by the publication of Barbara Cassin's *Dictionnaire des intraduisibles* (published in English as *Dictionary of Untranslatables*) and Emily Apter's *Against World Literature: On the Politics of Untranslatability*. Among the reactions of translation study scholars, it was Lawrence Venuti who accused Apter of "hijacking" translation. Baer (2020) explains that, despite the fact that both Venuti and Apter aim to challenge and resist the appropriation of other cultures by a hegemonic Anglophone West, "the way they conceptualize translation's role within that project is almost diametrically opposed, with Venuti placing the power to 'foreignize' in the hands of the translator and Apter situating untranslatability in a discrete set of words" (p. 146). While Venuti stresses the role of the translator, Apter's (2008) emphasis is on the "effect of the noncarryover that carries over nonetheless, or that transmits at a half-crocked semantic angle, endows the Untranslatable with a distinct symptomology" (p. 587). Baer (2020) argues that Apter is less nuanced than Cassin "who acknowledges that incommensurability runs across languages and so defines untranslatables not as unique instances of untranslatability but as 'symptoms of difference', which inspire repeated attempts at translation" (p. 146). As such, the point is not that words in themselves are untranslatable but rather they contain "symptoms of difference" (Baer, 2020, p. 146), which translators can deal with and which can inspire multiple translations:

> In other words, the problem with untranslatability from a Translation Studies perspective is not that it posits something as absolutely incommensurable and so incapable of being translated – Cassin does not claim that, in fact arguing that untranslatables inspire repeated translation – but that it implies the easy commensurability of everything that is not an untranslatable. This is why I prefer Cassin's description of the untranslatable as a symptom of widespread incommensurability rather than Apter's positing of a resistant "semantic nub."
> (pp. 146–147)

What follows then is that if the untranslatable is a symptom of widespread incommensurability, does it mean that in the current context translation of Chinese poetry into English suffers from widespread incommensurability? This study will contribute to the discussion of "untranslatability" by examining how translators deal with problems in the practice of translating poetry. Given the availability of Chinese poems in English and related material, the focus of my analysis has so far been on English translations of poetry by Jiang Hao 蔣浩, Jidi Majia 吉狄馬加, Yang Mu 楊牧, Ye Mimi 葉覓覓, Liu Waitong 廖偉棠, and Xi Xi 西西. To better understand the perspective of the translator, I have consulted translator's notes and essays about the translation process or the translator's experience. The aim of this study is to analyze the translator's perception of the poet's characteristics and solutions to the translation problems that translators encounter. This will help understand how much is related to the different cultural systems of English and Chinese and, in Sun's (2017) words, how "successful and less successful efforts have been made to translate the untranslatable" (p. 101).

Studies about the translations of poetry from Chinese into English include both those about translating classical or premodern Chinese poetry as well as about translating modern and contemporary Chinese poetry. Relevant for the practice of translating Chinese poetry are studies that impart knowledge about the historical development or evolution in translation, such as Yeh's (2016) "Inventing China: The American Tradition of Translating Chinese Poetry," in which she argues that "Pound started an American tradition of translating Chinese poetry that has been so influential that several generations of poets and translators are compelled to engage with it in one way or another" (p. 293). But also a comparative study such as "Nineteen Ways of Looking at Wang Wei" by Eliot Weinberger (2016), whose critical reading of each translation of "Deer Park" is illuminating for the different translation strategies, and as he writes,

> In its way a spiritual exercise, translation is dependent on the dissolution of the translator's ego: an absolute humility toward the text. A bad translation is the insistent voice of the translator – that is, when one sees no poet and hears only the translator speaking.
>
> (p. 8)

The discussion about the role of the translator has always been important.

When it comes to practical experience of translating modern/contemporary Chinese poetry, there are several articles by well-known poetry translators, including Klein (2018), who in his discussion of the question of Hong Kong and Mainland Chinese Sinophones illustrates his argument by using his translations of poems by Liu Waitong and Cao Shuying. Admussen (2019) discusses the embodiment in the translation of Chinese poetry by looking at Jennifer Feeley's translations of Xi Xi, Austin Woerner's of Ouyang Jianghe, and Ming Di and Jennifer Stern's of Liu Xia. Lingenfelter (2014) writes about the problems and solutions when translating poems by Yang Mu. Feeley (2017) explains the different methods of translating wordplay in Xi Xi's poetry. Yeh (2018) discusses aspects of nature, classical tradition, and music in Yang Mu's poems in her introduction to *Hawk of the Mind: Collected Poems*. Mair (2014) introduces the challenging concepts and perspectives in the poetry of Jidi Majia, whose work is rooted in the Nuosu tradition. Based on these and other articles that discuss the characteristics of the work of these poets, I will examine the translator's individual approach to translation of Chinese modern poetry.

The Central Quality of the Source Text

In the following sections, I will explore what is perceived as the special feature or the central quality of the source text of the poet whose work the translators (chose to) translate and how that influences their individual approach to translation. It appears that usually it is exactly that special feature or central quality that is the most challenging to translate because the translator has set himself the task to convey this characteristic to the target reader. Based on the six Chinese poets mentioned previously, I look into the individual approaches of Denis Mair, Ming Di, Andrea Lingenfelter, Steve Bradbury, Jennifer Feeley, and Lucas Klein. Although this is only a limited set of data, the analysis gives some insight into different types of individual approach of each translator.

Daoist Aspects

In the translator's introduction to Jiang Hao in the volume *New Cathay, Contemporary Chinese Poetry 1990–2012*, Ming (2013) identifies Daoist aspects as a special feature of Jiang Hao's poetry.¹ She explains that the poet felt a responsibility to return to tradition because he found that Chinese poetry in the 1970s and 1980s was too much influenced by the West (Ming, 2013). She furthermore notes that in his poems "every little detail leads to retrospection, with a Daoist outlook" (Ming, 2013, p. 111) and explains that

> his diction is clearly Daoist, which can look and sound almost ungrammatical in modern Chinese. Although sometimes criticized as pedantic or "overeducated" by people who feel confused by a first reading of his work, Jiang Hao is praised by many others who appreciate the classical resonance of his poetry.
> (pp. 111–112)

Although Ming Di does not explain how Jiang Hao expresses this Daoism in his outlook and diction, this is undoubtedly an aspect of Jiang Hao's work that she perceives as the central quality of his work that has to be rendered to the readers.

The way these Daoist aspects are conveyed can be seen in the three poems by Jiang Hao included in the collection: "A Pebble," "*from* Book of Sin," and "The Shape of the Ocean." (Jiang, 2013, pp. 113–116). Taking a closer look at the latter, some grammatical problems can be found in the English version, for example, inconsistent use of the (in)definite article: the shape of an ocean, ocean's shape, and the shape of ocean; the use of "this" when referring to two bags of ocean water should be "they." There is an incomplete question, "You don't believe?" In the last line, the word for "shape" is translated into "image," which is confusing given that the keyword in the poem is "shape" (Jiang, 2013, p. 113). Later though, another version of "The Shape of the Ocean" translated by Ming Di and Frank Stewart was published in *Mānoa* in 2019, which is grammatically correct. Among the many changes, the problem with the (in)definite articles is solved, the incomplete question is fixed, and the word "image" in the last line is now "shape."

It appears that only concrete Daoist concepts in the poem can be translated, such as the idea that fish are not fish in the early version: "two non-fish will soon swim out" (Jiang, 2013, p. 113) changed into "two not-fish are about to emerge" (Jiang, 2019, p. 48) in the later version, and the denial in the early version: "You affirm, you deny; then you non-affirm, and non-deny" (Jiang, 2013, p. 113) changed into "you say yes, then no; then not-yes, not-no" (Jiang, 2019, p. 48) in the later version. By contrast, the Daoist style in terms of grammar, in particular syntax, is untranslatable, and the translator can only focus on semantics, in particular meaning and the relation between words. The only way to let the reader know about Daoist aspects of the poet's work is to explain this in translator's notes or in the introduction to Jiang Hao or his biographical details by stressing that Jiang has a Daoist outlook and Daoist diction, which Ming Di indeed did.

Nuosu Culture

For Denis Mair the central quality of Jidi Majia's poetry is his minority background. Hence, his focus is on rendering the tribal sensibility of the Nuosu. This is primarily reflected in Mair's (2014) selection of the poems, which are all about or refer (in)directly to his Nuosu identity. A good example is Mair's (2014) selection of poems in the collection *Rhapsody in Black*, which are all related to the Nuosu people and their culture.[2] Mair (2014) explains in his "Translator's Note" that the title of the collection, after the title of a poem, sums up two important aspects of Jidi's poetry:

> His work is rooted in the tribal traditions of his people, which he sums up with the word "blackness," partly because they call themselves the Nuosu ("Black Tribe"). At the same time, he embraces worldwide currents of thought, using a fluid succession of moods and reflections to express modern sensibility (as in George Gershwin's *Rhapsody in Blue*).
>
> (p. xiii)

Given this, what Mair (2014) calls "dual orientation" (p. xiii), the translator is confronted with a new culture, a minority culture quite different from Chinese culture. Therefore, it shows that the translator spared no effort to familiarize himself with the Nuosu culture, as evidenced in the 26 footnotes to the poems, among which 19 are about Nuosu culture, including the meaning of colors, religious aspects, myths, headdress, dance, and musical instruments. The remaining seven give information about more general topics, such as Chinese history, Tibet, and a poet from Martinique. Despite the fact that these notes provide "the useful material for delving into native interpretations" (Bender, 2014, p. 204), as reviewer Bender (2014) writes, "in a few instances somewhat more information would have been useful" (p. 204). Previously in 2012, Mair had already published the article "Son of the Nuosu Muse: The Poet Jidi Majia" in *Chinese Literature Today*, which is part of a special section focused on the diversity of Nuosu Yi poetry and poetics. This article contains Mair's (2012) observations of Jidi Majia's homeland during their trip to Liangshan Yi Nationality Autonomous Prefecture.[3] All these so-called "paratexts," including introductions, footnotes, and essays, are helpful for a better understanding of the Nuosu minority and Jidi Majia's poetics.

In terms of translation strategy: some words that are specific to Nuosu culture are transliterated; for example, the religious figure *bimo* is introduced in the poem "Vigil for the *Bimo*" (Jidi, 2014, p. 41) 守望畢摩, and the poem is dedicated to a Nuosu ritualist. *Bimo* is the pronunciation in standard Chinese, not Nuosu dialect. This poem is mentioned in the "Translator's Note" where Mair (2014) explains that "the poet's connection to his tribal homeland is everywhere woven into his metaphoric language" (p. xiv). It is not only Nuosu culture that Mair (2014) explains but also the natural environment; for example, where Mair is more concerned with the context of topography, he notes that while he was translating this poem he recalled a washed-out road on his trip to Sichuan, therefore he added the adjective "flash" in "flash floods" "to appeal to the reader's topographic imagination" (p. xiv). For Mair (2014), it was important to give an all-around picture of the Nuosu and their surroundings. In Bender's (2014) opinion, the fact that Mair had traveled to Butuo and experienced firsthand Nuosu culture was a great asset to the translation process and enabled him to connect with Jidi's vision. And he writes, "This ability to really touch the cultures surrounding the work of ethnic poets in China (or indigenous poets anywhere) is one of the great challenges of translating culture-bound poetry" (Bender, 2014, p. 204). This immersion in the Nuosu minority and rendering it to the target reader was Mair's individual approach as translator.

Innovation

A similar strategy is deployed by Steve Bradbury in his translation of Ye Mimi's poetry, in the sense of immersion and bringing as much of the source text across as possible. As reviewer Stenberg (2016) explains, Bradbury "usually takes a different route in his translations, matching the poet in terms of innovation and daringness" (p. 102).[4] For Bradbury, "innovation" is the major characteristic of Ye Mimi's work, and it is clear from the poems that he tries to retain this effect in the target text. For example, the change of nouns into verbs in the poem "His Days Go by the Way Her Years" 《他度日她的如年》 (Ye, 2014, pp. 29–30):

她頭髮他的胸膛他晴朗她的情郎
有一天大家都會變做土壤
他度過一艘船
她山過一個夜晚

she hairs his chest he heartens her sweetheart
one day every living soul will turn to soil
he ocean fleets a vessel
she mountain passes a night

In English too, Bradbury changed the nouns into verbs just like the original Chinese. These are nouns that don't normally work as verbs, neither in Chinese nor in English, so for readers of both versions, they may strike as odd. In English, however, the effect is even more prominent because of verb conjugation.

Another example is the literal translation of the structure with the adverb "yue" 越 . . . 越 . . . as in: 越車越遠, which Bradbury translates as "The More Car the More Far" (Ye, 2014, p. 21), and also the phrase 他越是太陽她越是月亮 "the more he is the sun the more she is the moon" from the poem "His Days Go by the Way Her Years." (Ye, 2014, p. 30) It looks ungrammatical, but because it is so unusual, the reader will know it is done on purpose. Moreover, this is the aspect of Ye Mimi's work that Bradbury wants to render into the target language, because it is the central quality of the source text.

Shape-shifting Lyricism

More focused on poetic devices is the translation strategy deployed by translator Andrea Lingenfelter for her translations of Yang Mu's poetry.[5] As she explains,

"Yang Mu's fluid syntax and pivotal line breaks create a sort of shape-shifting lyricism that is both very challenging and rewarding to translate" (Lingenfelter, 2017, p. 78). By pointing out these two characteristics, it is clear that for her, these are the "central quality" in Yang Mu's poetry that need to be rendered in the target text. Hence, in her translations of Yang Mu's poetry, Lingenfelter (2014) follows the source text closely but makes adjustments for the readers to understand the theme of the poem or where "Chinese and English syntax may be at odd" (p. 60). An example of making adjustments to understand the theme of the poem is when Yang Mu alludes to Chinese literary tradition, which he is known for. An example that Lingenfelter (2014) discusses is the poem "Since you went away" (pp. 678–740), which shows engagement with the Tang-dynasty poet Zhang Jiuling. In this poem, she translates the character *can* 殘 into "neglected" instead of the more often used equivalent of "broken" or "damaged" in the last line "The full moon wastes away, while indoors// stands a long-neglected loom" (Yang, 2018, p. 164). Lingenfelter (2014) argues that Chinese readers will understand the concept of a woman who has neglected her loom is a metaphor to her lover's neglect of her. In other words, the translator tried to bring this context to English readers by deviating from the more literal meaning and introducing the theme of the abandoned woman. The way in which Lingenfelter deals with translating Chinese cultural tradition is to help the English reader, whereas Chinese readers of the original will understand the association without help. Her solution is to incorporate the explanation or reference in the translation, there is no need for footnotes or comments in the translator's introduction.

An example of adjustments for line breaks, as Lingenfelter (2014) explains, "many modern poets use enjambment, the practice of breaking a line mid-phrase, in order to amplify meanings, enliven rhythm, or create surprising twists" (p. 58). She gives examples to show that Yang Mu is no exception. The first example from the poem "Afternoon of a Gladiolus" shows that the same enjambment can be used in the translation; in other words, it works fine in English to retain the word order and cause similar effects of interruption, suspense, and surprise. Lingenfelter (2014) concludes that "the grammar and syntax of English and Chinese are in harmony" and "a translation can easily preserve the sequence of words and images of the original without disturbing Yang Mu's expressive line breaks" (p. 60). However, the second example from "Since you went away" (Lingenfelter, 2014, p. 60) shows that

> Chinese and English syntax may be at odds. When sentence structure doesn't map easily from one language to the other, a translator may be forced to choose between the literal, transcribed meaning and the original sequence of images and enjambment.
>
> (p. 60)

Although she admits that other translators might approach this issue differently, she found that enjambment can be so central to the experience of reading Yang Mu's poetry that she tried to preserve his enjambments wherever possible. In sum, Lingenfelter is led by what she perceives "the central quality" of Yang Mu's poetry. She follows Yang Mu's style closely and only makes adjustments if it doesn't work in English.

Political Significance

Lucas Klein is also concerned with the effect on the reader, and he writes that his ethic as a translator of contemporary Chinese poetry is "to give the reader both what the poet says and how she or he says it" (Klein, 2017, p. 32). In his discussion about Hong Kong and Mainland Chinese sinophones, Klein (2018) stresses the political significance of Liu Waitong's poem "Over the Counter-Revolution" (鳩鳴之詩).[6] While this poem is written in the style of the *Shijing* 詩經, the *Book of Odes*, which is the earliest collection of Chinese poetry dating from the eleventh-seventh century bc, Klein (2018) explains that "it also refers in its title to current events surrounding Occupy Central" (p. 150), the street protest in Hong Kong at the end of 2014 also known as the "Umbrella Movement." Klein (2017) explains that at the time of the protests, people from the mainland were bused to Hong Kong to participate in the counter-protest movement. Among them was one woman who denied any political motivation or nationalist devotion in an interview. She claimed that she "wanted to have fun" (p. 150) and planned to "go shopping," or *gouwu* 購物 in Chinese and *gau wu* in Cantonese. This word 購物 was rewritten as the homonym of 鳩鳴 (sound of birds hooting). The title of the poem 鳩鳴之詩 means literally "the poem of sparrows hooting," but because of the historical context, Klein translated it as "Over the Counter-Revolution," simultaneously referring to the political events and to go shopping. In the poem, as Klein (2017) explains, he translated the sound of the sparrows as "Cheap, cheap" (pp. 150–151) in connection with *gouwu*.

Further down in the poem, the sentence "A revolution *is* a dinner party" mocks Chairman Mao, who wrote the opposite, "A revolution is not a dinner party," and who wrote instead: "A revolution is an insurrection, an act of violence by which one class overthrows another" (Klein, 2017, p. 151). From the comments provided by Klein, it shows that in the process of translating Liu Waitong, much attention was given to the interpretation and rendering of the political meaning and intention of the poet. Hence, the translator's approach to the poem originates in getting the political message across. The same goes for poems published elsewhere, for example, the four poems by Liu Waitong that Klein translated and published on the hkprotesting.com site, which also have strong political significance.[7]

Wordplay

For translator Jennifer Feeley, the central quality of Xi Xi's poetry is wordplay. She explains that "Xi Xi uses wordplay as a rhetorical device, often for humorous effect" (Feeley, 2017, p. 46). She argues that instead of dismissing wordplay as "untranslatable," she believes that "they inspire the translator to conjure up creative solutions in English" (p. 46). Some critics and translators find this unacceptable because changes in meaning and structure will inevitably occur, but for

Feeley (2017), "in translating Xi Xi's poetry, not translating the wordplay leads to even greater loss" (p. 50). Therefore, she chooses "to create a new environment" (Feeley, 2017, p. 50). She introduces new phrases where there is no wordplay, that fit the tone of the poem and echo the musicality of the Chinese original (Feeley, 2017, p. 52). Where Feeley (2017) aims to imitate the visual effect of the poem, at the same time she also makes sure that the quality of the poem, which is a mouthful to read out loud in Chinese, she makes a mouthful to read in English (p. 55). Feeley is more concerned with the effect that the translated poetry has on her readers rather than linguistic accuracy or so-called faithfulness to the ST although she does consult with the poet when making changes.

An example from the poetry collection *Not Written Words* by Xi Xi (2016), translated by Jennifer Feeley, can be found in the song-like poem "Round and Round a Tree We Go" 《繞著一顆樹》 where the translator adds words to enhance rhythm and rhyme (Xi, 2016, pp. 76–79). The first stanza for example (Xi, 2016, 76–77):

繞著一顆樹
繞圈子
是哲學的遊戲

Round and round a tree we go
going round in circles
in our philosophical game of to and fro

Literally it says: move around a tree, move in a circle, it is a philosophical game. The English translation is adapted to the target language readers to make it read more fluently and sound like a song: "Round and round" creates a rhythm, and by adding "to and fro" to the end of the last line, it rhymes with the last word "go" of the first line.

Further down in the fifth stanza (Xi, 2016, pp. 76–77), she adds words for rhyme effect:

我在車站等巴士
車子來了，人人爭先
把我擠到最後

When I'm waiting for a bus
and it finally comes, there's such a scramble, such a fuss
I'm smushed and pushed to the back of the line

Literally it says: I'm waiting at the [bus] stop for the bus, the bus arrives, everyone tries to be first, I'm pushed to be last. The words "such a fuss" are presumably added to rhyme with "bus" in the first line. This kind of translation practice is what Ezra Pound calls "translating the 'cantabile' or song-like values of a poem" (Venuti, 2016, p. 190; Pound, 1954, p. 196). Feeley selected words that created "a certain meter or rhythm, a sound effect that might accompany the communication of meaning" (Venuti, 2016, p. 190). For Feeley (2017) it is not about finding the right equivalent:

> In poetry translation, exclusively aiming for so-called equivalence – long controversial in translation studies but stubbornly present in everyday discourse – is not effective, especially when wordplay is a central quality of the source text. The translator has many more tricks up her sleeve. In translating Xi Xi, I have made my choices, and others will make theirs – in reading and hearing my translations, or writing and speaking their own. Xi Xi's poetry allows, encourages and positively invites multiple interpretations and hence multiple translations.
>
> (p. 70)

Hence, the translator's approach is based on wordplay, because that is perceived as the central quality of the source text. The way Feeley translates, there is no need to aim for "equivalence" and "loyalty" in the conventional sense, and there is more room for creativity so that the effect of the target text is similar to that of the source text.

Each of these characteristics are either bringing "new thought," like Daoist aspects, Nuosu culture or political significance, or "new syntax/semantics," like innovation, lyricism, and wordplay. These are the decisive factors that make the poetry worth translating. They are the central quality of the source text that will influence the translator's approach and in turn lead to words or phrases that are difficult to translate.

Sometimes this focus on a special feature or central quality may come at the cost of minor losses, such as for example in Jidi Majia's poetry, where the focus is on introducing Nuosu culture. Some other aspects may have received less attention, such as the literary device of repetition in the poem "Vigil for the *Bimo*" (Jidi, 2014, p. 41). These four characters 守望畢摩 are repeated in stanzas 2, 3, and 4 in Chinese, but in English translation, they are deviating from the title: stanzas 2 and 4 have "To keep vigil for a *bimo*" and stanza 3 "Keeping vigil for a *bimo*." Although it is not necessary to retain repetition, in this case the original refrain-like usage could have been kept in English. Another example can be found in the poem "The Other Way" (Jidi, 2014, p. 13) 反差, where the four characters 另一個我 are first translated as "my other self" but the second time as "another one of me." Here, it would seem better to keep "my other self" in both instances, which would also alert the English reader to the same idea.

As for the innovation that Steve Bradbury introduces in English, it is an ingenious way to match the source text. Sometimes, however, as Stenberg (2016) argues, there are differences between the effect of the original Chinese compared to the effect of the English rendering on the readers because of linguistic differences.

> By checking against the original, one can usually see why Bradbury has done this; but in the near-absence of grammatical inflection in Chinese, the results

are often more radical in English than in Chinese, and leaps in the original are sometimes finessed to something more connected.

(p. 102)

Although Bradbury rendered Ye Mimi's style, the effect of the original Chinese style was amplified during the process of translation. Therefore, Bradbury's individual approach appears in fact to be "over-achieving" in his aim to match the "innovation" and "daringness" of the original. A similar case is discussed by Apter, who found the neologism in Gu Cheng's poetry odd. It is in the poem "Hidden Moon Alley" 《遮月胡同》 where Gu Cheng writes 絲本主義 instead of 資本主義 and is translated by Joseph R. Allen as "zapitalism" (Gu, 2005, p. 174). Apter doubts whether Gu's vision of "zapitalism" will "bequeath future modernisms" because it

> names a globality that functions as an Untranslatable for both Asian and Euro-American interpretive traditions. It thus challenges the way in which East-West comparatism is currently written into literary history and throws off the bipolar dynamic that has one world system competing against another in claiming primacy of first terms.
>
> (Apter, 2008, p. 596)

In other words, the meaning of this kind of neologism is unclear in both ST and TT. There is no tension between East and West, or Chinese and English. But she refrains from offering a better solution.

Conclusion

My findings show that the translator's individual approach depends, for the greater part, on their perception of the special feature or central quality of the source text. It is the decisive factor that is important for the translator to determine what to get across to the reader and how to do it. Although this is different for each poet's unique style as well as the individual translatorial style of the translator, there is a clear direction once the translator has identified the characteristic of a poet's work. In the end, it is the translator's personal perception of the "central quality" of the source text that dominates the translator's approach and strategy and finally the target text. For Jiang Hao, Jidi Majia, and Yang Mu, this sometimes leads to translation problems based on cultural differences that the translators explain and render in a domesticating way. For Ye Mimi, Xi Xi, and Liu Waitong, this sometimes leads to translation problems that occur at the semantic level based on linguistic differences, which the translators explain and recreate in a more foreignizing way.

Notes

1 Other translators of Jiang Hao's work are Thomas Moran, whose translations are included in the poetry collection *Push Open the Window: Contemporary Poetry from China* (Jiang, 2011) and Chenxin Jiang, whose translations were published in *Asymptote* (Jiang, undated) and *The Arkansas International* (Jiang, 2018).

2 Other translators of Jidi Majia's poetry include Jami Proctor Xu, who published *Words from the Fire* (Jidi, 2018), and Frank Stewart, who published *I, Snow Leopard* (Jidi, 2016).
3 Mair (2012, p. 75) explains how this trip helped him understand Jidi Majia's own poetics, which is based on a combination of Nuosu culture and foreign poetical influences from figures like Pablo Neruda and the poets associated with the negritude movement and the Harlem Renaissance movement.
4 This is a different method compared to the more conservative translator Todd Klaiman, who also translated Ye Mimi but in a less innovative and daring way. For example, in the poem "Keeping a 酉鬼" (養酉鬼), Klaiman keeps the Chinese characters in the translation and adds an explanation in the footnote: "The Chinese character 醜 (ugly) is composed of the two characters 酉 (5–7 pm) and 鬼 (ghost)" (Ye, 2014, p. 42). Although Klaiman did not create a similar image in English, his solution is also good because it shows that the characters *you* and *gui* are untranslatable, and without the transliteration, it has a foreignizing effect.
5 There are many translators who translated Yang Mu's works into English. On the Yang Mu website, besides *Hawk of the Mind*, as discussed in the current study, the two poetry collections, *No Trace of the Gardener* translated by Lawrence R. Smith and Michelle Yeh (Yang, 1998), and *Memories of Mount Qilai*, translated by John Balcom and Yingtsih Balcom (Yang, 2015) are displayed, as is the guide of Yang Mu's poetics *The Completion of a Poem: Letters to Young Poets* translated by Lisa Lai-ming Wong (Yang, 2017). Other translators of Yang Mu's poetry are Frank Stewart, Wen-chi Li, Joseph R. Allen, and Colin Bramwell.
6 A collection of Liu Waitong's poems in English translation was published in 2016 as *Wandering Hong Kong with Spirits*, translated by Enoch Yee-lok Tam, Desmond Sham, Audrey Heijns, Chan Lai-keun, and Cao Shuying (Liu, 2016a). His poems in the online *Pangolin House: An International Poetry Journal in English and Chinese* were translated by Diana Shi and George O'Connell (Liu, 2015–16). My translations of his poems have also been published in *Exchanges* (Liu, 2016b) and *Epiphany* (Liu, 2014).
7 The four poems are: "Two Million and One" (二百萬零一), "Reborn" (復活), "Words Spoken into the Wind" (逆風說的話), and "The Longest Summer" (最漫長的夏天) (Liu, 2020). Unfortunately, the sources of the citations in the last poem are omitted in the English translation. These could have been helpful for better understanding the context of the poem.

References

Admussen, N. (2019). Embodiment in the Translation of Chinese Poetry. In *Chinese Poetry and Translation: Rights and Wrongs*, edited by M. V. Crevel and L. Klein, 113–133. Amsterdam: Amsterdam University Press.
Apter, E. (2008). Untranslatables: A World System. *New Literary History 39* (3), 581–598.
Baer, B. J. (2020). From Cultural Translation to Untranslatability. *Journal of Comparative Poetics 40*, 139–163.
Bender, M. (2014). Review of Rhapsody in Black. *Chinese Literature: Essays, Articles, Reviews (CLEAR) 36*, 201–204.
Feeley, J. (2017). Can We Say an Ear of Cabbage: On Translating Wordplay in Xi Xi's Poetry. *Journal of Modern Literature in Chinese 14* (2)–*15* (1), 45–72.
Gu, C. (2005). *Sea of Dreams: The Selected Writings of Gu Cheng*, translated by J. R. Allen. New York: New Directions Books.
Jiang, H. (2011). Jiang Hao, Translated by Thomas Moran. In *Push Open the Window: Contemporary Poetry from China*, edited by Q. P. Wang, translations co-edited by S. L.-C. Lin and H. Goldblatt, 240–245. Port Townsend, WA: Copper Canyon Press.

Jiang, H. (2013). "A Pebble," "*from* Book of Sin," and "The Shape of the Ocean", translated by D. Ming. In *New Cathay, Contemporary Chinese Poetry 1990–2012*, edited by D. Ming, 113–116. North Adams, MA: Tupelo Press.

Jiang, H. (2018). Spring Festival Poem. Translated by C. X. Jiang. *The Arkansas International*. Retrieved from https://www.arkint.org/jiang-hao

Jiang, H. (2019). The Shape of the Ocean. Translated by D. Ming and F. Stewart. *Mānoa 31* (1), 48.

Jiang, H. (undated). Address. Translated by C. X. Jiang. *Asymptote*. Retrieved from https://www.asymptotejournal.com/poetry/jiang-hao-address/

Jidi, M. (2014). *Rhapsody in Black*, translated by D. Mair, foreword by S. J. Ortiz. Norman, OK: University of Oklahoma Press.

Jidi, M. (2016). *I, Snow Leopard*, translated by Frank Stewart, preface by Barry Lopez, afterword by D. Mair. Honolulu: Mānoa books/El León Literary Arts.

Jidi, M. (2018). *Words from the Fire: Poems by Jidi Majia*, translated by Jami Proctor Xu. Honolulu: University of Hawaii Press.

Klein, L. (2017). Strong and Weak Interpretations in Translating Chinese Poetry. *Journal of Modern Literature in Chinese 14* (2)–*15* (1), 7–43.

Klein, L. (2018). One Part in Concert, and One Part Repellence: Liu Waitong, Cao Shuying, and the Question of Hong Kong and Mainland Chinese Sinophones. *Modern Chinese Literature and Culture 30* (2), 141–172.

Lingenfelter, A. (2014). Imagine a Symbol in a Dream: Translating Yang Mu. *Chinese Literature Today 4* (1), 56–63.

Lingenfelter, A. (2017). Where You End and I Begin: Notes on Subjectivity and Ethics in the Translation of Poetry. *Journal of Modern Literature in Chinese 14* (2)–*15* (1), 73–105.

Liu, W. T. (2014). On Anhui North Lane I Kissed a Girl, translated by A. Heijns. *Epiphany: A Literary Journal* (winter issue), 33.

Liu, W. T. (2015–16). Poetry, translated by D. Shi and G. O'Connell. *Pangolin House: An International Poetry Journal in English & Chinese* (10). Retrieved from https://pangolinhouse.com/poets/liu-wai-tong/

Liu, W. T. (2016a). *Wandering Hong Kong with Spirits: Selected poetry of Liu Waitong*, translated by E. Y.-L. Tam, D. Sham, A. Heijns, L.-K. Chan and S. Y. Cao. Brooklyn, MA: Zephyr Press.

Liu, W. T. (2016b). Three Poems by Liu Waitong, translated by A. Heijns. *Exchanges* (fall issue). Retrieved from https://exchanges.uiowa.edu/issues/interstices/three-poems-by-liu-waitong/

Liu, W. T. (2020). Four Poems. Translated by L. Klein. *Hong Kong Protesting: A Cha Project*. Cha: An Asian Literary Journal. Retrieved from https://hkprotesting.com/2020/07/22/poems-liu-waitong/

Mair, D. (2012). Son of the Nuosu Muse: The Poet Jidi Majia. *Chinese Literature Today 2* (2), 75–77.

Mair, D. (2014). Introduction. In *Rhapsody in Black*, edited by M. Jidi, translated by D. Mair, foreword by S. J. Ortiz. Norman, OK: University of Oklahoma Press.

Ming, D, ed. (2013). *New Cathay, Contemporary Chinese Poetry 1990–2012*. North Adams, MA: Tupelo Press.

Pound, E. (1954). Calvacanti. In *The Literary Essays of Ezra Pound*, edited by T. S. Eliot, 149–200. New York: New Directions.

Stenberg, J. (2016). Review of A Moth Laid Its Eggs in My Armpit, and Then It Died and His Days Go by the Way Her Years. *Chinese Literature Today 5* (2), 101–103.

Sun, Y. F. (2017). Translatability. In *The Routledge Handbook of Chinese Translation*, edited by C. Shei and Z. M. Gao, 101–114. London and New York: Routledge.

Venuti, L. (2016). Hijacking Translation: How Comp Lit Continues to Suppress Translated Texts. *Boundary2 43* (2), 179–204.

Weinberger, E. (2016). *Nineteen Ways of Looking at Wang Wei*. New York: New Directions Books.

Xi, X. (2016). *Not Written Words*, translated by J. Feeley. Brooklyn, MA: Zephyr Press; Hong Kong: MCCM Creations.

Yang, M. (1998). *No Trace of the Gardener: Poems of Yang Mu*, translated by L. R. Smith and M. Yeh. New Haven: Yale University Press.

Yang, M. (2015). *Memories of Mount Qilai: The Education of a Young Poet*, translated by J. Balcom and Y. T. Balcom. New York: Columbia University Press.

Yang, M. (2017). *The Completion of a Poem: Letters to Young Poets*, translated by L. L.-M. Wong. Leiden: Brill.

Yang, M. (2018). *Hawk of the Mind: Collected Poems*, edited by M. Yeh. New York: Columbia University Press.

Ye, M. (2014). *A Moth Laid Its Eggs in My Armpit, and Then It Died*, translated by S. Bradbury and T. Klaiman, edited by B. Dao, S. K. Y. Chan, G. C. F. Fong, L. Klein, and C. Mattison. Baltimore, MD: Project Muse.

Yeh, M. (2016). Inventing China: The American Tradition of Translating Chinese Poetry. In *Reading the Past across Space and Time*, edited by B. D. Schildgen and R. Hexter, 285–295. New York: Palgrave Macmillan.

Yeh, M. (2018). Introduction. In *Hawk of the Mind: Collected Poems*, edited by M. Yeh. New York: Columbia University Press.

4 On the "Clamour of Voices" in Translation Anthologies of Contemporary Chinese Literature

Xiulu Wang

Introduction

As early as the eighteenth century, Chinese literature began to be translated sporadically into the English-speaking world. Often carried out by Western Sinologists, early literary translation projects focused primarily on Chinese classical works of literature. For a long time, Western scholars, translators, and general readers have remained quite indifferent, if not entirely oblivious, to contemporary Chinese literature.

With the rise of its national power in the twenty-first century, China has started to have an enhanced presence on the international stage. The world is also showing a keener interest in getting to know various aspects of contemporary China. Literature has long been regarded as a valuable window into the attitudes and values of a particular society and culture. Translation of contemporary Chinese literature, therefore, has started to gain some momentum in the last few decades. According to the annual report from *Paper Republic*, an online consortium of English translators of Chinese literature, 160 contemporary Chinese novels, 43 poetry collections, and 88 works of children's literature and/or picture books have been translated and published between 2016 and 2021.[1]

Most current studies on contemporary Chinese literature translation tend to focus on the international dissemination and reception of specific texts or individual authors. Translation anthologies of contemporary Chinese literature, however, have not yet received sufficient attention. This may have something to do with the longstanding bias against anthologies in literary studies. Jason Epstein, who was editorial director of Random House for 40 years, once commented that anthologies "are of little value in themselves. . . . They serve no literary purpose, usually find few readers and quickly go out of print" (Epstein, 2001, p. 139). For Epstein, anthologies are only a repackaging of literature and therefore are not creative in the way novels and poems are. But if we cast our eyes upon translation anthologies, the so-called originality of literary works might not seem that important.

Both translation and anthologies have a very practical dimension in themselves, and both can serve as promising tools for approaching literature. If, as Di Leo suggests, "anthologies chart courses through the literary world and are one of the primary ways through which we learn to navigate it" (Di Leo, 2007, p. 3), studies on

DOI: 10.4324/9781003368168-5

Chinese literature in translation should be giving equal, if not more, importance to translation anthologies than to translations of major Chinese authors' works. After all, compared to a full-length work by a single author, literature anthologies may encompass a broader range of topics, present a more diverse range of styles, tell more nuanced stories, and possibly appeal to a wider readership. They can, therefore, serve as a more effective means in China's quest for literary legitimacy and recognition in the international arena.

Taking literary anthologies as an important means of presenting the Other and projecting the relationship between different literary traditions, this chapter offers a historical overview of the publication and influence of contemporary Chinese literary anthologies in the English-speaking world, focusing on the political and poetic factors that have influenced and manipulated the production and reception of these anthologies. Motivated by a dissatisfaction with the tendency of literary anthologies to be politicized and an insistence that intercultural literary interactions should be primarily literary-oriented, this chapter draws on David Der-wei Wang's concept of "the clamour of voices" and makes a plea that translation anthology of contemporary Chinese literature should strive to construct a polyphonic literary space so as to accommodate the "the clamour of voices."

The Question of Criteria and What May Affect Them

Etymologically speaking, *anthology* is derived from the Greek word *anthologia*, where *anthos* means "flower" and *-logia* means "to gather" (Korte, 2000, p. 2). To put together an anthology is not only about "gathering." This might be what distinguishes an anthology from a textual database or a literary archive. Databases or archives usually seek to be comprehensive and even complete with regard to the topic concerned, but anthologies are much more selective in their choice of corpus. In many ways, putting together an anthology is similar to putting on a museum exhibition, in that both involve a process of selection, preservation, presenting, structuring, cultural narration, and intervention:

> Anthologies and collections can do for texts what museums do for artefacts and other objects considered of cultural importance: preserve and exhibit them, by selecting and arranging the exhibits, project an interpretation of a given field, make relations and values visible, maybe educate taste.
> (Essman & Frank, 1991, p. 66)

Like objects in museums, texts in anthologies are selected and recontextualized in ways that may produce new ways of looking/reading and sense-making about a particular cultural tradition. In the compilation of an anthology, one of the first things an editor has to decide on is the criteria for the selection of texts. Karen Kilcup (2000, p. 37) identifies three traditional bases for textual selection in composing anthologies: "excellence, representativeness (and/or comprehensiveness), and interest." These three criteria may be valid for literary anthologies in general, but perhaps they are not the best starting point for a discussion of contemporary

Chinese literary anthologies. The criterion of "excellence," according to Kilcup, may refer to "the best that's been thought and said" (ibid). Contemporary Chinese literature, however, has not yet been adequately translated and read.[2] Compared to the massive amount of English literature being constantly translated into other languages, much less literature has been translated into English. When it comes to Chinese literary translation, "the number is minuscule" (Qi, 2022, p. 23). If contemporary Chinese literature has not yet been sufficiently translated, it probably has not yet been adequately "thought and said" as well. The criterion of "excellence" becomes rather dubious. The relatively marginal position of contemporary Chinese literature within the English-speaking world could lead to the other two criteria – representativeness and interest – being reduced to mere hollow rhetoric as well. After all, how does one endeavor to present a literary tradition that the vast majority of readers are not yet familiar with, do not comprehend, and are not even all that interested in learning about?

André Lefevere (1945–1996) may have provided us with a more viable approach. "The putting together of anthologies" is, according to Lefevere, a common form of "rewriting," an umbrella term that includes a diversity of literary phenomena such as translation, interpretation, criticism, and historiography (Lefevere, 1985, p. 233). In *Translation, Rewriting and the Manipulation of Literary Fame*, Lefevere (1992) presents a systematic and comprehensive theory of rewriting. Anthology is again explicitly listed as a form of creative rewriting, which is subject to contextual motivations and constraints:

> Whether they produce translations, literary histories or their more compact spinoffs, reference works, anthologies, criticism, or editions, rewriters adapt, manipulate the originals they work with to some extent, usually to make them fit in with the dominant, or one of the dominant ideological and poetological currents of their time.
>
> (Lefevere, 1992, p. 8)

At the core of Lefevere's discussion of manipulation is "a double control factor" underlying the operation of the literary system and the mechanism of its interaction with other subsystems in a given cultural context. The first control factor mainly involves the professional within the literary system "where poetics is concerned," while the second refers to patronage that operates outside the literary system who is "usually more interested in the ideology of literature than in its poetics" (Lefevere, 1992, p. 15). In light of this "double control factor" that manipulates the literary system, we can start by examining the factors from both within and outside the literary system that influence the text selection in anthologies of translated contemporary Chinese literature.

Where Literature and Politics Meet

Lionel Trilling once famously and dramatically described his work as a cultural critic as taking place at the "dark and bloody crossroads where literature and politics meet" (Trilling, 1950, p. 10). More than half a century later, we might say that crossroads have a whole new look to them. Today, the entanglement of literature and politics is no longer seen as a dire apocalyptic prophecy but as a general reality that one has perhaps learned to cope with. For example, Martin Puchner, the general editor of the *Norton Anthology of World Literature*, notices the "worldly" nature of "world literature" and proposes a new concept of world literature as "appropriated, adopted, distorted, used, and abused by the world" and as something "not discrete, delicate, and benign, but embraced by the world, is made for the world, and put in the service of worldly purposes." This worldly world literature, as Puchner (2011, p. 258) points out, is situated right at the crossroads of literature and politics.

Translation anthologies perhaps constitute one of the most prominent categories of texts in the "worldly world literature." The dissemination of contemporary Chinese literature in the English-speaking world, in particular, has been rather susceptible to external conditions and constraints, such as transnational relations, geopolitics, and ideologies of different eras. For a long period during the Cold War, communist China was perceived in the West as a formidable antagonist, an immediate threat, and perhaps one of the evil enemies of modern times. The politico-ideological tensions between China and Western countries were also explicitly reflected in the literary field. Many English translation anthologies of contemporary Chinese literature published in the U.S. during this period highlighted social maladies or controversial themes portrayed by Chinese authors. The titles of several translation anthologies published during this period seem to have echoed such a belligerent political agenda:[3]

- *Bitter Harvest: The Intellectual Revolt behind the Iron Curtain* (Stillman, 1959)
- *The Wounded: New Stories of the Cultural Revolution 77–78*. (Barmé & Lee, 1979)
- *Wild Lilies, Poisonous Weeds: Dissident Voices from People's China* (Benton, 1982)
- *Fragrant Weeds: Chinese Short Stories Once Labelled as 'Poisonous Weeds'* (Jenner, 1983)
- *People or Monsters and Other Stories and Reportage from China After Mao* (Link, 1983a)
- *Stubborn Weeds: Popular and Controversial Chinese Literature After the Cultural Revolution* (Link, 1983b)
- *Roses and Thorns: The Second Blooming of the Hundred Flowers in Chinese Fiction 1979–1980* (Link, 1984)
- *Seeds of Fire: Chinese Voices of Conscience* (Barmé & Minford, 1986)
- *New Ghosts, Old Dream: Chinese Rebel Voices* (Barmé & Jaivin, 1992)

Peppered with highly suggestive and metaphorical terms, such as iron curtain, wound, wild lilies, poisonous weeds, thorns, monsters, and ghosts, these titles have considerable potential to incite Western readers' imagining of an exotic, dangerous, and antagonistic alien land. Most of these anthologies indeed provided narratives about China that Western readers have come to expect: an exaggerated portrayal of social darkness and corruption, a bitter denunciation of political oppression, or the suffering stories of dissidents who embraced Western ideals.

Take, for example, the three story collections compiled by Perry Link, which have been regarded as the best examples of Chinese literary anthologies of the period. Among the three, *Stubborn Weeds* is "a volume of the most controversial pieces and of political humor," *People or Monsters* is a collection of reportage writings "portraying ineradicable corruption and injustice throughout the Communist Party establishment," and *Roses and Thorns* is a collection of short fiction with an "equally hard-hitting" sense of socio-political critique (Kinkley, 2000, p. 244). Link is a scholar with considerable literary attainment and a decent knowledge of contemporary Chinese literature, but the scholarly thinking he was most concerned with when compiling these anthologies revolved around the sociology of Chinese reading and state control mechanisms of literature. Viewing China as traumatized by dictatorship and sectarian violence, Link preferred to select works that would reflect such social realities rather than those of literary merit. In fact, he admits that "popular and controversial" are two criteria for text selection, and some stories included may even "frustrate the reader who is seeking literary art" (Link, 1983b, p. 25). "Cries From Death Row," a short story included in *Stubborn Weeds*, is a case in point. Written by Jin Yanhua and Wang Jingquan, two little-known writers, the story was originally published in the January issue of *Guangxi Wenyi* (later renamed *Guangxi Wenxue*) in 1980. In the early 1980s, several short stories depicting the misery of the Cultural Revolution were published in successive issues of this literary journal, but none of them gained high acclaim from the Chinese literary community. They were not only considered as "falling several years behind the emergence of similar works of 'scar literature'" but also were criticized for "their obvious traces of imitation in terms of ideological content and crudeness in terms of artistic skills" (Jiang, 2008, p. 79). But the reason for choosing such a poorly written work, Link explains, is that the story can "give the Western reader a sense of the kind of sensationally accented stories of woe that were commonly told" (Link, 1983b, p. 26). It can only be said that this way of selecting text tends to reinforce the commonly perceived image of Communist China as a threat to Western values and democracy.

The impact of antagonistic politics on the selection of material for translation has been attenuated with the end of the Cold War. In the age of globalization, however, the ideological manipulation of text selection for translation has unfolded in new and more subtle ways. Howard Goldblatt, an influential and prolific translator of contemporary Chinese literature and the co-editor of *The Columbia Anthology of Modern Chinese Literature* (1995), once commented in an interview that sex, politics, and crime are the themes that are most likely to attract American readers to contemporary Chinese literature (Ji, 2009, p. 47). Goldblatt's observation can be partially substantiated in the growing number of translation anthologies of Chinese women writers or about Chinese women in the new era. For example,

- *The Rose Colored Dinner: New Works by Contemporary Chinese Women Writers* (Liu et al., 1988)
- *The Serenity of Whiteness: Stories By and About Women in Contemporary China* (Zhu, 1991)
- *I Wish I Were a Wolf: The New Voice in Chinese Women's Literature* (Kingsbury, 1994)
- *Red Is Not the Only Color: Contemporary Chinese Fiction on Love and Sex between Women, Collected Stories* (Sieber, 2001)

When introducing to Western readers the work of Chinese women writers or about Chinese women, issues of gender and sexuality are frequently foregrounded and so are their relations to politics. Within these stories, there is a lingering presence of the old-fashioned sentiments of victimized Oriental women. Some of these anthologies, as Kinkley describes, "help satisfy curiosity, but are unexciting" (Kinkley, 2000, p. 272). Recurring themes in these collections include contemporary Chinese women's lives under the emotional and physical privations of communism, their struggle against traditional patriarchalism in the quest for equality and freedom, their awakening to self-consciousness and exploration of personal sexuality, as well as various implications all these may have for modern Chinese political life. These stories of modern Chinese women and their lives are placed once again under the Western gaze. As Jiang Zhiqin observes, English anthologies of contemporary Chinese women writers often embody a "western narcissistic perception of its own culture, which in essence is the confirmation of one's self-identity through the appropriation of the Other" (Jiang, 2016, p. 91). In a similar vein, Qi Lintao argues that there is an "Orientalist mindset" at work, in which the image of China is politicized, exoticized, or even commodified. Consequently, China is once again not represented as "what it is" but "what the receivers want it to be" (Qi, 2022, p. 22).

The prevalence of ideological or political manipulation behind the text selections can have a constraining or even detrimental effect on the general cause of translation of contemporary Chinese literature. One of the biggest problems that can arise from either the Cold-War confrontational politics or from today's neo-Orientalist mindset is a tendency to lead to a homogeneous understanding of China and its contemporary literary landscape. The underlying impulse behind any schemes of literary translation projects should be the desire "to promote different national literatures and the effect to create diversity, not homogeneity, at supra-national level" (Cronin, 2003, p. 56). When dealing with contemporary China, the critical focus of the West on political dissent and contestation has not been particularly effective. It is difficult to imagine what better intercultural understanding and engagement would result from mere adherence to the political primacy in the international literary dialogue. Ideology is, fortunately, only one element of the "double control factor" operating on the literary system. There is also the internal element of literary professionals who act as a somewhat counterbalancing force in the mechanism of literary production.

Poetics Matter

Most often, the compilers of Chinese literature translation anthologies are academics[4] with a professional interest in Chinese literature, such as Sinologists, translators, literature scholars working in departments of East Asian languages or comparative literature in Western universities or research institutions. These people are not only readers with literary sophistication but also actors with a substantial amount of linguistic and cultural capital. In Even-Zohar's terms, they are "power holders" and "free agents" who are capable of engaging in "cultural planning" and bringing changes to "an extant or a crystallizing repertoire" (Even-Zohar, 2002, p. 45). When these professionals put together anthologies, they might not choose works of mere exotic interest nor yield completely to the existing ideological imperatives. Most likely, they choose, to the best of their knowledge, literary works that have specific literary merits, that are representative of a certain literary trend or phenomenon, and that might better reflect recent or ongoing events and their repercussions in the Chinese literary field.

These professionals' keen observation of the contemporary Chinese literary scene has led them to pay particular attention to the emergence and flourishing of avant-garde literature in China after the 1980s. The new wave of avant-garde literature was a rather complex trend, mixing a reaction against mainstream realism, a critical borrowing from Western modernist thinking, a curiosity about absurd material and bizarre narratives, and an eagerness to experiment with various innovative writing techniques. Compared to the literary works of New China in the preceding 30 years or so, the avant-garde literature of the 1980s has clearly turned away from the political imperatives to concentrate on the realm of aesthetics. Instead of taking writing as an "anxiety-ridden political act," the avant-gardists see literature as an experimental site for expressing a lighter existence of being. As these young avant-gardists "flaunted the lightness of being as a mere instance of improvisation in narration" (Wang, 1998, p. 2), they also embark on a bold exploration of the narrative apparatus, carrying out subversive experimentation with modes of expression as well as the language itself. This trend has evolved and achieved amazing success not only in novels but also in shorter literary genres such as poetry and short story. The new wave of innovative writings in shorter forms provide ideal corpus material for literary anthologies. Consequently, the English-speaking world in the late 1980s saw several quite remarkable translation anthologies featuring the Chinese avant-garde writings of the time. Kinkley (2000, p. 257, added emphasis) is quite pleased to note that the "reader now has a choice of good works, most excellently translated, in several anthologies; *the day of the socially driven collection is for now over.*" Among these "excellently translated" anthologies are several collections of translated contemporary Chinese poetry, including the following:

- *Trees on the Mountain: An Anthology of New Chinese Writing* (Soong & Minford, 1984)
- *The Red Azalea: Chinese Poetry since the Cultural Revolution* (Morin, 1990)
- *A Splintered Mirror: Chinese Poetry from the Democracy Movement* (Finkel & Kizer, 1991)
- *Anthology of Modern Chinese Poetry* (Yeh, 1992)
- *Out of the Howling Storm: The New Chinese Poetry* (Barnstone, 1993)

The poets in these collections, including Bei Dao, Jiang He, Gu Cheng, Duo Duo, Mang Ke, Yang Lian, and others, were emerging figures at that time. Many of them have since become renowned icons of contemporary Chinese poetry. Developed as a reaction against political-moralizing uses of literature, Misty poems celebrate freedom of individual expression, both in form and content. According to Leo Ou-fan Lee, contemporary Chinese poetry in the 1980s saw "a diversity of extreme sensibilities, a polyphony of new voices clamoring to be heard, a raw energy and a defiant spirit that can no longer be contained by any official campaigns" (1990, p. xxvii).

The diversity and polyphony are also reflected in short stories anthologies of the same time. Take, for example, *Spring Bamboo: A Collection of Contemporary Chinese Short Stories* (Random House, 1989). Translated and edited by Jeanne Tai, the anthology includes 11 short stories chosen from the works of the new generation of Chinese writers, including Zheng Wanlong, Han Shaogong, Wang Anyi, Chen Jiankong, Li Tuo, Zhaxi Dawa, Shi Tiesheng, Mo Yan, Ah Cheng, and Zhang Chengzhi. In the "Introduction," Leo Ou-fan Lee acknowledges the diverse and experimental writing style of these writers and commends their exploration of new ways of literary expression:

> These new writings, exemplified by the stories in this collection, are notable not just for the striking absence of ideology and politics, but also for their ambitious attempts to explore new idioms and to experiment with plot characterization and language.
>
> (Lee, 1989, p. xvii)

This anthology of short stories, as Lee suggests here, is primarily driven by literary rather than political or social motivations. A similar case in point is *Running Wild: New Chinese Writers* (Columbia University Press, 1994). Co-edited by Jeanne Tai and David Der-wei Wang, this collection includes Chinese short stories and novellas written in the later 1980s and early 1990s by writers from China's mainland, Taiwan, Hong Kong, and overseas. At a rather sensitive point in history, there was hostile speculation and fear in the West about the China of the time. Rather than pander to or reinforce such hostility, the editors of this anthology made an intentional effort to posit a new image of China, "a China defined not by geopolitical boundaries and ideological closures but by overlapping cultures and shared imaginative resources" (Wang, 1994, p. 238). Wang urges the reader to appreciate the stylistic inventiveness, lyrical inclination, and playful wit of these end-of-the-century Chinese fictions and, more importantly, to be aware of a Chinese literature that is on the verge of "letting all of its voices speak" (ibid 258).

Obviously, one cannot be so naive as to think that the choices made by literature scholars are free from the influence of particular ideological conceptions. In his theory of rewriting, Lefevere explicates very clearly that professionals "frequently rewrite works of literature until they are deemed acceptable to the poetics and the ideology of a certain time and place" (1992, p. 14). At a time when there were severe ideological confrontations between East and West, even scholars like Perry Link gave political considerations precedence over poetic choices. Currently in the era of globalization, however, the East-West antagonisms have to some extent subsided, while cooperation and mutual understanding are increasingly becoming the prevalent themes. The selection of Chinese literature for translation should also be adjusted accordingly to this changing context. Choosing a careful balance between political criteria and poetic considerations is a challenging task, which requires practical wisdom, prudence, and dexterity. But the bottom line is that the compilers of literary anthologies should not be oblivious to the current state of development in the contemporary Chinese literary system, which as David Der-wei Wang observes, is increasingly characterized by the articulation of a multiplicity of voices and experiences. The selection of material for the translation anthologies, therefore, needs to accommodate this plurality so that the "clamour of voices" will be heard rather than silenced by political stereotypes and prejudices.

Accommodating the "Clamour of Voices"

The "clamour of voices," as used in this chapter, is a term coined by David Der-wei Wang, the aforementioned co-editor of *Spring Bamboo* and also a highly influential scholar and critic of contemporary Chinese literature. In 1988, Wang published his own essay collection on Chinese literary production of the 1930s and the 1980s under the title of 眾聲喧譁, which in literal translation would be "the clamour of voices." In the introduction to this collection, Wang acknowledges that his title originates from Bakhtin's lexicon "heteroglossia" and describes it as an endeavor to draw attention to "the inevitable constraints, differentiation, contradictions, revisions, innovations, and other phenomena occurring in the process of using language and communicating meaning" (Wang, 2014, p. 381). Intrigued by the concept of "heteroglossia" and its inherent emphasis on pluralism, openness, and defiance of conventional perceptions, Wang advocates a more nuanced and dialectical approach to the study and construction of literary history:

> To reassess the canon of masters and classics; to search for divergent subjects, styles, and ideologies; and to tease out the unexpected "origins" of an author's creative intention are the tasks we need to undertake persistently.
>
> (ibid)

In other words, a literary historiography that allows for "heteroglossia" would seek to break away from the extant paradigm and to destabilize the broader network of relations between highbrow and lowbrow, between traditional and experimental, and between canonical and popular.

After the initial use by David Der-wei Wang, the expression "clamour of voices" became a very popular catchphrase and gradually evolved to be a prominent theme in contemporary Chinese literary studies. A fitting example of celebrating the "clamour of voices" in writing literary history would be *A New Literary History of Modern China* edited by David Der-wei Wang (2017) himself. Regarding his editorial vision and format, Wang lists several underlying sources of influence, which include, in addition to the Chinese tradition of mutual illumination of literature and history, a wide range of postmodernist elements such as Walter Benjamin's "constellation," Mikhail Bakhtin's "heteroglossia," Michel Foucault's "genealogy," and Gilles Deleuze's "assemblage" (Wang, 2017, p. 8). Putting together 161 essays contributed by 143 authors, this massive volume explores a wide spectrum of topics concerning modern Chinese literary and cultural dynamics. The tremendous variety, though "befuddling, and sometimes contradictory" (Larson, 2018, p. 181) does make enough of a "clamour."

While David Der-wei Wang has managed to retain the polyphony of voices in his anthology of contemporary Chinese literary history, we would like to make a similar plea here for the compilation of literary anthologies. After all, an anthology itself inherently bears both the commitment to and expectation of a plurality of voices. It is, however, important to keep in mind that Bakhtinian ideal of polyphony and heteroglossia is not simply a juxtaposition or quantitative accumulation of independent viewpoints but rather necessarily involves their "engaged co-existence" (Sidorkin, 2005, p. 283). The multiple voices or viewpoints are not just simultaneously there: they need to engage with each other in conversation or dialogue.[5] This is exactly why databases or archives might not be seen as polyphonic, even though they encompass many voices. Once a text is selected to be a constitutive part of the anthology, it enters a new network of textual relations that was totally absent at the time of its original production. Anthologizers should endeavor to provide a space where different perspectives assemble into a new network of "engaged co-existence," where the logic through which texts have been produced and used in their original context can speak to and placate with the logic through with the same texts are going to be received and understood. As such, this new textual space would "creates a meaning and value greater than the sum of meanings and values of the individual items taken in isolation" (Frank, 1998, p. 13).

Another common misconception about polyphony or heteroglossia is that the emphasis on the multitude of voices dispenses with the need for coherence altogether. Polyphony or heteroglossia, however, carries with it a conceptual sense of unity, which is what Dostoevsky's novels unfold for Bakhtin: "a plurality of consciousnesses, with equal rights and each with its own world, combine but are not merged in the unity of the event" (Bakhtin, 1984, p. 6). Such unity is a unity of a plurality and of a manifold. Perhaps musicians know best the diverse and unifying qualities of polyphony. Mahler, for example, comments on the random sounds of a forest festival as the archetype of his polyphony:

> Do you hear that? That is polyphony and that is where I have got it from. . . . Exactly like that, coming from quite different sides, this is how the themes must be completely distinct in their rhythmic and melodic character (anything else is merely something written in many parts, disguised homophony); it requires that the artist should organize it and unify it into a congruous and harmonious whole.
>
> (cited in Adorno, 1992, p. 15)

In distinguishing polyphony from "something merely written in many parts" and "disguised homophony," Mahler emphasizes the importance of artistic organization and makes clear the quest for wholeness behind polyphony. These two elements – artistic organization and a unity of a plurality – are also absolutely essential in our advocacy for editorial vision that prioritizes the "clamour of voices" in the compilation of anthologies of contemporary Chinese literature.

Constructing a Polyphonic Space: *By the River* as a Case Study

When it comes to the articulation for a "clamour of voices" in compiling translation anthologies of contemporary Chinese literature, sizeable anthologies may come to mind as ready and apparent examples of allowing for a plurality of literary voices to be expressed and intersect.[6] It is, however, also important to keep in mind that the potential of polyphony does not depend on how many voices or how loud they are but how well these voices are organized and connected. To better illustrate this point, this chapter chooses a smaller translation anthology as an example, that is, *By the River: Seven Contemporary Chinese Novellas* (Tulsa: University of Oklahoma Press, 2016).

Co-edited by Charles A. Laughlin, Liu Hongtao, and Jonathan Stalling, *By the River* is a beautifully edited collection of seven novellas written by Jiang Yun, Xu Zechen, Han Shaogong, Chi Zijian, Fang, Li Tie, and Wang Anyi. While all the authors featured in this collection are highly regarded in contemporary Chinese literary circles, their international recognition varies. When asked in an interview about the selection of texts in this anthology, Charles Laughlin, one of the editors, explained that this collection is a joint project involving scholars from both China and U.S. and that the seven novellas were all recommended by Chinese scholars (Wang, 2018, p. 68). Some Western readers may feel suspicious and distrustful of the official Chinese perspective behind the selection of texts, but such doubts are not exactly warranted. On the whole, contemporary Chinese literature has not been studied in depth even among Western Sinologists. Some Western scholars may be familiar with one or more Chinese contemporary authors, but few have read enough contemporary Chinese literary works to be able to grasp them in a broader context. In contrast, Chinese scholars in related fields have much more comprehensive experience in reading these texts. Their selections may be weighted toward works that are officially recognized in China, but official recognition does not necessarily imply that the literary quality of the works is inferior to that of a text selected by a Western Sinologist.

The seven novellas included in *By the River* are justly representative of the finest Chinese literary writings in this genre, with a considerable richness and diversity in terms of the themes and settings of the stories, the styles and techniques of writing, as well as the identity, including gender identity of the authors. The seven novellas appear to be separate stories, depicting unrelated people and events in different regions of China and at different stages of contemporary history. The editors, nevertheless, find two elements to bind them together into an "engaged co-existence" in this collection: one is the uniqueness of genre, best characterized by the interest in depicting the minutiae of the everyday, and the other is the image of "river," which appear in most of the stories in this collection.

It is common to use genre as a principle of organization in anthologizing literature. As the subtitle suggests, *By the River* focuses on a very distinctive literary genre, novella. Few Chinese novellas have been translated and published in English. One of the reasons behind the editors' decision to publish this collection is an intention to enhance English readers' awareness of this genre, which is, though slightly marginal in the West, "the mainstay of modern Chinse fictional art" (Laughlin, 2016, p. vii). Despite the very different trajectories and current state of development of novella in both Chinese and Western literary traditions, the editors see the possibility and significance of engaging them. In the introduction, Laughlin reviews the development of the novella in Europe, particularly in Germany and how German literature may have influenced and inspired the Chinese novella in terms of both narrative techniques and themes. To illustrate its unique value in terms of literary expression, novella is also compared with two other popular narrative genres, namely, the novel and the short story. Compared with full-length novels involving grand narratives that usually span a wide range of scenes and settings, novellas are more suited to depicting the lives of individuals at present. The added length of novellas also allows them to delve deeper than short stories into the detritus of ordinary life. Or as the editors of the anthology put it, "they plumb the depths of the psychic and mythic beneath the surface of the everyday" (Laughlin, 2016, p. xii). At a time when "much of the Chinese fiction that has been influential in translation shares an almost obsessive fascination with the distant past and sometimes outrageous and gratuitous violence" (ibid, xi–xii), the editors of *By the River* see the necessity and exigency of presenting China in a way that is less exaggerated and more in tune with the present reality. The genre choice of this anthology, therefore, is made not randomly but in response to and in conjunction with a multitude of voices: China and Europe, past and present, novels and short stories, and even different gender perspectives. As the readers begin to go through these stories, they would find themselves entering an intricate and manifold network of significance, which enables but not dictates extra layers of meaning and ambiguity to emerge in their interpretation of the texts.

Another thread that runs through the collection is the image of the river: "rivers appear in most of the stories, lending the grouping an unexpected coherence" (Laughlin, 2016, p. xi). In straightforward terms, rivers are constantly present, serving as a backdrop or a scene in which these stories take place, thereby connecting the separate stories together. But a more subtle layer of coherence lies in the fact that the recurring image of the river has also become a poignant and promising narrative anchor for the editors to voice the story they wish to tell. In the "Introduction" to this anthology, Laughlin speaks of the anthropological significance of rivers, which is worth quoting here at some length:

> This recurrence of the river image is no coincidence: rivers are the lifeline of human community. They offer an entry and exit point between the hometown and the world outside, allowing for both chance encounters and final farewells. But they are also the scene of communal domestic activities like bathing and washing clothes with all the attendant joking and gossip. Even if in the twenty-first century rivers in more urban landscapes no longer play such a practical community role, this universal social legacy confers an archetypal quality on them that draws characters toward them for contemplation and emotional transactions.
>
> (Laughlin, 2016, p. xi)

The "river" is seen as a background to the everyday lives of ordinary people. There may not be much dramatic happening by the river, but the mundanities of life can also have profound power. The anthropological implications and associations behind the image of the river are entwined and juxtaposed within the stories in the collection to constitute a thriving unity of the diverse experiences of ordinary people in contemporary China. As the readers move through the book, story by story, they walk into a river of experiences. They witness the diversity of landscapes and customs, encounter ordinary Chinse man and women, and get to know them by their peculiarities and eccentricities. They hear their everyday whispers, low but clear, just like the river's rippling song. There might be no powerful currents and crashing waves in the river, but in subtle ways, the "river" reveals some of the most profound aspects of contemporary Chinese reality.

The previous examination of the editorial vision behind *By the River* goes to show that our plea for translation anthologies to highlight a "clamour of voices" does not necessarily mean that we should strive to edit larger collections, to include more literary works, or to tell louder stories. Of course, editors may need to make a conscious effort to broaden the range of their selections and to cultivate a more embracing literary enthusiasm. But what matters most is the need to construct connections between texts, to construe new textual networks that allow the final collection to articulate a "clamour of voices" while at the same time reflecting an underlying unity.

Conclusion

Both translation and anthology have traditionally been described as secondary, derivative, and mechanical, but both are increasingly recognized as important forms of cultural rewriting. Translation anthologies not only serve as sourcebooks of representative literary works from another culture, but also participate in the construction of cultural and literary images of the Other for its reader. They tend to, however, "offer a potted social history of the source culture" and thus have "a potential for both challenging and reinforcing prejudices or stereotypes" (Barnaby, 2002, p. 86).

In recognition of the important role of translation anthologies in cultural construction and intervention, this chapter proposes an editorial vision for translation anthologies that is oriented toward highlighting cultural diversity and respecting literary heterogeneity. With regard to the compilation of translation anthologies of contemporary Chinese literature, we have borrowed from David Der-wei Wang's concept of "clamour of voices" as a guideline for editors to disrupt certain established politicized editorial biases and to present a more diversified image of Chinese literature. In retrospect, the original formulation of this phrase is inextricably linked to the carnival of Chinese avant-garde literature from the 1980s onwards. The Chinese literary scene today is not the same as it was in the 1980s, but the literary ideals that emphasize detachment from politics, diversity, and creativity have not dissipated. David Der-wei Wang's emphasis on the "clamour of voices" can be perceived as essentially in line with a liberalist view on literature:

> The job of criticism would seem to be, then, to recall liberalism to its first essential imagination of variousness and possibility, which implies the awareness of complexity and difficulty. To the carrying out of the job of criticizing the liberal imagination, literature has a unique relevance, not merely because so much of modern literature has explicitly directed itself upon politics, but more importantly because literature is the human activity that takes the fullest and most precise account of variousness, possibility, complexity and difficulty.
> (Trilling, 1950, p. xii)

If literature embodies "variousness, possibility, complexity and difficulty," it is only natural that translations of literature should also retain those qualities and that literature anthologies should amplify those qualities as well.

David Damrosch, one of the leading scholars in the field of world literature, conjures that "future anthologies of world literature must find new and better ways to manage the tensions between the reader's world and the worlds we read about" (Damrosch, 2000, p. 19). Translation anthologies, as a site of intercultural encounter and dialogue, allow the reader to traverse between their own world and the world of the Other. We would hope that they be pleased to see both worlds full of diverse possibilities, clamorous voices, and polyphonic resonances.

Notes

1 See Paper Republic website for details: https://paper-republic.org/project/year-end-roll-call/
2 This is even true for Mo Yan, the Nobel Prize-winning novelist, whose writings have received more newspaper reviews and scholarly attention, but "they were still not widely read in the U.S." For more information on the reception of contemporary Chinese

literature in the West, see Cui Yanqiu 崔艳秋. *Translation and Dissemination of Modern Chinese Novels in the US since the 1980s* 八十年代以来中国现当代小说在美国的译介与传播. Doctoral dissertation. Jilin University, 2014.
3 For a more comprehensive survey of Chinese literary translation anthologies in English, see Kinkley, Jeffrey C. "APPENDIX: A Bibliographic Survey of Publications on Chinese Literature in Translation from 1949 to 1999." In *Chinese Literature in the Second Half of a Modern Century: A Critical Survey*. Eds., Chi Pang-Yuan and Wang David Der-wei · Bloomington, IN: Indiana University Press, 2000: 239–286.
4 Translation projects initiated by Chinese state institutions are not included in the current discussion.
5 For Bakhtin, dialogue is both a fact of life and an ideal to strive for. Dialogue defines the very nature of life: "To live means to participate in a dialogue: to ask questions, to heed, to respond, to agree and so forth" (1984, p. 293). The world thus merges into an open-ended, multi-voiced, dialogical whole.
6 As the first comprehensive anthology of modern Chinese literature in English translation, the text selection of *The Columbia Anthology of Modern Chinese Literature (1995)*, for example, is hailed as "expert, including both the socially dissident 'nativist' fiction and newer, more avant-garde works from Taiwan, including several 'classics' (to evoke that oxymoron again) as well as post-Mao literature from the mainland, and emphasizing younger writers and experimentalism rather than early 1980s new realism" (Kinkley, 2000, p. 257).

References

Adorno, T. W. (1992). *Mahler: A musical physiognomy*. Chicago, IL: Chicago University Press.
Bakhtin, M. (1984). *Problems of Dostoevsky's poetics*. Minneapolis, MN: University of Minnesota Press.
Barmé, G. & Jaivin, L. (Eds.) (1992). *New ghosts, old dreams—Chinese rebel voices*. New York: Times Books.
Barmé, G. & Lee, B. (Eds.) (1979). *The wounded: New stories of the Cultural Revolution 77–78*. Hong Kong: Joint Pub. Co.
Barmé, G. & Minford, J. (Eds.) (1986). *Seeds of fire: Chinese voices of conscience*. Hong Kong: Far Eastern Economic Review.
Barnaby, P. (2002). Scotland anthologised: Images of contemporary Scottish identity in translation anthologies of Scottish poetry. *Scottish Studies Review*, 3(1), 86–99.
Barnstone, T. (Ed.) (1993). *Out of the howling storm: The new Chinese poetry*. Middletown, CT: Wesleyan University Press.
Benton, G. (Ed.) (1982). *Wild lilies, poisonous weeds: Dissident voices from people's China*. London: Pluto Press.
Cronin, M. (2003). *Translation and globalization*. London: Routledge.
Damrosch, D. (2000). World literature today: From the old world to the whole world. *Symplokē*, 8(1–2), 7–19.
Di Leo, J. R. (2007). Introduction to focus: Anthologies and literary landscapes. *American Book Review*, 28(2), 3.
Epstein, J. (2001). *Book business: Publishing, past, present and future*. New York: Norton.
Essman, H. & Frank, A. P. (1991). Translation anthologies: An invitation to the curious and a case study. *Target*, 3(1), 65–96.
Even-Zohar, I. (2002). Cultural planning and cultural resistance in the making and maintaining of entities. *Journal of Humanities*, 14, 45–52.
Finkel, D. & Kizer, C. (Eds.) (1991). *A splintered mirror: Chinese poetry from the democracy movement*. San Francisco, CA: North Point Press.

Frank, A. P. (1998). Anthologies of translation. In M. Baker (Ed.), *Encyclopaedia of translation studies* (pp. 13–16). London: Routledge.

Jenner, W. J. F. (Ed.) (1983). *Fragrant weeds: Short stories once labelled as poisonous weeds*. Hong Kong: Joint Publishing Company.

Ji, J. 季进. (2009). The writing of pluralistic literary history: A study of modern Chinese literature abroad 多元文学史的书写 – 海外中国现代文学研究论之一. *Literary Review 文学评论, Vol. 2009*(6), 190–193.

Jiang, J. 江建文. (2008). The origins of new age literature in Guangxi 广西新时期文学之发轫 *Southern Cultural Forum 南方文坛, Vol. 2008*(6), 78–82.

Jiang, Z. 姜智芹. (2016). Contemporary Chinese literature spreading overseas and the shaping of China's image. 中国当代文学海外传播与中国形象塑造. In J. Yao 姚建斌 (Ed.), *Studies on the communication of contemporary Chinese literature abroad 中国当代文学海外传播研究* (pp. 81–92). Beijing: Beijing University Press 北京大学出版社.

Kilcup, K. L. (2000). Anthologizing matters: The poetry and prose of recovery work. *Symplokē, 8*(1–2), 36–56.

Kingsbury, D. B. (Ed.) (1994). *I wish I was a wolf: The new voice in Chinese women's literature*. Beijing: New World Press.

Kinkley, J. C. (2000). APPENDIX: A bibliographic survey of publications on Chinese literature in translation from 1949 to 1999. In P. Chi & D. D. Wang (Eds.), *Chinese literature in the second half of a modern century: A critical survey* (pp. 239–286). Bloomington, IN: Indiana University Press.

Korte, B. (2000). Flowers for the picking, anthologies in (British) literary and cultural studies. In B. Korte, R. Schneider, & S. Lethbridge (Eds.), *Anthologies of British poetry: Critical perspectives from literary and cultural studies* (pp. 1–32). Amsterdam: Rodopi.

Larson, W. (2018). Review: A new literary history of modern China, edited by David Der-wei Wang. *The China Journal, 79*, 181–182.

Lau, J. S. M. & Goldblatt, H. (Eds.) (1995). *The Columbia anthology of modern Chinese literature*. New York: Columbia University Press.

Laughlin, C.A. (2016). Introduction. In C. A. Laughlin, H. Liu, & J. Stalling (Eds.), *By the river: Seven contemporary Chinese novellas* (pp. vii–xii). Tulsa, OK: University of Oklahoma Press.

Lee, L. O. (1989). Introduction. In J. Tai (Ed.), *Spring bamboo: A collection of contemporary Chinese short stories* (pp. xi–xvii). New York: Random House.

Lee, L. O. (1990). Introduction. In E. Morin. (Ed.), *The red azale: Chinese poetry since the cultural revolution* (pp. xv–xxvii). Honolulu, HI: University of Hawaii.

Lefevere, A. (1985). Why waste our time on rewrites? The trouble with interpretation and the role of rewriting in an alternative paradigm. In T. Herman (Ed.), *The manipulation of literature: Studies in literary translation* (pp. 215–243). London: Croom Helm.

Lefevere, A. (1992). *Translation, rewriting & the manipulation of literary fame*. London: Routledge.

Link, P. (Ed.) (1983a). *People or monsters? And other stories and reportage from China after Mao*. Bloomington: Indiana University Press.

Link, P. (Ed.). (1983b). *Stubborn weeds: Popular and controversial Chinese literature after the cultural revolution*. London: Blond & Briggs.

Link, P. (Ed.) (1984). *Roses and thorns: The second blooming of the hundred flowers in Chinese fiction, 1979—1980*. Berkeley: University of California Press.

Liu, N. et al. (Eds.) (1988). *The rose-colored dinner: New works by contemporary Chinese women writers*. Hong Kong: Joint Publishing Company.

Morin, E. (Ed.) (1990). *The red azalea: Chinese poetry since the cultural revolution*. Honolulu: University of Hawaii.

Puchner, M. (2011). Teaching worldly literature. In T. D'haen, D. Damrosch, & D. Kadir (Eds.), *The Routledge companion to world literature* (pp. 255–264). New York: Routledge.

Qi, L. (2022). Construction and consumption of otherness: A (neo-)orientalist study of English translations of contemporary Chinese literature. In J. Zhao, D. Li, & R. Moratto (Eds.), *Chinese literature in the world: New frontiers in translation studies* (pp. 19–38). Singapore: Springer.

Sidorkin, A. (2005). Carnival and dialogue: Opening new conversations. In B. H. Banathy & P. M. Jenlink (Eds.), *Dialogue as a means of collective communication* (pp. 277–288). New York: Kluwer Academic/Plenum Publishers.

Sieber, P. (Ed.) (2001). *Red is not the only color: Contemporary Chinese fiction on love and sex between women, collected stories*. Lanham, MD: Rowman and Littlefield.

Soong, S. C. & Minford, J. (Eds.) (1984). *Trees on the mountain: An anthology of new Chinese writing*. Hong Kong: The Chinese University Press.

Stillman, E. (Ed.) (1959). *Bitter harvest: Intellectual revolt behind the iron curtain*. New York: Praeger.

Trilling, L. (1950). *The liberal imagination: Essays on literature and society*. London: Mercury Books.

Wang, D. D. (1988). 眾聲喧譁: 三十到八十年代的中國小說 *Zhongsheng xiuanhua: Sanshi yu bashi niandai de Zhongguo xiaoshuo*. Taipei: Yuanliu.

Wang, D. D. (1994). Afterword: Chinese fiction for the nineties. In D. D. Wang & J. Tai (Eds.) *Running wild: New Chinese writers* (pp. 238–258). New York: Columbia University Press.

Wang, D. D. (2014). Preface to heteroglossia. In S. Y. Chang, M. Yeh, & M. Fan (Eds.), *The Columbia sourcebook of literary Taiwan* (pp. 381–382). New York: Columbia University Press.

Wang, D. D. (2017). Introduction: Worlding literary China. In D. D. Wang (Ed.), *A new literary history of modern China* (pp. 1–28). Cambridge, MA: The Belknap Press of Harvard University Press.

Wang, J. (1998). Introduction. In J. Wang (Ed.), *China's avant-garde fiction: An anthology* (pp. 1–14). Durham, NC: Duke University Press.

Wang, X. 王岫庐. (2018). Diversified narratives of contemporary and poetic translation 当代中国故事的多元讲述与诗意翻译. *Chinese Translators' Journal* 中国翻译, *39*(2), 67–71.

Yeh, M. (Ed.) (1992). *Anthology of modern Chinese poetry*. New Haven and London: Yale University Press.

Zhu, H. (Ed.) (1991). *The serenity of whiteness: Stories by and about women in contemporary China*. New York: Ballantine Books.

5 Repositioning *The Injustice to Dou E* in a Global Generic Context

Ersu Ding

The Injustice to Dou E (窦娥冤) by Guan Hanqing is a masterpiece of Chinese drama that has been translated into English many times by different people, as is reflected in the multiple variations of its title in the target language: *The Injustice Done to Tou Ngo, Injustice to Tou O, Snow in Midsummer*, and *The Injustice to Dou E*. Despite enormous stylistic differences between the various English translations and adaptations of this text, one thing remains fairly constant in the process of cultural translation; that is, these translated texts are always anthologized either as a representative piece of a particular historical period or as a sample of its author's literary oeuvre. The former situation, for instance, applies to *Six Yuan Plays*, where *The Injustice Done to Tou Ngo* is selected as an exemplary piece of dramatic literature that characterizes the culture of Yuan Dynasty of China (Liu, 1972, pp. 115–158), whereas the latter situation can be found in *Selected Plays of Kuan Han-ching*, where *Snow in Midsummer* is anthologized as a constituent part of Guan Hanqing's overall theatrical craftsmanship (Guan, 1958, pp. 19–47).

To a large extent, the selection of *The Injustice to Dou E* in English translation anthologies is well justified both in terms of the quality of the work and its author's great importance in the history of Chinese letters. Although not much is known about his personal life, Guan Hanqing has been widely regarded as "the father of Chinese theatre" (West & Idema, 2010, p. 2). He wrote approximately 60 some dramatic texts in his life, but only a small number of them survived the wreck of time. His subject matters are extremely wide-ranging, covering all aspects of social life under the rule of Mongols, who took over China for about a century (1271–1368). Nevertheless, Guan Hanqing is better remembered for the impressive women characters he puts on stage, sharing with audiences of different generations the travails they have to go through in life as the most oppressed group in Chinese societies of old.

One such character, of course, is the forever memorable Dou E, whose undeserved suffering and death have moved the heart of Chinese theatergoers for centuries. Presented as the protagonist in the play, Dou E loses her mother at the age of 3 and is sold to a moneylender, Mistress Cai, as a child bride so that her father, Dou Tianzhang, can go to the capital to participate in the imperial examinations in an effort to glorify his ancestry. After she grows up, she only enjoys two years of brief conjugal happiness before her husband dies of a terminal disease, leaving

DOI: 10.4324/9781003368168-6

behind Mistress Cai and Dou E to fend for themselves in this harsh world. It happens that a crooked local physician owes money to Mistress Cai, but instead of making the payment, he plans to kill the latter to escape his debt. The physician's action is accidentally thwarted by the arrival of an old man surnamed Zhang and his vicious son, Donkey. As "saviors," these two men coerce Mistress Cai to not only marry the father herself but also agree to a marriage between Dou E and the son. Mistress Cai eventually succumbs to the pressure, but Dou E refuses to comply, which leads to a series of events where Father Zhang (instead of Mistress Cai, who is the real target) is mistakenly killed by his son. Donkey Zhang then falsely accuses Dou E of poisoning his father with mutton soup and gives her a choice of either marrying him or facing prosecution in court. Being a person of integrity, Dou E opts for the latter, not knowing that Donkey Zhang would bribe the local official to adjudicate the lawsuit in his favor. While in court, Dou E is tortured by the corrupt official who wants to extract a false confession, but she firmly holds her ground despite repeated thrashings on her frail body. Only when the official threatens to torture her mother-in-law for a desired testimony does she agree to put her fingerprint on the paper of "admission." Dou E is speedily executed but not before she makes her three exonerating oaths: first, if she is innocent, her blood from decapitation would spill onto the white flag high above; second, if she is innocent, there would be instant snow in midsummer to cover her corpse; third, if she is innocent, there would be a three-year draught in the district where she is wronged. All these oaths are materialized, which leads to the arrival of her father, now a disciplinary official from the central government, who not only rehabilitates her reputation but also punishes the wicked who are involved in her case.

It is obvious that Dou E suffers more than the average portion of human misery with the early death of her mother, painful separation from her father, sudden death of her young husband, blackmail from her marriage seeker, and ridiculous imputation of murder in court, but what really "moves heaven and shakes earth" (感天动地) derives more from how she adheres to the traditional Chinese moral principles of chastity and filial piety amidst all these adversities. As is mentioned earlier, after Donkey Zhang and his father accidentally save Mistress Cai from murder, they demand marriage from both the old lady and her daughter-in-law. Under the threat of being strangled to death, Mistress Cai is about to give in to Father Zhang's demand, but Dou E stands firm on the Confucian ethic of "three obligations and four virtues" (三从四德). The following is what she says to her mother-in-law (Mair, 2000):

> Now your knot of hair is as white as snow,
> How can you wear the colorful silk veil?
> No wonder people say,
> You cannot keep a grown girl at home.
> Now you are about sixty years of age,
> Isn't it said that "when middle age arrives, all is over"?
> With one stroke, you mark off the memories of former love;

Now you and this man act like newlyweds.
To no purpose you make people split their mouths with laughter.

(p. 682)

When Mistress Cai later persuades her to accept the marriage proposal from Donkey Zhang, Dou E is equally blunt and expresses her clear objection to marrying another man (Mair, 2000):

One horse cannot wear two saddles.
When your son was alive we were married for two years;
Yet now you ask me to marry another.
This is indeed something I cannot do.

(p. 690)

She refuses to remarry certainly because she is a loyal person who remembers the happy days with her late husband but also does it for the sake of defending the good reputation of the Dou family. At a later point in the play, she proudly announces that "in our Tou family for three generations there has been no male who has broken the law, and for five generations there has been no woman who has remarried" (Mair, 2000, p. 704). All these textual details reveal Dou E's strong sense of chastity, which was very much emphasized and respected in traditional Chinese societies.

Apart from being a "chaste woman" (贞女), Dou E is also portrayed as a "filial person" who performs family duties on behalf of her deceased husband. In fact, the entire play of *The Injustice to Dou E* is an adaptation of an ancient Chinese legend titled "The Filial Woman of Donghai" (东海孝妇), which can be traced back to as early as Han Dynasty (206 bce – 220 ce). As the story goes, there was a very filial woman in Donghai who continued to take care of her mother-in-law long after her husband died. The latter was so touched by her daughter-in-law's devotion to her well-being that she, being quite advanced in age, hanged herself in order not to encumber the younger generation anymore. The old woman's daughter, however, went to court and accused her in-law of killing the mother. The corrupt official in charge of the case wanted a quick closure to the lawsuit and cruelly tortured the filial woman until she succumbed to the charge. Immediately after the execution of the filial woman, a severe three-year drought began to plague the rural district where heinous injustice was done. A higher-level official was thus dispatched to the affected area to investigate the case and was told that the woman looked after her mother-in-law for more than a decade after her husband's death and was known far and wide for her selfless filial dedication. The new official went to sweep the tomb of the wrongly executed woman, and this immediately brought rain to the area, which led to a bumper harvest of crops that year. As is obvious from this brief summary, *The Injustice to Dou E* draws heavily from "The Filial Woman of Donghai," including the three famous oaths that are not mentioned here, but the main emphasis in both texts is on filial duties that are expected of the younger generation. Like the legendary woman from Donghai,

Dou E becomes a widow at the age of 19 but continues to look after her mother-in-law as her moral obligation. Her diligence in this respect is in full exhibition when she makes mutton soup for Mistress Cai, who falls ill due to the marriage demands from Donkey Zhang and his father. More indicative of her filial quality is how she falsely admits to the murder charge in court in order to save her mother-in-law from physical torture, which could easily cripple Mistress Cai for the remainder of her life. Even after she is dead, Dou E's spirit still worries about the well-being of her mother-in-law. This is shown in the scene where she meets her father as a ghost and raises two requests, the satisfaction of which would put her roaming soul to rest. She first asks her father to rehabilitate her reputation as an innocent person and then implores him to take care of Mistress Cai, who now has no children left to perform the duty. All these details are meant to show that Dou E is a very filial woman, which further enhances the cathartic effect of pity and fear aroused by Guan Hanqing's masterpiece.

As is well-known, the concept of catharsis consisting of pity and fear was first proposed by the Greek philosopher Aristotle in relation to tragic drama. "A tragedy," he says in his *Poetics*,

> is the imitation of an action that is serious and also, as having magnitude, complete in itself; in language with pleasurable accessories, each kind brought in separately in the parts of the work; in a dramatic, not in a narrative form; with incidents arousing pity and fear, wherewith to accomplish its catharsis of such emotions.
>
> (Barnes, 1984, p. 2320)

Although 2,000 years apart, Aristotle's definition of tragic drama seems a perfect description of *The Injustice to Dou E* as well as many other dramatic works that were produced by Chinese playwrights of the same historical period. Nevertheless, the generic or sub-generic identity of the text has seldom if at all been mentioned in the institutional practice of anthologizing *The Injustice to Dou E* for its English readers.

There are several reasons why *The Injustice to Dou E* is not presented as a piece of tragedy to its Western readers. First among them is the pervasive misbelief or misconception among scholars both in the West and the East that tragic art does not exist outside of Hellenic and Elizabethan theaters. Albert Camus, for one, is of the view that tragedy is "one of the rarest of flowers," and it has blossomed only twice in the long history of Western civilization: once in ancient Greece and another time in Renaissance Europe (Camus, 1970, p. 298). His mission as a playwright, of course, is to resuscitate this classic art so that it will blossom one more time in the twentieth century. George Steiner holds the same opinion that tragic drama prospered first in ancient Greece and then in Renaissance England, Spain, and France, but after Pierre Corneille and Jean Racine, it fell into oblivion due to the erosion of such Enlightenment ideologies as science and technology that believe in the ultimate perfectibility of man and society. More specifically, in the eye of Greeks of fifth century bce, the misery and suffering of this world were caused by the jealous and callous gods of Olympia, who incessantly fought amongst themselves, victimizing innocent humans along the way, and there was little that human beings could do to take control of their fate or destiny. For the subjects of Queen Elizabeth and King Louise XIV, who were trying hard to break free from the yoke of Christianity that had dominated Europe for well over a dozen centuries, suffering was always linked to the innate flaw in human nature that incurred the primal fall from grace in the first place. Once again, human beings were not masters of themselves but playthings in the hand of nature, be it in the form of human desire or ambition this time around. In contrast to their Greek and Renaissance counterparts, modern men and women who are influenced by the Enlightenment movement of the eighteenth century attribute the mishaps and injustices they encounter to the existing social fabric built by generations of tyrants and exploiters. Since social ills are caused by humans themselves rather than supernatural or transcendental forces, they certainly can be fixed by changes in education or improvements in material circumstances. Such confidence in human capability is inimical to tragedy and is particularly reflected in contemporary theater where villains reform and "lovers and heroes walk hand in hand at the close of the story" (Steiner, 1961, p. 136). Such a "happy finale" in drama together with many other social factors led Steiner to pronounce that tragedy is dead in the modern era, hence the title of his influential book *The Death of Tragedy*.

It must be pointed out that for Steiner, tragic art has not just perished in the West in the modern period because of inhospitable circumstances; it has never existed outside the West for similar social and ideological reasons. "All men are aware of tragedy in life," so says he in the opening paragraph of the previously mentioned book.

> But tragedy as a form of drama is not universal. Oriental art knows violence, grief, and the stroke of natural or contrived disaster; the Japanese theatre is full of ferocity and ceremonial death. But that representation of personal suffering and heroism which we call tragic drama is distinctive of the western tradition.
>
> (Steiner, 1961, p. 3)

Here, in addition to "happy ending" in a dramatic work that he deems fatal to tragic art, Steiner has added another culprit for the absence of tragedy in the East, that is, lack of heroism on the part of the tragic protagonist.

Whether or not it is due to the influence of George Steiner's very popular monograph, viewing oriental culture as devoid of tragic art has become the dominant theoretical position taken by most scholars in the field of literary studies. So much so that it has even infiltrated into university textbooks and encyclopedic entries. What follows, for example, is a quotation from a relevant entry in the most prestigious *Encyclopedia of Britannica*:

> In no way can the importance of a conceptual basis for tragedy be better illustrated than by a look at other drama-producing cultures with radically

different ideas of the individual, human nature, and destiny. While the cultures of India, China, and Japan have produced significant and highly artistic drama, there is little here to compare in magnitude, intensity, and freedom of form to the tragedies of the West. In Buddhist teaching, the aim of the individual is to suppress and regulate all those questioning, recalcitrant, rebellious impulses that first impel the Western hero toward his tragic course. The goal of nirvana is the extinction of those impulses, the quieting of the passions, a kind of quietus in which worldly existence ceases. Western tragedy celebrates life, and the tragic hero clings to it: to him, it is never "sweet to die" for his country or for anything else, and the fascination for Western audiences is to follow the hero – as it were, "from the inside" – as he struggles to assert himself and his values against whatever would deny them.

(Sewall & Conversi, 2021, December 20)

The title of this encyclopedic entry is "Absence of Tragedy in Asian Drama," and its authors (Leonard W. Conversi and Richard B. Sewall) obviously agree with George Steiner that there is no real tragedy in the East, including China. Like Steiner, these two scholars pinpoint the fighting spirit of the tragic protagonist ("to assert himself and his values against whatever would deny them") as a hallmark of tragedy and find it lacking in Oriental culture due to its Buddhist tendency to "to suppress and regulate all those questioning, recalcitrant, rebellious impulses that first impel the Western hero toward his tragic course." Toward the end of this quote, a third and new feature of tragedy is broached by Conversi and Sewall, that is, the Western tragic hero never finds it sweet to die for his or her country or for anything else.

Looking at the whole picture, we now have three major dramatic qualities that are deemed to be missing in oriental drama: a hero who refuses to give up, an individual who deems it not sweet to die for others, and a catastrophe that ends the protagonist's struggle. None of these assumed requisites, however, is sufficiently convincing for us not to grant tragic status to Guan Hanqing's *The Injustice to Dou E*.

First of all, unlike the diagnosis made by Steiner and his followers about Oriental tragic protagonists being passive in their suffering, Dou E exhibits all the signs of a heroine who wages battles not just against fate and destiny but also against evil forces in society. It is true that she is not a rebel in the sense of opposing dominant social ideologies or challenging conventional rules of conduct, but her firm stance on following what she believes to be the right moral principles is nothing short of being admirable. In our earlier discussion of the plot, we have already seen how she bravely assumes the responsibility of taking care of her mother-in-law after her husband dies and never shuns such filial duty during and even after her life. More impressive is her courage to stand up to the bully of Donkey Zhang and his father by first rejecting their marriage proposals and then being willing to go to court in the hope of finding justice when she is falsely accused of murder. Incessant torture in the courtroom cannot make her change her mind except when it is applied to her mother-in-law who is advanced in age and frail in body. Last but not least, shortly before she is executed for a crime she never committed, she wants the entire world to know her innocence by making three truth-revealing oaths. Her courage and bravery in doing all these things is second to none, which clearly defies the characterization of Oriental drama made by the likes of George Steiner.

In fact, we can even counter-argue, as Terry Eagleton does so well in his *Sweet Violence: The Idea of the Tragic*, that "not all tragedies portray suffering as ennobling" (Eagleton, 2003, p. 31). In other words, there are also tragic works in the Western tradition where, instead of being presented as admirable characters with a fighting spirit, the protagonist is more of a passive bearer of suffering and pain, who reveals little or no positive moral qualities. One good example of such tragedy from the Hellenic period is *The Women of Trachis* by Sophocles, where the protagonist Heracles howls like a wounded animal without showing any sign of dignity toward the end of the play. Nor does his suffering originate from a noble source; rather, it results from the erosion of his flesh caused by a robe that his wife Deianeira sent him by mistake. A modern version of "pathetic" rather than sublime tragedy can be found in Eugene O'Neill's *Mourning Becomes Electra*, where the Mannon family suffer and die one after another. None of the characters in the play has an ideal to live or die for except the never-ending incestuous relationships across three generations that keep haunting the house until the death of its very last member. One can hardly find a heroic spirit in any of them, which is said to be "distinctive of the western tradition" by George Steiner. Such being the case, there is all the more reason to propose that *The Injustice to Dou E* be read as a piece of tragic art.

The second argument for the absence of tragedy in Asian drama is that Oriental dramatic protagonists find it worthwhile to suffer and die for other people. The proposition is put forward by Leonard W. Conversi and Richard B. Sewall in "Absence of Tragedy in Oriental Drama," but no explanation is offered as to why. Dou E certainly fits this category of dramatic figures who willingly sacrifice themselves to the well-being of others. At the age of 3, she is definitely too young to make a decision to become a child-wife so that her father can pursue his dream of glorifying their ancestry, but when she is 19, she certainly does not have to live in widowhood and continue to look after her mother-in-law following the death of her husband. Nor does she have to "admit" to the murder in court to save Mistress Cai from being tortured, which leads to her own decapitation. The fact that she chooses to do these things for the sake of others makes her character even more noble and her suffering and death more tragic. In fact, a similar play of sacrifice can be found in *Iphigeneia at Aulis* by Euripides, where the eponymous character, after much struggle together with her parents, willingly gives up her young life so that the Greek fleet can proceed on their military journey to conquer Troy. It is equally a sacrifice for Agamemnon and Clytemnestra, who love their daughter Iphigeneia very much and yet have to give priority to the interest of the state to which they belong. In addition to these, Terry Eagleton finds a tragic sacrificial character in Jesus Christ as presented in the *New Testament*. Here is what he has to say:

> If Jesus finally submits willingly to death, it is only because he seems to see it as unavoidable. We do not know why he felt this way, and no doubt neither

did he. But it appeared the only path left open to him, given the way of the world and what we may speculate was his disappointment over the relative lack of impact of his mission in Galilee. It was probably not as effective, for example, as his mentor John the Baptist's, at least as far as crowd-pulling went. And for him to have felt this way about his death is to say that his crucifixion is tragic. Since he was not, as far as we can judge, insane, it is not what he would have chosen had the decision been his own, which he did not consider it was. His death is a sacrifice precisely on this account. Sacrifice is not a matter of relinquishing what you find worthless, but of freely surrendering what you esteem for the benefit of others.

(Eagleton, 2003, p. 35)

We can say that, like Jesus Christ, Dou E is not a masochist who seeks pain for the sake of pleasure but a lover of life who does everything in her power to avoid suffering. Only when she sees it as unavoidable does she willingly surrender what she values for the benefit of others. The fact that she suffers and dies for the well-being of her mother-in-law makes her a tragic heroine in every sense of the word.

The third argument for the absence of tragedy in Oriental drama is related to the structural feature of "happy ending," which for many theorists and playwrights is fatal to tragic art. *The Injustice to Dou E* indeed concludes with the realization of an impartial cosmic law in the name of heaven. The following is the last word of the play uttered by Tou E's father, Dou Tianzhang (translated as Tou T'ien-chang in the next section), as he reads out the final verdict of the case:

I am Tou T'ien-chang. The ghost who has just been here is my wrongly slain daughter, Tuan-yun. Now all of you listen to the sentence. Donkey Chang, who murdered his own father and attempted to seduce a widow, deserves to be sentenced to "slicing alive." Take him to the marketplace, nail him on a "wooden donkey," and let him be sliced one hundred twenty times and die. T'ao Wu, who has been promoted to the post of governor, and the clerks in his department, all responsible for the wrong handling of criminal law, should each receive a hundred strokes and never again be employed in the government service. Sai Lu-yi should not have repudiated his debt, tried to strangle a citizen, or mixed poison that cost a human life. He is to be permanently exiled to a malarial district to work under the surveillance of military authority. Mistress Ts'ai is to come to stay in my house. The guilt of Tou O is to be cleared.

(Mair, 2000, p. 712)

Here, as in many other Oriental dramas, justice is eventually served by rehabilitating the innocent (Dou E and Mistress Cai) and punishing those who are guilty (Donkey Zhang, the local official Tao Wu, and the pharmacist), which expresses a very popular Chinese belief that "virtue will be duly rewarded and vice punished" (善恶有报). For many literary critics, however, "where there is compensation, there is justice, not tragedy" (Steiner, 1961, p. 4). This pronouncement, once again, is made by George Steiner, and he does so in relation to the well-known story of Job narrated in the Old Testament of the Bible. The biblical story begins with Job being a wealthy man with a large family and extensive flocks, but as the plot deepens, he not only loses most of his properties but also his servants and ten children due to various invasions and catastrophes. He is also made to suffer terrible skin sores by God, who is testing the faith of his subject. After a few more twists and turns during which he meditates on the meaning of existence and man's relationship with God, Job receives blessing once more from God for keeping his faith in the entire process and is made twice as rich as before. For Steiner, it is happy ending like this that robs any literary work of its tragic status. Most literary theorists today share Steiner's view on this issue. Paul Allen, for example, defines tragedy as "a story with an unhappy ending that is memorably and upliftingly moving rather than simply sad" (Eagleton, 2003, p. 2). F. L. Lucas, for another, tells us that tragedy has had three meanings: for the ancients, it meant serious drama; for medieval people, it meant a story with unhappy close; for modern men and women, it means a drama with an unhappy close (Lucas, 1972, p. 25). To make the issue more relevant to the discussion of *The Injustice to Dou E*, we turn to a Chinese scholar Zhu Guangqian, who holds a similar view:

> Interest in Chinese drama generally lies in what Aristotle calls "Peripetia", but seldom in the final catastrophe. Open any unknown play at random, no matter what a painful situation in which the principal personages find themselves, you may be sure that they will be all right in the end; what you want to know is how they manage to come to the happy ending. The total impression of a piece is seldom gloomy. More than five hundred plays were written in the Yuan Dynasty alone (i.e. in a period of less than a century), but not a single one of them can be properly called a tragedy.
>
> (Zhu, 1987, p. 209)

What the nay-sayers fail to see, however, is that "happy ending" is actually a common occurrence both in Greek tragedy and its Renaissance successor. Aeschylus, for example, ended his famous trilogy *Prometheus* with the establishment of a civil tribunal where all future family feuds are to be peacefully resolved. Sophocles, arguably the best tragedian ever, also wrote a piece titled *Philoctetes*, where the titular character agrees to rejoin his comrades in the Greek army after much physical pain and emotional sulking. Euripides is said to be the most tragic of all three Greek tragic poets, but even he managed to finish one-third of his plays with happy ending. Shakespeare is undoubtedly the most representative writer of Renaissance tragedy, but he certainly concluded *Romeo and Juliet* with a reconciliation between two feuding families and ended *Macbeth* with condign punishment for the usurper. In France, Pierre Corneille and Jean Racine are believed to be the rearguards of classical Western tragic art, but they produced far more optimistic endings than pessimistic ones in their tragic works such as *Horace* and *Esther*. If the epithet "tragic" can be applied to these Western dramatic texts, there is no reason why it should be denied of works like *The Injustice to Dou E*, which contains "a tiny tail of jubilation" (欢乐小尾巴).

The fact that happy ending occurs both in Western and Chinese dramas of woe suggests that it should not be viewed as an enemy to tragedy but rather as a different structural manifestation of tragic art. Indeed, it has been very well argued by some scholars that even if a dramatic work strikes a sanguine note at the end, it does not mean that the work in question is not tragic. Terry Eagleton offers the following explanation, which is rather convincing:

> Many tragedies end with the dispensation of justice; what is tragic about them is that so much bloodshed should have proved necessary to attain it, or that there should be crimes which call for such stringent penalties in the first place. The Book of Job is Steiner's example of a narrative of justice rather than tragedy; but even if Job is finally comforted, was it not tragic for him to suffer so much affliction in the first place? Why should it be true that all's well that ends well?
>
> (Eagleton, 2003, p. 139)

Applying this piece of exposition to *The Injustice to Dou E*, we can say that even though Dou E's reputation as a chaste and filial woman is rehabilitated and her persecutors duly punished in the end, the outcome cannot compensate for the untold suffering she has to go through in her life. Nor can the justice that Dou E's father restores to the community bring back the life that his daughter lost at such a young age, which makes the play very tragic. As one contemporary American scholar puts it very well: "What is decisive (about tragedy) is not the end but whether we participate in tremendous, terrifying suffering" (Kaufmann, 1968, p. 181).

As was pointed out earlier, echoing the sentiment expressed by Albert Camus and George Steiner, most scholars today are of the view that tragedy as a form of art has witnessed only two periods of prosperity in its entire history of development: one in ancient Greece of fifth century bce and the other in Renaissance Europe of the sixteenth and seventeenth centuries, but there are also theorists like Raymond Williams who try to expand the history of tragedy into the modern era where playwrights such as Henrik Ibsen and Arthur Miller continue to narrate stories of human suffering. "The most striking fact about modern tragic theory," Williams says in his *Modern Tragedy*, which was written as a rebuttal of Steiner's fallacy of the death of tragedy,

> is that it is rooted in very much the same structure of ideas as modern tragedy itself, yet one of its paradoxical effects is its denial that modern tragedy is possible, after almost a century of important and continuous and insistent tragic art.
>
> (Williams, 1966, p. 46)

With a comprehensive study of tragedians across the Atlantic Ocean ranging from Henrik Ibsen to Bertolt Brecht, as indicated in his table of contents, Williams has sufficiently proven that tragic art is not only not dead but very much alive in the modern period.

The same discrepancy exists between Steiner's denial of tragic art in Oriental cultures and the actual history of Chinese drama since the middle of the thirteenth century. With a trade route through West Asia all the way to Europe initiated by the new Mongol rulers, Yuan Dynasty of China experienced a brief period of economic prosperity, which created a huge demand for theater in some major cities like Dadu (now Beijing) and Lin-an (now Hangzhou). There were many entertainment corners called "washe" (瓦舍), which offered dramatic performances for theatergoers all day long and all year-round. The subject matters of Yuan theater were wide-ranging, including those on the pain and travail of human existence. According to one recent calculation, of the 150 plus extant Yuan plays, one-sixth of them are tragic works (Xie, 1995, p. 202), but they were called "dramas of woe" (苦戏) rather than "tragedy," which was a technical term imported from the West at the turn of the twentieth century. Whichever way they were named, the Yuan Dynasty of China witnessed a small surge of tragic drama of its own, including *Autumn in Han Palace, The Orphan of Zhao, The Story of Pipa*, and *The Injustice to Dou E*. Like Guan Hanqing's work we have been discussing in this paper, many of classical Chinese dramas do contain a happy finale but remain very sad in their overall dramatic mood. Some of them, as the first two plays listed here, portray characters who sacrifice their life either for the country or for other people, which is considered by Chinese to be all the more tragic. By repositioning these works as members of the tragic genre in the global context, we can definitely better appreciate them not only as representative works of a particular period or a specific individual writer, but also as different manifestations of tragic art as a universal language of human agony. That way, it offers us one more dimension of literary art where playwrights from the East and the West exchange views on the most fundamental moral and political issues that are often reflected in tragedy.

References

Barnes, J. (1984). *Complete works of Aristotle, volume 2: The revised Oxford translation*. Princeton, NJ: Princeton University Press.
Camus, A. (1970). *Lyrical and critical essays*. New York: Vintage Books.
Eagleton, T. (2003). *Sweet violence: The idea of the tragic*. Malden, MA: Blackwell Publishing.
Guan, H. (1958). Selected plays of Kuan Han-Ching. Shanghai: New Art and Literature Publishing House.
Kaufmann, W. (1968). *Tragedy and philosophy*. Princeton, NJ: Princeton University Press.
Liu, J. E. (1972). *Six Yüan plays*. Baltimore, MD: Penguin Books.
Lucas, F. L. (1972). *Tragedy: Serious drama in relation to Aristotle's poetics*. London: Chatto & Windus.
Mair, V. H. (2000). *The shorter Columbia anthology of traditional Chinese literature*. New York: Columbia University Press.
Sewall, R. B., & Conversi, L. W. (2021, December 20). *Tragedy*. Retrieved from www.britannica.com/art/tragedy-literature/Absence-of-tragedy-in-Asian-drama
Steiner, G. (1961). *The death of tragedy*. London: Faber and Faber.

West, S. H., & Idema, W. L. (2010). *Monks, bandits, lovers, and immortals: Eleven early Chinese plays*. Indianapolis, IN: Hackett Publishing Company.

Williams, R. (1966). *Modern tragedy*. Stanford, CA: Stanford University Press.

Xie, B. 谢柏梁. (1995). *A global history of tragic drama* 世界悲剧文学史. Shanghai: Shanghai Art Publishing House 上海文艺出版社.

Zhu, G. (1987). *The psychology of tragedy*. Hong Kong: Joint Publishing Co.

6 Translating Traditional Chinese Opera for the Stage

The Cult of *Qing* and the English Script of *The Peony Pavilion* (*The Young Lovers' Edition*)

Wenjing Li

1. Introduction

Theater translation is the focus of this chapter, which examines the translation of Tang Xianzu's most famous play, *The Peony Pavilion*. It analyzes the translation strategies employed in the English script of an edition of *The Peony Pavilion* tailored to a modern audience and then focuses on how the concept of *qing* is represented in the English script. Although Tang Xianzu is a well-known playwright in China and sometimes dubbed the Shakespeare of the Orient, he never gained a truly international status of prestige. The fact that he is much less well-known worldwide may be ascribed to a multiplicity of reasons. This is partly due to the lackluster reception of Tang Xianzu's works in the global market. This case study of a successful adaptation of his play may provide insight into the future rewriting of Chinese literature via translation, particularly in the context of theatrical production.

2. *The Peony Pavilion* and Its Historical Context

Subtitled *The Return of the Soul*, *The Peony Pavilion* is a classic work of Chinese literature and a timeless romantic comedy written in 1598 by Ming dynasty playwright Tang Xianzu. Originally written to be performed as *Kunqu* opera, one of the genres of traditional Chinese theatrical art, *The Peony Pavilion* has since become successful with reading audiences as well. It is also considered one of the most famous Chinese plays in the West. Often referred to as the *Romeo and Juliet* of the East, *The Peony Pavilion* depicts the passionate love story of a young woman, Du Liniang, who dies of lovesickness only to be brought back to life to seek love with a young scholar, Liu Mengmei. Her emotive force assisted her in transcending her fictitious position in the feminine imagination, much as Du Liniang's love ultimately overcame death in the play.

Since H. Acton's first selected translation was published in *T'ien Hsia Monthly* in 1939, the play has been translated into English in more than 23 different versions in English (Zhou, 2015, p. 40), involving various modes of translation, such as complete translation, selected translation, and theatrical adaptation for surtitles. Among all Chinese classical dramas, it has the largest number of translated

DOI: 10.4324/9781003368168-7

versions into English (Chang & Zhang, 2020, p. 35), attracting the attention of translation scholars. Among the most studied English versions are the translations by the American Sinologist Cyril Birth, Chinese translator Guangqian Zhang, and/ or Rongpei Wang (e.g., Wei, 2011). Translation scholars are interested in translation strategies for tackling cultural-linguistic problems, such as the translation of allusions (Tao, 2013), cultural images (Zhang & Cao, 2018), and translation strategies in terms of purposes (Chang & Zhang, 2020).

One of the most recent translations is the English version of the play script *The Young Lovers' Edition* (further referred to as the YLE), jointly reproduced by Kenneth Hsien-yung Pai, a world-renowned writer originally from Taiwan, and a team of scholars and *kunqu* artists from mainland China, Hong Kong, and Taiwan. This edition was produced for performance with the aim of reviving the traditional Chinese theater, *kunqu* opera, for modern audiences. Since making its debut in Taiwan in 2004, the YLE has traveled both domestically and internationally, performing 232 times in ten years (till 2014) (Pai, 2014a). The performance was well received by Western audiences (See Dougill, 2008; Lei, 2011; Winn, 2006), commended as "a theatrical triumph" (Lam, 2006) and "a beautiful and curious spectacle" (Hutera, 2008). Although there have been some researches on the play's successful mass communication and adaptation strategies, its translation has not received much attention.

English surtitles are provided for international audiences in both the Western and Hong Kong tours so that they can follow the plot and better appreciate the performance on stage. The script was translated by Lindy Li Mark, professor emerita of anthropology and translator of *kunqu* musical drama. The script (Chinese text with English translation) of YLE was published with minor revisions by Digital Heritage Publishing Limited in Hong Kong in 2008, along with a translator's introduction to the translation strategies, the *kunqu* music, and the play.

The positive reviews of the YLE's overseas performance stand as a clear indicator of the success of English surtitling. This chapter first examines the translation strategies of the English surtitles of the music drama and then focuses on the English representation of a key concept of the play, *qing*, to hopefully shed light on the translation of traditional Chinese literature for theatrical productions.

3. Translation Strategies of the English Script of the YLE

3.1 Purpose and Translation Strategies

Theater Translation

Discussions of theatrical translation are inextricably linked to the purpose of translation. Whether the translated text is to be read as written literature or used as a script for a stage, performance is a crucial factor in the choice of translation strategies. In the latter case, theatrical performativity is foregrounded by the translator. It is necessary to distinguish between drama text (in its strict sense) and theater text. Simply put, the dramatic text is the printed theatrical text for reading, while the theatrical text refers to its production for performance. Although the two terms are sometimes used interchangeably by some translation scholars (e.g., Windle, 2011), they indicate two main forms of translation of theatrical texts, namely, reading on the page or performance on the stage. In translation studies, theatrical translation falls into the category of literary translation (as do most Shakespearean translations) (Bassnett, 1991, p. 106), whereas theatrical translation is considered an integrated part of a multidimensional stage spectacle.

The discussion of theatrical translation used to focus on "performability," a popular criterion of theatrical translation. It has been denounced by Susan Bassnett as "hypothetical" and "non-existent" (Bassnett, 1985, p. 102, 1991, p. 102). This is especially true of traditional Chinese opera, which consists largely of verses for singing to specific tunes (called *qupai*). However, with the development of technologies, most theaters nowadays offer surtitles (i.e., translated or transcribed libretti and spoken parts projected above the stage or displayed on a screen) during a performance. The significance of surtitling is so great that it transcends the conventional polarization between "readability" and "performability" and between the written text and the performance as in the translation of the sung text.

Features of Surtitling Translation

Surtitle translation is a type of screen translation and shares the same characteristics of audiovisual translation (AVT). It is part of a multimodal production, and the verbal text is presented to the audience together with audio and visual elements. Like subtitling in films, surtitling can be described as written, additive, immediate, transient, and synchronous. Translation strategies for subtitling and surtitling are largely influenced by these features, as well as by spatial and temporal constraints on surtitling lines. That is the length of each line and the time it remains on the screen are constrained by various factors such as the width of the screen, the speed of utterances, and the average reading speed of the audience. Under these circumstances, in the translation of surtitles, as noted by Gambier, "fidelity is subordinated to the communicative needs of an audience" (Gambier, 2003, p. 185). Faithfulness to the source text and the literariness of the target text may have to give way to readability and accessibility when necessary. In other words, due to the constraints of space, a surtitle is a condensed version of the original text because a lengthy text projected on a screen over a short period of time can be a serious distraction.

The translator must also take into account the degree of difficulty of the words and phrases used in order to help the audience understand what is said and sung on stage while working within these constraints. In this regard, an immediacy of comprehension is required, and the theater audience has a limited amount of time to process the information presented to them. For this reason, the translator must find a way to overcome linguistic and cultural differences that might hinder immediate comprehension of the target text. In traditional Chinese opera, this is even more of a challenge, considering the extensive use of culturally loaded words, allusions, metaphors, etc. It may be possible to learn more about subtitling classical Chinese operas by looking at how the script of *The Young Lovers' Edition of The Peony Pavilion* is translated for the stage. This opera is a successful example of introducing *Kuqu* opera to international audiences.

3.2. Translation Strategies Used in the YLE

The ST Adaptation

The source text of the YLE was adapted with the aim of reviving the traditional art of *kunqu* opera for modern audiences. According to producer Hsien-Yung Pai, three key principles are followed in their "rearranging"[1] of *The Peony Pavilion*: (1) abridging without alteration, (2) retaining classic excerpted scenes, and (3) focusing on romantic "love" as the main theme (Pai, 2014a). The original 55 scenes were cut down to 27 to accommodate a modern stage presentation, which contributed to its successful reception. The poetic libretti were not changed, and the classical scenes were retained. The translation is based on the adapted version. The first two adaptation principles make it possible to compare different translated versions of the classical scenes of the play so that the features of surtitle translation can be revealed. Therefore, this section focuses on the translation strategies rather than the adaptation/rearranging strategies in the YLE.

Layout: Line by Line Translation

As noted by Lindy Li Mark in her preface to the script, the translation of the abridged edition is "better suited to present-day theatre technology," compared to the widely recognized complete translation by Cyril Birch (Tang, 1980) (Li, 2014, p. 7). Limited by the space of the project subtitles, "the lines are shorter, the language simpler, more concise, and accessible" (Li, 2014, p. 7). The guideline is consistent with the features of screen translation as discussed in the previous section. It also allows the audience to focus more on the stage.

Example 1

The Original Text

> 但願那月落重生燈再紅。
> 但願那月落重生燈再紅。

The YLE

> May the waning moon return,
> May the light of life rekindle.

(Tang, 2014, p. 53)

These are the last words of Liniang before she died of longing for love. The line is sung twice in the performance. As can be seen in the example, the repetition is simplified in English surtitling, which is a common reductive approach in screen translation.

Simple and Direct Expressions

As discussed earlier, in order for the audience to immediately understand the plot without being distracted from the stage performance, surtitles tends to be short and concise, and direct expressions are preferred than complicated ones.

Example 2

The Original Text

> 可知我常一生兒愛好是天然。
> 恰三春好處無人見。
> 不提防沈魚落雁鳥驚喧。
> 則怕的羞花閉月花愁顫。

The YLE

> You know that all my life, I love to be beautiful;
> Like the early spring that no one sees,
> Startled by my beauty, fish dive, swans land, birds take flight.
> Flowers blush, the moon hides, and blossoms tremble.
>
> (Tang, 2014, p. 30)

Birch's translation[2]

> – You see, it has been
> always in my nature to love fine things.
> And yet, this bloom of springtime no eye has seen.
> What if my beauty should amaze the birds
> and out of shame for the comparison
> "cause fish to sink, wild geese to fall to earth,
> petals to close, the moon to hide her face"
> while all the flowers tremble?
>
> (Tang, 1980, p. 44)

For this part, the surtitling is notably simpler compared with Birch's version for obvious reasons. Some accessibility improvements are made to facilitate easy comprehension. As can be observed, the English translation of the YLE contains four lines corresponding to the Chinese lines, represented by simple and concise expressions if compared with Birch's version: "early spring" vs. "the bloom of springtime"; "swans land" vs. "wild geese to fall to earth"; "the moon hides" vs. "the moon to hide her face."

Similarly, simple and direct sentence structures are made in the YLE: "Startled by my beauty, fish dive, swans land, birds take flight. Flowers blush, the moon hides, and blossoms tremble." While in Birch's version, a much more complicated syntax is used: "What if my beauty should amaze the birds and out of shame for the comparison 'cause fish to sink . . . ' while all the flowers tremble?" The YLE's version is obviously more accessible to theater audiences.

Dealing with Allusions and Culture-loaded Words

Allusions and culture-loaded words are mostly unknown to foreign audience without further explanation. The translator adopts several methods to overcome this difficulty.

Example 3

The Original Text

> 既然這女子是慕色而亡，
> 貶在**燕鶯隊**裏去吧。

The YLE

> Since this woman died longing for romance,
> banish her to **rebirth** among **the birds and bees**.
> (Tang, 2014, p. 58)

This line is from the "Judge" of the Hell who is deciding the path of reincarnation for Du Liniang after her death. The word "rebirth" is added to the English version to support the notion of reincarnation after death, which is well-known and accepted in ancient China. Without such addition, the intended meaning might be unclear to the English audience. The metaphor "燕鶯隊" (*yingyan dui*), which literally means "a flock of orioles and swallows" and refers to female entertainers or prostitutes in ancient China, is rendered as "the birds and bees." The audience would likely be perplexed by this because they might find it meaningless, or they may associate it with the metaphorical story of "the birds and the bees" in English, which is commonly used to explain the mechanics and results of sexual intercourse to children. Though the original metaphor is appropriated by the translator, the association with "birds" and "sex" is kept, and the use of "banish" makes it clear that this path of reincarnation is a punishment for the heroine's longing for romance. The English line is still concise and accessible to the audience.

Example 4

The Original Text

> 門兒鎖，
> 放著這**武陵源**一座。

The YLE

> Behind locked gates,
> Lies **this enchanted spring.**
> (Tang, 2014, p. 62)

The translator appropriates some references to make direct comprehension possible. "武陵源" (*Wulingyuan*) is a commonly used allusion in ancient poems, referring to places with beautiful scenery where people live in seclusion. Here the word is used to describe the desolate garden where the romance begins. This allusion is omitted in the translated version because it is assumed that international audiences are unlikely to be able to make sense of it. Instead, the translator has changed the indirect reference to the actual description of the scenery, "the "enchanted spring." This is a viable strategy.

Example 5

The Original Text

寸草心怎報得春光一二。

The YLE

> How can my heart, **a mere weedling**,
> reply the debt of parental sunshine.
> (Tang, 2014, p. 17)

Birch's translation

> How can this heart, mere wisp of straw,
> give thanks for light by loving parents shed.
> (Tang, 1980, p. 7)

This line comes from Liniang when she is called to meet her parents. The metaphor "寸草心" (*cuncao xin*, the inch-long grass) and "春光" (*chun guang*, sunlight of spring) are taken from a well-known Chinese poem by a Tang Dynasty poet, Meng Jiao. The original line "誰言寸草心, 報得三春暉" ("Who says that the heart of inch grass, might be able to repay the sunlight of full spring") is an expression of the son's gratitude to his mother's love. The two images of grass and spring sunlight are kept in the English surtitles of the YLE with their connotation explicified, "my heart, a mere weedling" and "parental sunshine," so that the audience does not get lost in the unfamiliar metaphors. Birch's version, "How can this heart, mere wisp of straw, give thanks for light by loving parents shed," does not offer a direct access, and the target audience (not reader) may find it a little difficult to follow within a limited amount of time.

Puns and Wordplays

When translating puns and polysemous words, the translator generally refrains from maintaining or recreating puns and humorous effects so that the audience would not be distracted from the main plot of the play and the appreciation of the performance.

Example 6

The Original Text

> 柳夢梅：
> 喜的一宵恩愛。
> 被功名二字驚開。
> 好開懷這御酒三杯。
> 放著四嬋娟人月在
>
> 麗娘：
> 立朝馬五更門外。
> 聽六街里喧傳人氣概。
> 七步才，
> 登上了寒宮八寶台。
> 沉醉了九重春色。
> 便看花十里歸來。

The YLE

> Liu Mengmei:
> Glad for **one** night of wedded bliss,
> Broken up **again** by scholarly ambitions.
> Happily here, **3** cups of royal brew,
> That grace perfect companions: **Flower, willow, moon, and you.**
>
> Liniang:
> When at dawn, I hear horses halt at the palace gate;
> When I hear people cheer in the streets and lances;
> That is when, your quick talent for poetry,
> Will have raised you to Moon Palace heights.
> When you are flush with the wine of royal acclamation,
> I shall greet your return in the parade of Triumph.

(Tang, 2014, pp. 94–95)

In example 6, each of the lines contains a number: one night, two characters, three cups, four plays, five shifts, six avenues, seven steps, Eight Treasures terrace, ninth spring colours, ten miles. Some of them are allusions and culture-loaded words that need further explanation for foreigners. This numerical scheme is a kind of the aesthetic appeal of the traditional Chinese poems and verses. When it comes to the third line, which coincides with and corresponds to "three cups," the audience's expectation is aroused and satisfied. The poetic form is distinguished by the numerical order, the implementation of which in the verse is a pleasure to read. The previous partially literal back translation gives a taste of the pleasure experienced by the source reader.

The English translation of the YLE has made a half-hearted attempt to reproduce the numerical scheme, but only up to line three. This is understandable. Although it is not technically impossible to reproduce the scheme, it may prove to be a thankless task: the target reader may not find it aesthetically pleasing because of their different cultural and poetic tradition. Though the numerical scheme is not followed, an interesting addition can be found in line 4, where the translator abandons the original allusion of "四嬋娟人月" (*sichanjuan renyue*, four plays of talented females in ancient China, you and moon), and replaces it with familiar images from the story of *The Peony Pavilion*: "flower, willow, moon, and you."

4. The Concept of *Qing* and Its Representation in the English Script of the YLE

4.1 Qing *in Late Ming Literature*

Appropriately, in discussing the translation of *The Peony Pavilion*, a lucid understanding of the central theme of *qing* can be underpinned by taking into account its various interpretations and translations in different situations, especially in the context of surtitling.

"*The Peony Pavilion* is all about *qing*," remarked Ming dynasty Xiqu critic Wang Siren when summarizing "Four Dreams in the Camellia Hall," Tang Xianzu's four major plays (Wang, 2011, p. 1). In the play, the female protagonist, Du Liniang, is enchanted by the splendid blossoms in the springtime garden and has a dream in which she has a flaming romance with the young scholar Liu Mengmei. Du Liniang withers and dies of her lovesickness. Three years later, Liniang's dream lover appears, and she is resurrected with his help. The whole story is driven by "*qing*," the mysterious power that transcends the boundaries of life and death and is beyond the logic of *li* (理, principle or reason). Just like Tang's words in his inscription of *The Peony Pavilion*, "You never know when something that is absolutely impossible according to reason/principle will turn out to be something absolutely possible according to love" (第雲理之所必無, 安知情之所必有耶).

By the late Ming dynasty, Neo-Confucianism had developed into a major philosophical school (宋明理學, *Song-Ming lixue*, the principle of *li*/reason) and was institutionalized by imperial China. By "preserving the Heavenly Principle" (存天理, *cun tianli*) and "eliminating human desire" (滅人欲, *mie renyu*), the orthodoxy had imposed a rigid and repressive code of ethics on people. Against this background, the concept of *qing* emerged as an anti-hegemonic literary theme to resist the *li* (以情抗理, *yiqing kang li*) in the late Ming dynasty. Some of the writers of late Ming literature, in this so-called "cult of *qing*" movement, made *qing* a central theme in fiction and drama and extolled it as the highest human value to be celebrated (Huang, 1998, p. 161). Popularity adds to the complexity of this notion. Huang fruitfully explores the development and implications of *qing*, as well as its intricate association with several other terms such as *li* (理, reason), *xing* (性, innate nature), and *yu* (欲, desire) (Huang, 1998). According to Huang's study, *qing* and *xing* often overlap in meaning in traditional Chinese philosophical discourse, and when broadly defined, *qing* contains the meaning of *yu*. Because of the frequent pejorative use of *yu*, which can also be construed as "lust" by Confucian thinkers, *qing* became "a convenient alternative term for *yu* and thus blurred the distinction between the two terms" (Huang, 1998, p. 161). All these different implications of the concept of *qing* can be found in Tang's masterpiece, *The Peony Pavilion*, in which the word *qing* can be understood in different contexts as "feelings," "love," "desires," "passions," "sentiment," etc., or all of them together.

4.2 *The Concept of* Qing *in* The Young Lovers' Edition

As a representative figure among the late Ming literati who believes that "the world is always for *qing*, and *qing* gives birth to poetry" (世總爲情, 情生詩歌) (Tang, 1935), Tang Xianzu's *The Peony Pavilion* stands as a manifesto of the "cult of *qing*." In this section, we will take a close look at how the concept of *qing* is represented in the English surtitles of *The Young Lovers' Edition*.

As noted in the producer's preface of the YLE, one of the three basic principles in their "rearrangement" of the script is to "focus on romantic 'love' as the main theme" (Pai, 2014a, p. 5). Under this overarching principle of adaptation, the 27 scenes that were shortened from the original 55 are divided into three sections, titled "Love in Dream," "Love between Man and Spirit," and "Love in the Human Word" respectively. As a result, the adapted play emphasizes the theme of love in terms of its story line. Based on this general understanding, let us now take a closer look at its translation.

Example 7

The Original Text

情不知所起,
一往而深。
生者可以死,
死可以生,
夢中之情何必非真。

The YLE

Where does **love** arise?
It wells up from the deep.

> **For love,** the living can die.
> **For love,** the dead can revive.
> Let **love in dreams** be real, or unreal.
> (Tang, 2014, p. 15)

Birch's translation

> **Love** is of source unknown, yet it grows ever deeper.
> The living may die of **it**, by **its** power the dead live again.
> And must **the love** that comes in dream necessarily be unreal?
> (Tang, 1980, p. ix)

Tang's philosophy of *qing*, known as "至情觀" (*zhi qing guan*), that is, the ultimate/extreme/supreme of *qing*, is eloquently presented in his own preface, as shown in the following example 7. Most English translations of this part use the word "love" as an equivalent, as does Birch's version and the YLE. The difference with the YLE is the emphasis on "love" through the repetition of "for love" in lines 3 and 4, thus highlighting "love" as the ultimate drive of the story.

Although the abridged version focuses on the theme of love, the word *qing* has complex implications in various contexts of the play. The two sometimes contradictory implications of *qing*, that is, "*qing* as lofty romantic sentiments and *qing* as physical desires" (Huang, 1998, p. 183) are fully exploited in the story. It is clear that the exact meaning of *qing* is context dependent. The original Chinese word *qing* is treated differently in translation and can be divided into two broad categories.

1. *Qing* as romantic sentiment

Depending on the context, the original Chinese word is treated differently in translation. The most commonly seen:

Example 8

The Original Text

> 姐姐, 咱一片**閑情**愛煞你哩！

The YLE

> Lady, my heart is filled with love for you.
> (Tang, 2014, p. 33)

In example 8, the word *qing* is used in phrase "閑情" (*xian qing*, romantic love) and in the surtitle is immediately followed by the verb "愛" (*ai*, love). Then we have "Lady, my heart is filled with love for you."

Example 9

The Original Text

> 漫道**柔情**著意關, 牡丹亭畔**春夢**殘

The YLE

> For whom **tender feelings** spring;
> By the peony pavilion, **love dreams** wane.
> (Tang, 2014, p. 42)

When the same character *qing* is preceded by "柔" (*rou*, soft), and thus 柔情 (*rou qing*), it is rendered as "tender feelings." In the same line, "春梦," literally meaning "spring dream" but actually alluding "sex dream," is interpreted as "love dream," which is rather appropriate considering the theme of the play. In Chinese, the word *chun*, meaning spring, also bears complicated implications such as the season spring, youth, and sex. It is often used in association with *qing* and thus worth the discussion related to *qing*. It will be discussed later in this section.

Example 10

The Original Text

> 生和死, 孤寒命。
> **有情**人叫不出**情**人應。

The YLE

> In life and death, lonely is my fate.
> **The loved one** answers not **the lover**'s call.
> (Tang, 2014, p. 67)

The corresponding translation of "生和死, 孤寒命。 有情人叫不出情人應" is "In life and death, lonely is my fate. The loved one answers not the lover's call." In terms of formal length and rhythm, the translated version matches the original fairly well. At the same time, the use of "the loved one" and "the lover" highlights the romantic relationship between the couple.

Example 11

The Original Text

> 劉夢梅：
> 喜個甚樣人家？
> 麗娘：

但得個秀才**郎情傾意愜**。
劉夢梅：
小生倒是個**有情**的。
麗娘：
是看上你年少**多情**，
拖逗俺睡魂難貼。

The YLE

> Liu Mengmei:
> What kind of person do you like?
> Liniang:
> A young scholar, **romantic and devoted**.
> Liu Mengmei:
> I am indeed **a romantic one**.
> Liniang:
> I admired your **youthful affection**,
> Hovering about my slumbering soul.
>
> (Tang, 2014, p. 80)

It is worth noting that "love" is not the only choice here when *qing* is used to refer to romantic sentiments. In the dialogue between Liu Mengmei and Du Liniang, expressions such as "romantic and devoted" and "youthful affection" are chosen instead of "love" or "the loved." A multitude of ramifications of *qing* in translation can be unpacked to reveal the features and variables in relation or response to individual contexts.

2. *Qing* as physical desire

Apart from the lofty register of love, physical desire, that is, *yu* (desire) is also an important aspect of the concept of *qing* as we introduced in the previous section. It includes sensualized thoughts and sensualized descriptions.

Example 12

The Original Text

沒亂裏**春情**難遣

The YLE

> I know not why, **thoughts of passion** will not subside.
>
> (Tang, 2014, p. 32)

The English translation of "沒亂裏春情難遣" in the YLE is "I know not why, thoughts of passion will not subside." The Chinese phrase "春情" (*chun qing*) refers to love between men and women and consists of two characters, each of which can also be a single word. Separately, *chun* means spring, and *qing*, among other possibilities, as indicated earlier, affection. But once they are combined into one phrase, it carries an implication related to sensual desire, which is different from "*xian qing*" and "*rou qing*" discussed earlier. In Birch's version, it is "From turbulent heart these springtime thoughts of love will not be banished" (Tang, 1980, p. 46). In this case, the ostensible inclusiveness of the meaning is fully captured and rendered in the translation. However, "springtime thoughts of love" is somewhat perplexing for readers, even though the explanatory phrase "turbulent heart" is provided by the translator. What is the connection between "springtime" and "thoughts of love"? It is probably unreasonable to expect the target reader/audience to make sense of this. It is also not suitable for an audience to process this elaborate translated version in the theater. "Spring" in Chinese can be a sextually charged word. In its crude form, it refers to sexual desire, as in animals making calls, and this often happens in spring.

Example 13

The Original Text

甚良緣,
把**青春**拋得遠。
俺的**睡情**誰見。

The YLE

But what good is marriage,
If the **youth of springtime** is cast aside:
Who can see **my desire** as I sleep?
(Tang, 2014, p. 32)

As noted in the previous section, "springtime" seems to be a difficult concept to be translated. In the YLE, "青春" (*qing chun*, green spring) is rendered as "the youth of springtime," while in Birch's translation, it is "this springtime of my youth." In both versions, the word *chun* is eagerly retained. But in fact, only "youth" should suffice. In the surtitle version, the omission of "springtime" seems reasonable. Not entirely clear is the translation of "睡情" (*shui qing*). The YLE version reads "my desire," while Birch's version "sleeping form." Literally, the word means "sleeping love." This requires some interpretation on the part of the translator, which has led to different translation versions.

Example 14

The Original Text

一點**色情**難壞。
再世爲人。
化作了兩頭分拍。

The YLE

> Your unwavering love
> Wrought my resurrection.
> Now there is this second beginning.
> (Tang, 2014, p. 93)

In this example, the phrase "色情" (*se qing*) consists of two characters, in which *se* means beautiful appearance, and *qing* means the affection or desire aroused by it. Together, the phrase means the affection, as well as behavior, including sex, that are caused by physical attraction. In the translation, it becomes "your unwavering love," which is clearly romanticized by the translator, probably with an intention to highlight the theme of love.

Though at some point, the English script of the YLE renders *qing* as physical desire, it is also quite clear that the translator tends to highlight the romantic aspect of the concept and tone down the reference to physical desire when it is possible.

4.3 The Translation of Chun: *A Word Closely Related with* Qing

As mentioned earlier, *chun* (spring) is closely related with *qing* and appears frequently in Tang's original drama. In *The Peony Pavilion*, Liniang's story begins in a spring garden, where her natural desire and self-consciousness as a young woman are awakened by the blooming flowers in the abandoned garden. Thus, *chun* has become one of the key words intimately related to the theme of *qing* and, in particular, to express the more physical aspect of *qing*. Her maid is named Chunxiang (spring fragrance) and plays a very important role in Liniang's journey of self-discovery. She is the one who leads her to the spring garden. Chunxiang is the symbol of the natural world in the play, while Liniang's tutor, the old scholar Chen Zuiliang, represents the world of reason and principle. Therefore, it is also interesting to look at the English translation of this equally complicated word, *chun*, in the YLE.

When *chun* and *qing* are combined to form the phrase *chun qing*, as illustrated in example 12 (spring love/desire), it signifies love between men and women and usually sensual love. *Chun xin* (spring heart) literally means "the heart of spring" but actually means the desire for love. Similarly, *si chun* (thinking of spring) means "harboring the amorous thoughts of spring, being lovesick or longing for love," depending on the context. *Huai chun* (spring in heart) refers to a young girl's love for the opposite sex.

Example 15

The Original Text

> 春香, 我欲成詩一首,
> 暗藏**春色**, 提於畫上。

The YLE

> Chunxiang, I want to inscribe a poem
> on this portrait, alluding to **love**.
> (Tang, 2014, p. 46)

In example 10, Liniang tells her maid Chunxiang after she paints her own portrait that she wants to write a poem on it. The phrase "春色" (*chun se*) literally means "spring scenery" and is commonly used as a metaphor to refer to youthful appearance of a beauty. In the YLE, it is explicified as "love," while it is "spring yearnings" in Birch's version, a more indirect reference to the theme of the play.

Before the love dream in the play, there are numerous references to *chun*, the natural season of spring. After the dream, the references revolve around love and/or desire. In the English transcript of the YLE, *chun* is alternately translated as "longing," "desire," "love," and even "spring desires." The contextualized translation of *chun* attempts to capture the corresponding meanings in different combinations and situations. The linguistic and cultural situations in the original are fluid, but it is this fluidity that creates a sense of dynamism. Both *qing* and *chun* are polysemous words and, in their changing variables, highly evocative and tantalizing analogies and metaphors. Due to the nature of surtitling, some degree of simplification is unavoidable. Despite the precarious situations of surtitle translation, international audiences are generally well able to enjoy the artistic production of the *Kunqu* form of this play.

4.4 Brief Discussion

Translation, especially in the case of theater surtitling, necessitates explication. Although this necessity is undeniable, it undermines the potential poetic style of the original. However, as indicated at the beginning of this chapter, the YLE is undoubtedly a theatrical text and takes the form of surtitling. Brevity and concision are required of the translator. Since inclusiveness is necessarily dispensed with, the most important thing is to capture the essential content of the original. Although it cannot be denied that the artistic dynamics of the verbal text are diluted as a result, the overall communicative effect, including singing, dancing, and artistic stage performance, can well compensate for the obvious inadequacy of the translation. In this regard, the translational interpretation of the meaning of the lyrics and their cultural intertextuality play an essential role in highlighting the implicitness of many parts of the source text and contributing to the manifestation of the concept of *qing* and *chun* in the translation. In general, many of the essential features of the fluid poetic language are captured with precision and luminosity. The interpreted interaction between the word and the stage must be encapsulated in a concise form. In the case of surtitling, it is often sufficient to make the meaning clear, which should help avoid distractions.

5. Conclusion

Surtitling is a reflection of the multidimensional aggregates as an essential part of the cross-cultural experience of the international audience. The translation is an interplay between performativity and "readability," the latter meaning that the translated libretto text takes a condensed form in this context, and it is easy to read and not too distracting. There is no doubt that the experience of understanding dramatic scenes can be significantly heightened by surtitles, because reduced intelligibility, without the audience being able to follow the action and understand most of the details, seriously compromises the appreciation of opera performances. In other words, the stage action and singing, whose content is made intelligible to the target audience, provide a much better cross-cultural experience. The surtitles of *The Young Lovers' Edition* of *The Peony Pavilion* are successful in maintaining the poetic style of the original song lyrics, highlighting the romantic aspect, that is, love, of the concept of *qing*, which is the central theme of the drama. Although there is a tendency to simplify its variations in various situations and contexts, the international audience is well served and helped to understand the content of the original libretto text without significantly diluting their attention to the stage action. The related term *chun* is similarly well translated. In this way, potential cultural alienation is reduced, if not eliminated, for opera audiences, and the artistic enjoyment of *The Peony Pavilion* is thus made possible.

Notes

1 Instead of using "adaptation," Pai uses the word "rearrange" to describe their work on this classic play. The choice of words shows his respect of the original drama and the "abridge without alteration" principle.
2 Cyril Birch's version, an acknowledged complete translation of the play, is occasionally used for comparison in this section.

References

Bassnett, S. (1985). Ways through the labyrinth: Strategies and methods for translating theatre texts. In T. Hermans (Ed.), *The manipulation of literature: Studies in literary translation* (pp. 87–102). London and Sydney: Routledge.

Bassnett, S. (1991). Translating for the theatre: The case against performability. *TTR: Traduction, Terminologie, Rédaction*, *4*, 99–111. https://doi.org/10.7202/037084ar

Chang, J., & Zhang, Z. (2020). English translations of the Peony Pavilion, a traditional Chinese opera: Different strategies for different purposes. *Translation Review*, *106*(1), 35–49. https://doi.org/10.1080/07374836.2020.1720875

Dougill, D. (2008, June 8). *The Peony Pavilion; Sutra – David Dougill is transported by the exquisite beauty of Chinese opera*. Retrieved from www.thetimes.co.uk/article/the-peony-pavilion-sutra-36jnztq0j6n

Gambier, Y. (2003). Introduction: Screen transadaptation: Perception and reception. *The Translator*, *9*(2), 171–189.

Huang, M. W. (1998). Sentiments of desire: Thoughts on the cult of Qing in Ming-Qing literature. *Chinese Literature: Essays, Articles, Reviews (CLEAR), 20*, 153–184. https://doi.org/10.2307/495268

Hutera, D. (2008, June 5). *The Peony pavilion at Sadler's Wells*. Retrieved from www.thetimes.co.uk/article/the-peony-pavilion-at-sadlers-wells-cdchjbpggl8

Lam, A. (2006). *The deaths and lives of the Peony pavilion: The 16th-century Romeo and Juliet of China is revived, with a passion*. Retrieved from https://alumni.berkeley.edu/california-magazine/july-august-2006-indo-chic/deaths-and-lives-peony-pavilion

Lei, D. P. (2011). The blossoming of the transnational Peony: Performing alternative China in California. In *Alternative Chinese opera in the age of globalization* (pp. 98–141). London: Palgrave Macmillan.

Li, L. M. (2014). A short introduction to Kunqu music and the play. In *The Peony pavilion: The young lovers' eddition play script (Chinese text with English translation)* (2nd ed., pp. 7–14). Hong Kong: Digital Heritage Publishing Limited.

Pai, H.-Y. (2014a). Preface. In *The Peony pavilion: The young lovers' eddition play script (Chinese text with English translation)* (2nd ed., pp. 4–5). Hong Kong: Digital Heritage Publishing Limited.

Pai, H.-Y. 白先勇. (2014b, May 19). *Mu Danting*: Qingchun Kunqu Shinianlu.《牡丹亭》：青春昆曲十年路. *Guangming Daily* (p. 16). 光明日报.

Tang, X. 汤显祖. (1935). Erbo maguyou shixu 耳伯麻姑游诗序. In Z. Shi 施蛰存 (Ed.), *Wanming ershi jia xiaopin* 晚明二十家小品 (p. 69). Shanghai: Kwong Ming Book Store.

Tang, X. (1980). *The Peony pavilion: Mudan Ting* (C. Birch, Trans.). Bloomington: Indiana University Press.

Tang, X. (2014). *The Peony pavilion: The young lovers' eddition play script (Chinese text with English translation)* (L. M. Li, Trans.; 2nd ed.). Hong Kong: Digital Heritage Publishing Limited.

Tao, Y. (2013). The translation of allusions in the light of adaptation theory – a case study of Birch's English version of the Peony Pavilion. *Theory & Practice in Language Studies, 3*(7).

Wang, S. 王思任. (2011). *Pidian yumingtang Mudan Ting* 批点玉茗堂<牡丹亭>. Nanjing: Phoenix Publishing & Media.

Wei, C. 魏城璧 (2011). Lun Mudan Ting yingyi celüe de yunyong he juxian 论《牡丹亭》英译策略的 用和局限. *Studies in Culture & Art* 文化艺术研究, *4*(1), 162–168.

Windle, K. (2011). The translation of drama. In *The Oxford handbook of translation studies*, (pp. 153–168). Oxford: Oxford University Press.

Winn, S. (2006, September 19). *From a girl's dream springs an operatic experience ravishing to the ear and eye. At nine hours long, 'Peony' will fly by*. Retrieved from www.sfgate.com/performance/article/REVIEW-From-a-girl-s-dream-springs-an-operatic-2551497.php#taboola-3

Zhang, W., & Cao, Y. (2018). The loss of cultural image in literary translation – a case study of the English version of the Peony Pavilion. *Studies in Literature and Language, 17*(2), 66–69.

Zhou, Y. 周莹. (2015). Mudan Ting yingyi zongshu《牡丹亭》英译综述. *Journal of Hebei Radio & TV University* 河北广播电视大学学报, *20*(1), 39–41.

7 The Silence of Anxiety and Trauma in the English Translation of *Selected Stories of Xi Ni Er*

Yi-Chiao Chen

1. National Literature to the World

World literature denotes that a work of a nation circulates out into a broader world beyond its linguistic and cultural birthland (Damrosch, 2003). Present-day theorists divide the discussion of world literature into two major themes: (1) an investigation into the relationship between national literature and world literature and (2) an examination of how to become a part of world literature. As two instances of the first theme type, Hugo Meltzl (1846–1908) invests his lifelong effort in introducing and emphasizing foreign influences to the national literature for constructing the real-world literature system, while Damrosch (2003) delves into ways to deal with foreign literature and examines translation issues. Examples of the second theme type include Casanova (2004, 2005), Moretti (2000), and Apter (2006). These authors analyze the relationship between the center and the periphery and highlight that writers of peripheral societies must have their creations circulated in central societies for their works to be recognized as a part of world literature, allowing the status and readership of the works to be enhanced and broadened. For example, Casanova (2004, 2005) deems France to be a hegemony in literature in the late nineteenth and early twentieth centuries, so Paris was regarded as a central city for writers to seek an international reputation.

This concept can also be applied to the investigation of Singapore's national literature. As a relatively young nation, Singapore is an island inhabited by several ethnicities. When Sir Stamford Raffles of the British Empire landed on this island in 1819, there were only slightly more than 100 Malays and 30 Chinese (Purcell, 1967; Saw, 1969). Raffles seized the land from the Sultan of Johor and developed it to become a hub of trading for the empire, from which Singapore began its modernization, and a growing number of people relocated to this place. Nowadays, this country has more than five million residents, comprising 74.34% of Chinese, 13.42% of Malays, 9.03% of Indians, and 3.22% of other ethnic groups (Singapore Department of Statistics, 2020). The population composition entails a variety of tongues, and it also tells us that English, which is the lingua franca in present-day Singapore, is not the mother tongue of the locals, and the great majority of Singapore's literary works are written in Chinese or Malay. Therefore, local publishers strive to translate local classics

DOI: 10.4324/9781003368168-8

into English in an attempt to elevate local writings to global status and widen the readership.

The English translation of Singaporean Chinese literature is a practice that has been undertaken for decades. Wong Meng Moon and Wong Yoon Wah published *An Anthology of Singapore Chinese Literature* (1983) to offer access to non-Chinese readers and to facilitate the literary exchange inside Singapore. *Droplets* (2001), edited by André, and *Lychee Fragrance: The Selected Works of Chen Qing Shan* (2002), translated by Chen Minliang and Chen Minhua, are two books that promote Singaporean Chinese traditions and values and help today's Singaporean Chinese students learn their mother tongue. Wong Yoon Wah's writings, translated by Jeremy Tiang in *Durians Are not the Only Fruit* (2013), are seen as an attempt to introduce Wong's valuable life experiences and insightful opinions. In multiethnic Singapore and in the era of globalization, during which English has become the world's lingua franca, translation helps to gain a wider readership, not only within the island, but also across the world. Apart from readership, I believe that the efforts invested in rendering Singaporean Chinese literature to English are also for winning recognition from big overseas names and obtaining a global reputation. In my opinion, Casanova's center-periphery argument is also observed here. Unlike in her case, however, English plays the predominant role.

2. Xi Ni Er in Singaporean Chinese Literature

Flash fiction refers to short-short stories that are often fewer than 1,500 words and nowadays even becomes "the catchall term for any minuscule narrative" (Galef, 2016, p. viiii). According to Seah (2020), flash fiction has been mainstream in Singaporean Chinese literature because (1) present-day Singaporeans do not have sufficient time to read long novels, (2) English-dominated education results in a poorer command of Chinese among local residents, and (3) flash fiction has become a trend in the Chinese sphere since the 1980s.

Among all flash fiction writers, Xi Ni Er (the pseudonym of Chia Hwee Pheng) is one of the most recognized because he is the key figure in promoting flash fiction in Singapore and even in the Chinese-speaking world. To him, flash fiction is a format that is suitable for recording our lifestyles and experiences (lest we forget in the future) and for reviving our spirit (Jin, 2013). As Koh Hock Kiat (quoted in Zhu, 2018) comments, Xi Ni Er is a key figure that cultivates flash fiction in Singapore, and he endeavors to broaden this genre by introducing literary devices that have not been adopted in flash fiction writing, such as ballads, fables, and obituaries. As a talented, prolific, and influential writer, Xi Ni Er has received several prestigious literary awards, including the National Book Development Council of Singapore's Book Award, the Southeast Asian Writers Award, and Singapore's highest cultural award – The Cultural Medallion. Meanwhile, he is an honorary president of the Singapore Association of Writers.

Xi Ni Er is known for examining Singaporeans' shared habits, beliefs, ideologies, and collective memories and transforming his observations and reflections into mesmerizing Chinese poems and stories (Zhu, 2018). As Yue (1996) puts it,

Xi Ni Er receives high recognition because he stands out as a Singaporean writer who expresses his concerns for the humanities through an avant-garde writing style that features the previously mentioned literary devices and blends traditional Chinese literary culture with Singaporean elements.

Because Xi Ni Er is a representative writer in the field of Singaporean Chinese literature, his writings have been rendered into English to gain a global reputation and readership. Nevertheless, the Singapore-specific beliefs, ideologies, and memories embedded in the stories constitute translation challenges because the English context is remote from the Singaporean one. As world literature theorists put it, translation often smooths out some source elements in an attempt to maintain the readability of the target text, and this is like the translator bestows upon the source text a new life in a new language as it is its debut (Berman, 1992; Damrosch, 2003). Therefore, this paper considers it worthwhile to delve into and analyze the translation of Xi Ni Er's short stories to identify whether Singapore-specific elements are smoothed out.

3. Research Methodology

The research texts are 希尼尔小说选 (*Selected Stories of Xi Ni Er*, 264 pages), published by Singapore's The Youth Book Company, and its translation, *The Earnest Mask* (208 pages), published by Singapore's Epigram Books. *Selected Stories of Xi Ni Er* comprises 79 short stories written by Xi Ni Er over three decades (from the 1980s to the 2000s). The translators – Howard Goldblatt and Sylvia Li-Chun Lin – are prestigious literary translators who have previously dealt with many Chinese novels together, including Wang Chen-Ho's *Rose, Rose I Love You*, Li Ang's *The Lost Garden*, and Nobel laureate Mo Yan's *Shifu, You'll Do Anything for a Laugh*.

After the research materials are determined, I take the following step to understand Xi Ni Er's writing style and the themes that he touches upon in his *Selected Stories of Xi Ni Er*. I then categorize the stories in this publication into four themes: (1) traditional Chinese values and their retention/alteration in Singapore, (2) reflections on Chinese Singaporeans' attitudes to their mother tongue and culture, (3) indignation to World War II sufferings, and (4) the national identity of Singapore.

Subsequently, a close reading is undertaken to identify the preceding elements and characteristics in the source text and to establish how they are reconstructed in the English version. The examination enables us to understand whether elements or characteristics are likely to be left behind in the process of translation and become translation challenges.

4. Results and Discussion

Boase-Beier (2011, p. 167), under the belief that "literary reading is always far more than a mere decoding or understanding of meaning," contends that holocaust poetry has to trigger readers' emotions. Based on this argument, she highlights that those left unsaid in a poem (i.e., the silences) are what can force readers to step out of "a comfortable state of unknowing" (Boase-Beier, 2011, p. 168) and get to know and participate in the holocaust experience. Boase-Beier then advances to introduce Celan's poem, titled "*Espenbaum*," to investigate the silences within it and determine how to deal with them appropriately. From her discussion, we can understand that the silences in her example concern connotations and metaphors that are hidden between the lines.

Boase-Beier's argument shares a connection with the skopos theory, which deems translation to be a purposeful action to fulfill a desired effect, and the fulfillment of the effect is deemed to be the most important (Munday, 2010; Pym, 2010; Vermeer, 1989/2004). According to Boase-Beier (2011), Celan's poem can be examined on two levels: (1) the connotations and metaphors that are hidden between the lines and (2) the feelings of loss, grief, and regret that are generated by the hidden messages. Regarding the first level, the poem includes contrastive descriptions, such as (1) "the aspen tree can go from white to dark as the seasons change but my mother's hair can no longer change colour," (2) "the spring has returned to the land of Ukraine but my mother cannot return home," and (3) "the star forms a golden loop but my mother's heart was wounded by a lead bullet." The contrastive descriptions in this poem are introduced to imply the death of the mother, and the arousal of the previously mentioned feelings, if we analyze from the perspective of skopos theory, is the final effect that Celan wishes to realize among the target readers.

Investigating the *Selected Stories of Xi Ni Er* and its translation based on this concept, I observe that the translators have created a fascinating rendition that is faithful to the ST on the textual level. Nevertheless, translation challenges can be identified on the ideological level, which, like Boase-Beier's case, may obstruct the fulfillment of the desired emotions among readers. I categorize the identified challenges into two groups (anxiety and trauma) and discuss how they are silenced in the following sections.

4.1 Anxiety Over the Loss of the Mother Tongue and Culture

The Chinese language and culture in multiethnic Singapore is an issue that has been investigated by former scholars, such as Lee (2011, 2013), Quah (2009), and André (2006). Lee departs from the perspective of Singapore's Westernization and reveals how readers react to translated texts, the ideologies of which are different from theirs, and the existence of Anglophobic themes in Singaporean writings. Quah focuses on the status and role change of Chineseness in the Westernization of Singapore. André examines "multi-voiced" playwrights written by Singaporean writers of three different generations, and the findings reveal the social, cultural, educational, and power relations hidden behind words and sentences. The key concept shared by former studies is the anxiety triggered by the loss of the mother tongue and culture over the prevalence of English, and this is also a theme in which Xi Ni Er takes a strong interest.

Born in Singapore in 1957, Xi Ni Er went through tumults before and after the independence of the Republic of Singapore and witnessed a change in the linguistic landscape of the island. In the 1950s and 1960s, the political unrest caused by Konfrontasi led to not only the confrontation between Malaysia and Indonesia but also racial riots within the Malaya Peninsula, including Singapore. This incident resulted in the establishment of the Federation of Malaysia, which involved Singapore. Nevertheless, the federation did not merge well because Chinese-led Singapore had often been in discord with the Malay-led Malaysian central government, and race riots took place in Singapore. Eventually, Singapore became an independent republic in 1965.

Due to the preceding circumstances, the newly established republic determined to make all its national policies based on racial harmony, multilingualism, and equality, and English was thus adopted to be the official language of public administration, communication, education, and business (Mohanty et al., 2018; Tan, 2017; Wee, 2004). In addition, the Singapore government initiated the Speak Mandarin Campaign in 1979 to motivate Chinese Singaporeans who spoke different dialects to communicate in Mandarin so as to eliminate dialect barriers within the Chinese community. Looking into the language policy now, we must say that it has successfully enabled the ethnic groups of Singapore (mainly Chinese, Malays, and Indians, as indicated in Section 1) to communicate with one another easily, which has greatly facilitated understanding among ethnic communities; however, it has also altered the language landscape of once linguistically diverse Singapore. According to a survey conducted by the Department of Statistics Singapore (2020), 21,702 households in Singapore only communicate in English, while 4,945 households communicate in Mandarin and 4,439 households communicate in both. The data have revealed a stunning message that English has overtaken Mandarin to become the language most spoken at home in Singapore, where about 75% of the population is Chinese.

The preceding paragraphs have introduced the context in which Xi Ni Er grew up and have enabled us to understand why he is highly concerned about the Chinese race identity, the culture/root, and the language. Xi Ni Er writes to express his nostalgia to China, his mother land, and to show the feeling of anxiety over the fading of the Chinese language in the face of predominant English and over Chinese Singaporeans' indifference to their mother culture – these have become the major themes in his writings (Nan, 2012; Quah, 2009; Zhang & Teo, 2018). To make this point more concrete, I provide three excerpts from the three short stories in the next section. All examples come with not only official translations but also transliterations and back translations so that readers can gain a better understanding and investigate whether some messages are added to or omitted in the official translations.

- Example 1:

Original (Xi, 2007, p. 199)

换了以忌日（校长，是旭日）为背景的校徽，以示朝气蓬勃。（天啊！那不是'哈日'吗？）为了抛开旧文化传统的大包…包（是包袱），我们决定向过去说再见，决定不在同过去有任何瓜哥（瓜葛）。我们的校史就从搬来新镇算起，让过去 gone with the wind！

Transliteration

Huàn le yǐ jì rì (xiào zhǎng, shì xù rì) wéi bèi jǐng de xiào huī, yǐ shì cháo qì péng bó. (tiān ā! nà bú shì 'hā rì' ma?) wéi le pāo kāi jiù wén huà chuán tǒng de dà bāo ... bāo (shì bāo fú), wǒ men jué dìng xiàng guò qù shuō zài jiàn, jué dìng bú zài tóng guò qù yǒu rèn hé guā gē (guā gě). wǒ men de xiào shǐ jiù cóng bān lái xīn zhèn suàn qǐ, ràng guò qù gone with the wind!

Back Translation

Replace with death anniversary (principal, is rising sun) to be backdrop of school emblem to show vigour. (god! is it 'worship Japan'?) in order to ditch old cultural tradition big bag ... bag (is baggage), we decide face past say goodbye, decide no longer with past have any Gua Brother (connection). Our school history from relocate to new town calculate start, let past gone with the wind!

Official Translation (Goldblatt & Lin, 2012, p. 182)

The new school insignia used *jiri* (it was *xuri* – a rising sun, not death anniversary, Principal) as its backdrop, to show the vitality of the morning sun (Oh God, isn't that *ha-ri*, Japan-worshipping?). To shed the weighty bag ... bag (baggage) of old traditional culture, we are determined to say goodbye to the past, with which we no longer have any connectivity (connection). The history of our school begins with the day we moved to New Town, and we'll let the past be gone with the wind.

    Example 1 is an excerpt from the story titled "School's Anniversary," and the story describes the meeting in which all school staff gather to discuss how to celebrate the anniversary and who to invite. The principal in this story is a Chinese who mainly speaks English and possesses a poor command of Mandarin, so Xi Ni Er has him mistakenly adopt "*ji ri*" (death anniversary) to refer to "*xu ji*" (rising sun), not remember the term "baggage" (*bāo fú*, meaning "burden" in Mandarin), and finally give up and directly speak in English, "gone with the wind." The author also creates a connection between the rising sun and Japan's national flag, which features the red sun in the center; this is mentioned deliberately to imply Singaporeans' longtime resentment over Japan's occupation during World War II.

    Examining the translation, we can see that "not death anniversary" is additional information that the translators leave for the English readers to grasp the wordplay link between "*ji ri*" and "*xu ji*," and the term "*ha-ri*" is accompanied by a short note, "Japan-worshipping." Without the arrangements, it is quite likely that

English readers will be perplexed by this paragraph and cannot understand the punchline. Nevertheless, the readers will not realize that the principal eventually gives up and speaks English because the translation is already in English. From this example, it is noted that translators tend to intervene when plain translation causes confusion.

- Example 2:

Original (Xi, 2007, p. 24)

那时候我们都沉迷于歌仔戏。在三十周年的校庆里，每个班级都得呈献一个节目，我们被推选为演"荆轲刺秦王"的两大主角。
(*a sentence is omitted*)

"谁是金哥？"你问。
"就是那位大英雄！"我说。
"那么青王呢？"
"坏蛋一个。"
"做王的怎么会是坏蛋呢？"
"你问级任老师好了。"

Transliteration

nà shí hòu wǒ men dōu chén mí yú gē zǎi xì. zài sān shí zhōu nián de xiào qìng lǐ, měi gè bān jí dōu dé chéng xiàn yī gè jiē mù, wǒ men bèi tuī xuǎn wéi yǎn "jīng kē cì qín wáng" de liǎng dà zhǔ jiǎo.
(*a sentence is omitted*)

"shuí shì jīn gē?" nǐ wèn.
"jiù shì nà wèi dà yīng xióng!" wǒ shuō.
"nà me qīng wáng ne?"
"huài dàn yī gè."
"zuò wáng de zěn me huì shì huài dàn ne?"
"nǐ wèn jí rèn lǎo shī hǎo le."

Back Translation

that time we all indulge in singing opera. in thirtieth anniversary school celebration, every class must present a show, we are selected to play "Jing Ke assassinate Qin King" two major roles.
(*a sentence is omitted*)

"who is Jing Ke?" you ask.
"is that big hero!" I say.
"then Qing King who?"
"bastard one."

"be king person how can be bastard?"
"you ask teacher good."

Official Translation (Goldblatt & Lin, 2012, p. 24)

Back then we were both fans of Taiwanese opera. At our school's thirtieth Founder's Day, when each class was required to put on a performance, you and I were selected to play the main roles in "Jing Ke Assassinating the King of Qin".
(*a sentence is omitted*)

"Who's Jing Ke?" you asked.
"The hero," I said.
"Then who's the King of Qin?"
"The bad guy."
"How can a king be a bad guy?"
"Go ask the teacher."

Example 2 is extracted from the story titled "The Sword Goes Rusted," which centers on a class of students preparing a Chinese opera performance for the school anniversary. Jing Ke (荆轲) is an assassin at the end of China's Warring State Period, and the King of Qin (秦王) is the lord who unified the entire Chinese territory. In a short story on a school opera performance that is themed with this assassin, Xi Ni Er creates a scenario using a pun. When discussing the theme of this opera performance, a kid misunderstands 荆轲 (*jīng kē*, meaning "Jing Ke") as 金哥 (*jīn gē*, meaning "Brother Jin"), and 秦王 (*qín wáng*, meaning "the King of Qin") as 青王 (*qīng wáng*, meaning "green king"). The kid who asks the questions does not know these historical figures and so keeps relating the names to wrong interpretations. Through the use of homophonic puns, Xi Ni Er laments the loss of the mother culture among younger Chinese Singaporeans. Unlike the first example, the translators did not omit, add, or alter meaning in any part of this excerpt, and I hold that this is because a faithful translation does not cause any confusion here.

- Example 3:

Original (Xi, 2007, p. 138)

年代	学长	代表致词用语／（备注）
五十	霍元甲	国语（普通话, Chinese）
	许文强（强仔）	母语（粤语？）
六十	刘金妹（锦梅）	母语（不是方言）
	汪祖忠（Charles）	英语（Queen's English）
七十	William Chin K. S.	英语
	Susie Wong	英语（Singlish）

Transliteration

nián dài	xué zhăng	dài biăo zhì cí yòng yǔ/(bèi zhù)
wǔ shí	huò yuán jiǎ	guó yǔ (pǔ tōng huà, Chinese)
	xǔ wén qiáng (qiáng zǎi)	mǔ yǔ (yuè yǔ?)
liù shí	liú jīn mèi (jīn méi)	mǔ yǔ (bú shì fāng yán)
	wāng zǔ zhōng (Charles)	yīng yǔ (Queen's English)
qī shí	William Chin K. S.	yīng yǔ
	Susie Wong	yīng yǔ (Singlish)

Back Translation

year	school senior	representative speech language/(remarks)
50s	Huo Yuan Jia	National language (Putonghua, Chinese)
	Xu Wen Qiang (Qiangzai)	Mother tongue (Cantonese?)
60s	Liu Jin Mei (Jin Mei)	Mother tongue (not dialect)
	Wang Zu Zhong (Charles)	English (Queen's English)
70s	William Chin K. S.	English
	Susie Wong	English (Singlish)

Official Translation (Goldblatt & Lin, 2012, p. 125)

YEAR	NAME OF ALUMNUS	LANGUAGE(S) USED/REMARKS
1950	Huo Yuan Jia	Guoyu (Putonghua, Chinese)
	Xu Wen Qiang (Qiangzai)	Mother tongue (Cantonese?)
1960	Liu Jin Mei (Jin Mei)	Mother tongue (not dialect)
	Wang Zu Zhong (Charles)	English (Queen's English)
1970	William Chin K. S.	English
	Susie Wong	English (Singlish)

Example 3 is a selected part of the story titled "Roundabout." The story shows a list of alumni who are going to make a speech at the school anniversary celebration. This excerpt is more intricate than the previous two excerpts because it heterolingually involves English names and words and encompasses the names of a Chinese historical figure, 霍元甲 (Huo Yuan Jia); a TV series character, 许文强 (Hui Man-Keung); and a homophone, 汪祖忠 (Wang Zu Zhong) to imply 忘祖宗 (wàng zǔ zōng, meaning "forgetting the ancestors/ancestral root"). To begin, the Chinese names were all translated according to their Mandarin pronunciation. Nevertheless, 许文强 should not be called "Xu Wen Qiang" but "Hui Man-Keung" because his mother tongue is Cantonese, and this character is taken from a Hong Kong Cantonese TV series. Similar to the preceding two examples, the translators provided a faithful translation because the text was not confusing to the readers.

4.2 Anxiety Being Silenced

The story that involves Example 1 talks about how the principal and other teachers organize a celebration for the school's anniversary, the story with the second excerpt is about students seeking a sword that is suitable for their Taiwanese opera performance, and the last story encompassing the third example comprises a list of alumni who are going to make presentations at the school's anniversary. On the textual level, the translations for these three excerpts (and the whole stories) stand as solid as fluent texts, and English readers can understand the storylines easily. Nevertheless, on an ideological level, the anxiety that Xi Ni Er expresses over the loss of the mother tongue and culture among Chinese Singaporeans is silenced. Example 1 is used to criticize a social phenomenon in which a growing number of Chinese Singaporeans are educated in English and are so Westernized that they are no longer familiar with the Chinese language. To them, English is the key to climbing up to a higher social status (due to national policies), while Chinese cannot bring many pragmatic benefits. Likewise, Example 2 concerns the same phenomenon and points out that an English-based education, together with the Singapore government's curriculum design, has led to poor mother culture and historical knowledge among younger Chinese Singaporeans. Lastly, Example 3 lists six names in three different decades (the 1950s, 1960s, and 1970s), which correspond to the time the government adopted the bilingual policy in education (1966) and later enforced the language policy to take English as the language for work, education, and social interaction. It can be noted in the ST that the names in the 1970s have all become English, and the second name in the 1960s 汪祖忠 is in fact a Chinese homophone that implies 忘祖宗 (meaning "forget ancestry"), satirizing that Chinese Singaporeans have become too Westernized to remember their own roots.

All three stories center on school anniversary, whereas the themes, the most important ideas that Xi Ni Er wishes to deliver (i.e., the anxiety over the loss of Chinese language and culture), are hidden in the three excerpts. Revisiting the three translations from the perspective of the English readers, we note that these themes cannot be detected because (1) the heterolingual wordplay is not retained; (2) the stories, on the textual level, do not talk about the loss of the mother tongue and culture; and (3) it is unlikely that the English readers have knowledge of Singapore's turbulent past and pragmatic present. As a result, we can say that anxiety is silenced due to these three missing factors.

4.3 Trauma Caused by the Japanese Invasion

It is not uncommon to see writers compose based on traumatic experiences. For instance, China's Scar Literature poses a response to the harms and aftermaths brought by the cultural revolution, and the Holocaust literature pertains to the genocide operation undertaken by the Nazis. Writings of this theme are meaningful because they record the victims' voices while forming collective memories and motivating introspection.

As a crucial geopolitical spot, Singapore became an attack target when the Empire of Japan invaded Southeast Asia during World War II. To secure control of the conquered land, the Japanese military conducted the operation of "Sook Ching" (meaning "to purge"), in which numerous Singaporeans were killed, with a death toll between 5,000 and 50,000 (Gunn, 2007; Tay, 2015). Similar to the Holocaust in Europe, the Japanese massacre also caused trauma to Singaporeans and further formed collective memories among generations. Among them, Xi Ni Er composes a good number of poems and short stories to express his personal indignation and/or to depict Singaporeans' attitudes toward the Japanese. For instance, he writes a Chinese poem about Sarimbun Island, a place where the Japanese army landed to invade Singapore. In the poem, he phonetically translates Sarimbun to 始凌湄, and the three Chinese characters, respectively, mean "begin," "maltreat/bully," and "shore," that is, "the shore where the maltreatment began." Xi Ni Er's resentment over the Japanese invasion has become the theme in quite a few creations in *Selected Stories of Xi Ni Er*, and different from the discussion over anxiety, I would like to introduce one whole story here because it helps us understand the silence of trauma better in this way.

First published in 1987, "Major Yokoda" is a short story that talks about the grandson of a Japanese military official who flew to Singapore to visit the places that his grandfather had been to when he served as a military official during World War II. On this trip, he hired a Singaporean tour guide, and the two, representing the offspring of the perpetrator and that of the victim, held disparate understandings of the past. This story starts as follows:

Part 1

Original (Xi, 2007, p. 30)

我站在海山街口, 东张西望。
这一带的景物, 对我来说, 熟悉又陌生。

Transliteration

wǒ zhàn zài hǎi shān jiē kǒu, dōng zhāng xī wàng.
zhè yī dài de jǐng wù, duì wǒ lái shuō, shú xī yòu mò sheng.

Back Translation

I stand Hai Shan Street entrance, east look west look.
this area scenery, to me, familiar yet unfamiliar.

Official Translation (Goldblatt & Lin, 2012, p. 31)

I stood at the corner of Upper Cross Street, looking this way and that.
The scenery around me was familiar yet strange.

Said by the Singaporean tour guide, the two sentences locate the backdrop of this story on Upper Cross Street. The Singaporean then mentions the reason for his bad feelings toward Mr. Yokoda:

Part 2

Original (Xi, 2007, pp. 30–31)

不过，当社长告诉我，他的祖父当年曾经是"昭南市政会"的成员时，我对横田先生的到访，心灵上产生一种强烈的抗拒感。

Transliteration

bú guò, dāng shè zhǎng gào sù wǒ, tā de zǔ fù dāng nián céng jīng shì "zhāo nán shì zhèng huì" de chéng yuán shí, wǒ duì héng tián xiān shēng de dào fang, xīn líng shàng chǎn shēng yī zhǒng qiáng liè de kàng jù gǎn.

Back Translation

But when company head told me his father at that time was "Syonan City Council" member, I to Yokoda Mr visit, heart produces a strong repugnance sense.

Official Translation (Goldblatt & Lin, 2012, p. 31)

But a strong dislike for Mr. Yokoda rose up in me when the club director told me that Yokoda's grandfather had been a member of the Syonan City Council.

This is the first sentence in this story in which the Singaporean protagonist expressed his dislike of Mr. Yokoda, and from the translation, we only understand that such a bad feeling came merely from knowing the background of Yokoda's grandfather. After this statement, the two entered into a short conversation in which the Singaporean suggested that Yokoda should have visited Singapore with his grandfather because the grandfather could bring him to all places. Upon knowing that Yokoda's grandfather was already severely sick, the Singaporean responded as follows:

Part 3

Original (Xi, 2007, p. 31)

"不然，他会再度南下'进出'一番？..."我有点冲动地打断了他的话。

Transliteration

"bú rán, tā huì zài dù nán xià 'jìn chū' yī fān? ... " wǒ yǒu diǎn chōng dòng dì dǎ duàn le tā de huà.

Back Translation

"otherwise, he will again south down 'in out' once? ... " I somewhat impulsively interrupt his words.

Official Translation (Goldblatt & Lin, 2012, p. 32)

"Or maybe he could come south for another round?" I cut him off, feeling somewhat agitated.

Without being disrupted by the Singaporean's reply, the conversation continued, and Yokoda recalled that his grandfather said that the Japanese military came to Singapore to protect the islanders. This triggered an aversive feeling in the Singaporean because his victim grandfather's experience told a completely different story. The Singaporean had been indignant of what the Japanese army did during the war, and he even "thought of Nanking when we had lunch on Nankin Street" (Goldblatt & Lin, 2012). However, the Singaporean withheld the emotion until the end (also the culmination) of the story, when they walked past a memorial:

Part 4

Original (Xi, 2007, p. 32)

"我的祖父、八叔一家,都葬在这儿!"
"干什么?"
"他们都在当年'皇军进出'时,无辜被杀的!"
"无辜?"横田用惊慌的眼神看着我。
"这石碑,是对当年许许多多蒙难同胞的一种纪念与追悼。"

Transliteration

"wǒ de zǔ fù, bā shū yī jiā, dōu zàng zài zhè ér!"
"gàn shí me?"
"tā men dōu zài dāng nián 'huáng jun1 jìn chū shí, wú gū bèi shā de!"
"wú gū?" héng tián yòng jīng huāng de yǎn shén kàn zhe wǒ.
"zhè shí bēi, shì duì dāng nián xǔ duō duō méng nán tóng bāo de yī zhǒng jì niàn yǔ zhuī dào."

Back Translation

"my grandfather, eighth uncle one family, all buries here!"
"do what?"
"they all at that time 'imperial military in out' moment, innocently killed!"
"innocent?" Yokoda panic eyesight look me.
"this stone monument, is to that year many victimised fellow citizens a kind of commemoration and mourning."

Official Translation (Goldblatt & Lin, 2012, p. 33)

"My grandfather and my eighth uncle and his family are all in here."
"Why?"

"They were all innocent victims back when the Imperial Army 'passed through' the city."

"Innocent?" He stared at me with a look of panic in his eyes.

"This stone monument is a commemoration and mourning for the many victims of that time."

Upon hearing this, Yokoda asked about the number of casualties at that time and could not believe that what his grandfather said was not true, but the Singaporean did not give a concrete response. The story ends with Yokoda inviting the Singaporean to meet for a talk later that evening.

4.4 Trauma Being Silenced

Due to the word count limitation, I extracted only the trauma-related parts of this story. Similar to the discussion over anxiety-related examples, the translations of the four parts read very fluently, and we can easily understand the storyline. Nevertheless, by just reading the translation, it is quite likely that English readers will be perplexed by the first three parts:

1. Why did the Singaporean find Upper Cross Street familiar yet strange?
   Upper Cross Street is located in an area that is around the ground zero of the Sook Ching Operation (Roots, 2021; Thulaja, 2021). In the story, after a short conversation, the two walked to Pagoda Street and Chin Chew Street, which were also covered by the massacre. It is because of this that the Singaporean protagonist commented that the place is "familiar yet strange" – it is familiar because his parents often spoke of the massacre tragedy, and it is strange because he did not go through the incident in person, and the street landscape had already changed over the years.
2. Why was the Singaporean so indignant upon knowing the background of Yokoda's grandfather?
   After the Japanese army occupied Singapore, they changed the name of this island to "Syonan-to" (昭南岛), so the term is always connected with the Japanese Occupation Period and hence immediately reminds the Singaporean protagonist of what the Japanese did. Likewise, the Singaporean protagonist mentions Nanking because it is a city in China in which the Japanese conducted another slaughter. On top of that, the Syonan City Council was the ruling organization during that period, so the members were certainly deeply involved in the Sook Ching Operation.
3. Why did Xi Ni Er put "进出" in Part 3?
   This relates to a controversial action that the post-war Japanese government took to replace "[Japan] . . . invading China" (侵略中国) with "[Japan] . . . entering and leaving China" (进出中国) in their history textbooks (Liu & Li, 1997, p. 196; Zhang, 2009, p. 126). The Singaporean protagonist deliberately used this term in an attempt to bring forth this controversy and embarrass Mr. Yokoda, but the latter did not capture the irony because he was never told information like this in Japan.

Part 4 is relatively easy to comprehend because Xi Ni Er wrote a lot to describe how disparately the two persons understood the Japanese occupation of Singapore. Nevertheless, without background knowledge of the massacre, the English readers may wonder why the Singaporean protagonist was so agitated that he eventually decided to confront Yokoda.

The preceding paragraphs have explained the connection of this story with the trauma shared by elder Singaporeans, and it can be observed that all these expositions cannot be accessed in the translation itself. Reading the translation, the English readers get to know the agitation of the Singaporean protagonist, the different understandings of the two to the past, and their confrontation, but they remain unaware of the trauma, which is the factor that kindles the Singaporean protagonist's negative feelings and pushes him to confront the Japanese visitor and the core that Xi Ni Er endeavors to disclose. The silence on the trauma makes the English readers unable to sympathize with the Singaporean protagonist or feel empathy for Singapore's tragic past.

4.5 Research Implications

Having discussed the issue of silence and its importance, I must underscore that it is not the translator's failure if the themes do not come across; it is a dilemma that all translators of literary writings encounter occasionally. Facing this challenge, translators fall into a tug of war between producing faithful and fluent translations and adjusting the contents to convey the themes to the target readers; both options are supported by scholars and translators. The former option provides readers with content that is faithful, comprehensible, and with no interruption from supplementary add-ons. The latter option contextualizes the stories for the target readers so that they can capture both the textual and ideological messages that the original author wishes to deliver.

Although both options are reasonable, it is worthwhile to investigate the other side. That is, what solutions are available if we opt for the latter and overcome the translation challenges caused by the silence of anxiety and trauma? I have resorted to former theorists' translation strategies (Chesterman, 1997; Fawcett, 1997; Kaindl, 1999; Malone, 1988; Newmark, 1988; Pym, 2010) and identified useful methods.

First, translating original terms with analogous terms in the target culture can be an option. For example, replacing "the Sook Ching Operation" with "the Sook Ching Holocaust" may trigger stronger and desired emotions in English readers because "holocaust" reminds them of the one that took place in Germany and its cruelty. Second, the provision of annotations, preface, text analysis, and/or illustrations can be of help. Footnoting, although deemed by some scholars to be an interruption of reading flow (e.g., Sanchez & María, 2015; Zerby, 2003), can help amplify the meaning of the target text (TT), evoke an image, and provide the background knowledge that is necessary to comprehend the TT (Maniacco, 2021). Similarly, preface and text analysis can also help target readers identify the themes that the author wishes to convey or the issues to be discussed. Although nonverbal, illustrations can be more effective than words at delivering semiotic and ideational components (Chen, 2018; Painter et al., 2012). To me, illustrations are particularly useful when the source culture is remote from the target one, as there is a bigger gap in understanding. For example, English readers may possess less knowledge of the Japanese massacre than Korean readers. In such circumstances, annotations, prefaces, text analysis, and illustrations act as the effective means of communication that the translator can employ to interact with the target readers and help them capture the themes.

In addition, the silence identified in my research is different from that discussed by Boase-Beier (2011), although silences in both studies function as the key factor in triggering readers' emotions. To Boase-Beier, silences in the holocaust poetry are the hidden links between terms and between stanzas, waiting for readers to identify so that they will be able to step into the poetics of the poem. Comparatively, the silence that I observed in the examination is the phenomenon in which key themes are muted/invisible due to the missing of certain elements, mainly explanations of connotations and background knowledge of the incident. In addition, when concluding her examination, Boase-Beier (2011) points out that the successful delivery of thought (i.e., the links hidden in the silences) is far more important than other elements, such as lexical meaning, connotation, metaphor, and history. Contemplating the remarks based on the findings in my research, I agree that the conveyance of thought – that is, the attempt to trigger the same feelings in target readers and make them participate in the story – is an important goal that we seek to attain. Nevertheless, I contend that the realization of this goal is based on the successful rendition of the other elements that she mentions. Perhaps the difference in our attitudes derives from the text type difference in our research materials (poetry vs. flash fiction). In my research, expositions of historical background and connotations are indispensable if we wish to enable English readers to identify the silenced anxiety and trauma and further grasp the themes in Xi Ni Er's stories.

5. Concluding Remarks

Halbwachs (1992) proposes the term "collective memory" to denote the remembrances shared by a group of people, and this term was later extrapolated to various disciplines, including the sociocultural domain. Through examining *Selected Stories of Xi Ni Er*, we have identified four themes: (1) the traditional Chinese values and their retention/alteration in Singapore, (2) reflections on Chinese Singaporeans' attitudes to their mother tongue and culture, (3) indignation to World War II sufferings, and (4) the national identity of Singapore. These themes are collective memories shared among elder Chinese Singaporeans and facing a severe challenge as younger generations are losing awareness of them due to societal Westernization. Therefore, Xi Ni Er composed the stories in an effort to remedy the situation.

Investigating the publication and its English version to determine whether English readers can grasp these themes/collective memories, this paper has identified the silence of anxiety and trauma as the two translation challenges that are likely to be smoothed out if the translator employs the faithful translation strategy, the use of which, I would like to defend for the translators, is legitimate because this strategy provides the target readers with a translation that is fluent, comprehensible, and with no interruption in the reading flow.

Nevertheless, it is worthwhile for us to take a step to the other side and look into how to get the ideological themes across to the target readers. Iser (2006) proposes his concept of reception theory and points out, as Boase-Beier (2011) does, that text recipients should proactively decipher the ideas and contexts behind words, images, poetics, metaphors, etc., to grasp the meaning and the publication purpose of the text. Jauss's (1982) viewpoint on reception theory can be summarized to be that the text recipients understand the aesthetics of a text based on their own memories and experiences. The previous theorists' remarks reveal that being able to capture the themes (or the publication purpose) is an important gain for target readers. However, in the case of this paper, it is almost impossible for English readers to refer to their own memories to identify Singaporean themes/collective memories; the two cultures are simply too distant from each other. Therefore, this paper ends the research discussion with a proposal of possible solutions: analogy and the provision of annotations, preface, text analysis, and/or illustrations.

Finally, the findings and implications of this paper are not confined to the translation and analysis of Xi Ni Er's writings. In fact, the anxiety over the loss of the mother tongue and culture and the trauma caused by the Japanese invasion are two common themes among Singaporean writers (Jin, 2013; Tan, 2012; Teo, 2012), so this paper can serve as a reference to future researchers who wish to delve into other Singaporean translations and translators who encounter the same challenges.

References

André, J. S. (2006). Revealing the invisible: Heterolingualism in three generations of Singaporean playwrights. *Target: International Journal of Translation Studies*, *18*(1), 139–161.
Apter, E. (2006). *The translation zone: A new comparative literature*. Princeton, NJ: Princeton University Press.
Berman, A. (1992). *The experience of the foreign: Culture and translation in romantic Germany*. Stone Brook, NY: SUNY Press.
Boase-Beier, J. (2011). Translating Celan's poetics of silence. *Target*, *23*(2), 165–177.
Casanova, P. (2004). *The world republic of letters*. Cambridge, MA: Harvard University Press.
Casanova, P. (2005). Literature as a world. *New Left Review*, *31*(1), 71–90.
Chen, Q. S. (2002). *Lychee fragrance: The selected works of Chen Qing Shan* (M. Chen & M. Chen, Trans.). Singapore: Global Publishing.
Chen, X. (2018). Representing cultures through language and image: A multimodal approach to translations of the Chinese classic Mulan. *Perspectives*, *26*(2), 214–231.
Chesterman, A. (1997). *Memes of translation: The spread of ideas in translation theory*. Amsterdam: John Benjamins.
Damrosch, D. (2003). *What is world literature?* Princeton, NJ: Princeton University Press.

Department of Statistics Singapore. (2020). *Resident population aged 15 years and over*. Retrieved from https://tablebuilder.singstat.gov.sg/table/CT/17452

Fawcett, P. D. (1997). *Translation and language: Linguistic theories explained*. Manchester: St. Jerome.

Galef, D. (2016). *Brevity: A flash fiction handbook*. New York: Columbia University Press.

Goldblatt, H., & Lin, S. L. (2012). *The earnest mask. By Xi, Ni Er*. Singapore: Epigram Books.

Gunn, G. C. (2007). Remembering the Southeast Asian Chinese massacres of 1941–45. *Journal of Contemporary Asia*, *37*(3), 273–291.

Halbwachs, M. (1992). *On collective memory*. Chicago, IL and London: The University of Chicago Press.

Iser, W. (2006). *How to do theory*. Malden, MA; Oxford and Carlton: Blackwell Publishing.

Jauss, H. R. (1982). *Toward an aesthetics of reception*. Minneapolis, MN: University of Minnesota Press.

Jin, J. 金进. (2013). The city and people in the Singaporean writer Xi Ni Er's works 新加坡作家希尼尔笔下的"城"与"人". *Foreign Literature Studies* 外国文学研究, (3), 133–142.

Kaindl, K. (1999). Thump, Whizz, Poom: A framework for the study of comics under translation. *Target: International Journal of Translation Studies*, *11*(2), 263–288.

Lee, T.-K. (2011). The epistemological dilemma of translating otherness. *Meta: Journal des traducteurs/Meta: Translators' Journal*, *56*(4), 878–895.

Lee, T.-K. (2013). Translating anglophobia: Tensions and paradoxes of biliterate performances in Singapore. *Target: International Journal of Translation Studies*, *25*(2), 228–251.

Liu, S. 刘士田., & Li, Z 李志忠. (1997). Issue on Japan's compensation to China after the war 战后日本对华赔偿问题. *The Journal of Studies of China's Resistance War against Japan* 抗日战争研究, (3), 187–200.

Malone, J. L. (1988). *The science of linguistics in the art of translation*. Albany, NY: State University of New York Press.

Maniacco, V. (2021). An argument for footnotes: The special case of translating Tito Maniacco's *Mestri di mont* (2007). *Translation Review*, *110*(1), 15–30.

Mohanty, J., Choo, H., & Chokkanathan, S. (2018). The acculturation experiences of Asian immigrants in Singapore. *Asian Population Studies*, *14*(2), 153–171.

Moretti, F. (2000). Conjectures on world literature. *New Left Review*, *1*, 54–68.

Munday, J. (2010). *Introducing translation studies: Theories and applications*. London and New York: Routledge.

Nan, Z. 南治国. (2012). Visiting "the floating republic" – A way to interpret Xi Ni Er's writings 探访"浮城" – 希尼尔作品的一种解读. *Chinese Literature* 华文文学, (1), 183–196.

Newmark, P. (1988). *A textbook of translation*. New York: Prentice Hall.

Painter, C., Martin, J. R., & Unsworth, L. (2012). *Reading visual narratives: Image analysis in children's picture books*. Sheffield: Equinox.

Purcell, V. (1967). *The Chinese in Malay*. Oxford: Oxford University Press.

Pym, A. (2010). *Exploring translation theories*. London and New York: Routledge.

Quah, S. R. (2009). Performing Chineseness in multicultural Singapore: A discussion on selected literary and cultural texts. *Asian Ethnicity*, *10*(3), 225–238.

Roots. (2021). *Sook Ching Inspection Centre*. Retrieved from www.roots.gov.sg/places/places-landing/Places/historic-sites/sook-ching-inspection-centre

Sanchez, O., & María, T. (2015). The use of footnotes in literary translation. *Forum: Revue internationale d'interprétation et de traduction/International Journal of Interpretation and Translation*, *13*(1), 111–129.

Saw, S.-H. (1969). Population trends in Singapore, 1819–1967. *Journal of Southeast Asian History*, *10*(1), 36–49.

Seah, C.-T. (2020). Profundity in sublime words: Singapore Chinese history reflected in Xi Nier's flash fiction. *Journal of Nanjing University of Science and Technology (Social Sciences)*, *33*(3), 50–56.

St. André, J. (Ed.). (2001). *Droplets*. Singapore: Department of Chinese Studies at National University of Singapore.

Tan, C. (2017). Multiculturalism and citizenship. In O. S. Tan, E.-L. Low, & D. Hung (Eds.), *Lee Kuan Yew's educational legacy: The challenges of success* (pp. 127–137). Singapore: Springer.

Tan, C. L. 陈志锐. (2012). Looking into the construction of the bicultural homeland in Singaporean Chinese Literature from three texts 从三篇作品窥见新华文学双文化原乡的构建. *Chinese Literature* 华文文学, (2), 106–111.

Tay, F. (2015). Remembering the Japanese occupation massacres: Mass graves in post-war Malaysia. In A. Élisabeth & D. Jean-Marc (Eds.), *Human remains and identification: Mass violence, genocide, and the 'forensic turn'* (pp. 221–238). Manchester: Manchester University Press.

Teo, S. L. 张森林. (2012). The beginning of Singapore's scar literature 当代新加坡伤痕文学的发轫. *Chinese Literature* 华文文学, (2), 98–15.

Thulaja, N. R. (2021). *Cross street*. Retrieved from https://eresources.nlb.gov.sg/infopedia/articles/SIP_346_2005-01-26.html?s=Roads-Singapore

Vermeer, H. J. (2004). Skopos and commission in translational action (A. Chesterman, Trans.). In V. Lawrence (Ed.), *The translation studies reader* (pp. 227–238). London and New York: Routledge. (Original work published in 1989)

Wee, L. (2004). Singapore English: Morphology and syntax. In K. Bernd, B. Kate, M. Rajend, W. S. Edgar, & U. Clive (Eds.), *A handbook of varieties of English volume 2: Morphology and syntax* (pp. 1058–1072). Berlin: Mouton de Gruyter.

Wong, M. M., & Wong, Y. W. (Eds.). (1983). *An anthology of Singapore Chinese literature*. Singapore: Singapore Association of Writers.

Wong, Y. W. (2013). *Durians are not the only fruit* (J. Tiang, Trans.). Singapore: Epigram Bookshop. (Original works published in 1981, 2003, 2009, 2010, 2011, & 2013)

Xi, N. 希尼尔. (2007). *Selected stories of Xi Ni Er* 希尼尔小说选. Singapore: The Youth Book Company.

Yue, Y. 岳玉杰. (1996). On two young fiction writers in Singapore 新加坡新生代小说两作家论. *Journal of Huaqiao University (Social Science Edition)* 华侨大学学报: 哲学社会科学版, (1), 90–96.

Zerby, C. (2003). *The devil's details: A history of footnotes*. New York: Simon & Schuster.

Zhang, S. 张松建., & Teo, S. 张森林. (2018). Introduction: The trace of muse 导论：缪斯的踪迹. In S. Zhang 张松建 & S. Teo 张森林 (Eds.), *New national trend: Selected present-day Singaporean Chinese poems* 新国风：新加坡华文现代诗选 (pp. 1–30). Singapore: World Scientific.

Zhang, T. 张天明. (2009). On the studies of Japan's history textbooks from 1980 onwards 1980 年以来日本历史教科书问题研究述评. *The Journal of Studies of China's Resistance War against Japan* 抗日战争研究, (4), 126–135.

Zhu, C. 朱崇科. (2018). Considering the making of Singapore from the perspective of a person who is made in Singapore: On Xi Ni Er 从新加坡制造反思制造新加坡：希尼尔论. *Chinese Literature* 华文文学, (5), 61–70.

8 Silenced Interstitiality

Translated Hong Kong Literature in English and French Anthologies[1]

Maialen Marin-Lacarta

1. Introduction

In *Found in Transition: Hong Kong Studies in the Age of China*, Chu (2018) argues that Hong Kong culture is disappearing and that we should keep track of that erasure. This chapter aims at contributing to that goal, even more so now that China's new security law has been approved and Hong Kong citizens fear the fast erasure of this city's culture. Other scholars have contributed to giving visibility to marginalized literatures and cultures under the shadow of the great Chinese literature from Mainland China. The emerging field of Sinophone Studies was born and promoted by Shih Shu-mei for that reason. Shih (2008, 2011) argued for the use of this fruitful theoretical concept as a form of resistance to the hegemonic call of Chineseness. Sinophone Studies was "conceived as the study of Sinitic-language cultures on the margins of geo-political nation-states and their hegemonic productions" (2011, p. 710). In this sense, Sinophone literature includes a variety of works written in Sinitic languages in various locales and contexts, such as Sinophone Tibetan literature, Sinophone Hong Kong literature, Sinophone Taiwan literature, and Sinophone American literature, to name a few examples. What they all have in common is that they are produced in and from the margins. The Sinophone is a response to the problematic use of the term Chinese, which has been misused to equate language with nationality and ethnicity. As a consequence, official monolingualism has ignored and suppressed linguistic heterogeneity. The concept of Sinophone, in contrast, "evinces multilinguality not only in sound but also in script" (2011, p. 715).

Even within the context of Sinophone Studies and Hong Kong Studies, Hong Kong literature remains understudied, and it has received little attention not only in academia but also in the international literary market. The several academic monographs that focus on the uniqueness of Hong Kong culture often restrict their attention to cinema and popular music and overlook the fact that literature has the ability to create powerful images of cultures that are globally transmitted through translation. In the local scholarly scene, there has been a longstanding debate on how to define Hong Kong literature. This chapter contributes to the debate from a different perspective by looking at Hong Kong literature's global dissemination and its definition in the context of translation anthologies. More precisely, by focusing on multiauthored translation anthologies of Hong Kong literature, this chapter aims at investigating the way their paratexts shape and define Hong Kong literature. Through the analysis of the discourses of anthologizers found in the introductions of 24 English and 6 French anthologies, it broadens the understanding of Hong Kong literary identity; 12 English and 2 French anthologies focus exclusively on Hong Kong literature, while 12 English and 4 French anthologies also include authors from China, Taiwan, and the diaspora and, in a few cases, authors from other linguistic regions.[2]

Translation anthologies are typically used in comparative literature courses, influencing students' understanding of other literatures and cultures. They have a strong representational power, as demonstrated by Lefevere (1992), who considered both translations and anthologies as rewritings that frame our understanding of other cultures. Hong Kong literature translation anthologies in English and French are aimed at international audiences, and their editors are mostly motivated to compile these works because they wish to counter narratives that have been imposed from the outside. I argue that what I call a silenced and paradoxical marginalization is visible in the introductions to these anthologies. I demonstrate that in most anthologies, nothing is said about the marginal position of Hong Kong literature in the global literary landscape, and this position is reinforced by various attitudes and omissions. In addition, the silenced marginalization of Hong Kong literature is connected to the invisibility of translation. All anthologizers assume that Hong Kong literature is written in Chinese, and there is often no need to remind readers about the languages spoken and written in Hong Kong or about the fact that the selected works have been translated. Hong Kong literature's key interstitial features, such as its linguistic specificities (written not only in standard Chinese with Cantonese expressions and influenced by English grammar but also written in English) are also omitted. What translation and Hong Kong literature have in common is their interstitial nature: both are located in an in-betweenness, an interstitial zone, a vestibule to different cultures. This essential feature is silenced in the anthologies that I have analyzed.

Van Crevel (2008) and Yeh (1992) have argued that the margin (referring to Chinese poetry) can be where the most creative and powerful work happens. Van Crevel (2008, p. 49) also argues that the uniqueness of artistic creativity lies "in the fact that it isn't easily made to fit consensual truths, or financially quantified, or translated into palpable power over others." In a similar vein, I argue that marginality can be a way of approaching Hong Kong literature, and although this is usually the case in local debates and in the context of Sinophone studies, it is denied and silenced in anthologies aimed at an international audience.

Section 2 introduces the debate on the definition of Hong Kong literature, Section 3 reviews the literature on anthologies, Section 4 introduces the sources of this study, providing the context of their publication, and Section 5 and 6 focus on the findings and conclusions respectively.

2. Defining Hong Kong Literature: An Ongoing Debate

Although Hong Kong literature has developed for over 100 years, the study of Hong Kong literature started only in the 1970s (Wong, 2000, p. 935, 2008).[3] The study (and construction) of the identity of Hong Kong and its literature has been a key issue since the 1980s, with the beginning of Sino-British negotiations on the future of Hong Kong. Hence, it is not surprising that the proceedings of a conference held in 1999 at The Chinese University of Hong Kong opened with an article titled "Cultural Identity of Hong Kong Literature: Nativity, Nationality, and Cosmopolitanity" (Liu, 2000). Titles of conferences that have been held subsequently include "The Identity, Issues and Development of Hong Kong literature" (Leung, 2008) and "Backreading Hong Kong: Junior Scholars' Symposium on Hong Kong Literature and Culture", held yearly since 2017 with different themes. The study of Hong Kong literary identity continues to be the center of attention of many Hong Kong literature scholars.

Various authors have provided different answers to questions such as "what is Hong Kong literature" and "who are Hong Kong authors." Wong Wang-chi (2008) studied how various Hong Kong literary histories, anthologies, and other critical writings define the scope of Hong Kong literature and pointed out discrepancies. In the debate about which writers should be considered Hong Kong authors, the criteria have been – as Shih put it – "residency, sensibility and commitment" (Shih, 2008, p. 16). Leung (2008, pp. 7–8) reminded us that Hong Kong literature is multilingual (both in Chinese and English), and it can be written in three types of Chinese: classical Chinese (*wenyan* 文言), vernacular Chinese (*baihua* 白話), and Cantonese (*yueyu* 粵語). Leung (1989) also argued that these linguistic "impurities" are a reflection of the "impurities" of Hong Kong cultural identity. Chow (1998, p. 157) went further to assert that "[w]hat is unique to Hong Kong . . . is precisely an in-betweenness and an awareness of impure origins, of origins as impure."

The debate on the identity of Hong Kong extends to the way Hong Kong literature and culture should be studied. Most Hong Kong scholars have attempted to emphasize the uniqueness and specificity of Hong Kong culture (Wong, 2008; Leung, 1995; Chu, 2013). In contrast, Lo (2005, p. 16) assumed the "nonexistence" of Hong Kong and, instead of insisting on Hong Kong-ness, explored "Hong Kong's role in constructing Chineseness in the global age." In this same regard, Abbas's (1997) famous book explores the self-invention of Hong Kong as a culture of disappearance. By "disappearance," Abbas (1997, p. 7) did not mean "lack of presence" but an untheorized new form of culture. In the context of Sinophone studies, some scholars have denounced the marginalized position of Hong Kong literature vis-à-vis Chinese literature (Shih, 2008; Chow, 1993) and have even suggested that to "fold Hong Kong literature back to Chinese literature would be no more than a simple-minded but heavy-handed political gesture with no regard for history" (Shih, 2008, p. 16). In this sense, although recognizing the specificity of Hong Kong literature and the high critical value of Sinophone studies, Leung (2008, p. 8) argued that the history of Hong Kong literature is strongly connected to the history of Chinese literature and cannot be studied separately.

Some of the aforementioned studies reflect on theoretical issues (Shih, 2008); others review the historical construction of Hong Kong literary identity in anthologies, literary histories, and critical articles (Wong, 2008); while others study the identity of Hong Kong culture and literature by examining cultural products (Lo, 2005; Chow, 1998, 2011). To date, however, no publication has examined representations of Hong Kong literature in translation anthologies and the vital role played by anthologizers in shaping representations of Hong Kong and its literature that are globally circulated and that may influence local literary creation. Hence, this chapter strongly contributes to the debate on how the identity of Hong Kong and its literature are shaped by examining how anthologizers of translation anthologies present Hong Kong literature to an international audience. I demonstrate that as a consequence of omitting various key specificities of Hong Kong literature (such as its linguistic impurities and bilingual nature), its peripheral position and global connections, most of these anthologies fail to counter its marginalization.

3. Anthologizing and Translating as Sites of Representation

In the field of translation studies, systematic interest in translation anthologies is relatively recent and scarce (Essmann & Frank, 1991, p. 68; Frank, 1998, p. 13; Seruya et al., 2013, p. 1). Members of the Göttingen research project carried out several case studies on translation anthologies in the 1990s (Kittel, 1995), and since then the most influential monograph dedicated to this topic is *Translation in Anthologies and Collections* (Seruya et al., 2013). This volume covers different language combinations and genres and investigates key areas such as discursive practices in the text, peritext, and metatext of translation anthologies; the agency of the translator-anthologist; the interconnectedness between anthologizing, canonization processes, and image building; and issues of censorship.

The theoretical value of studying translation anthologies has been demonstrated by Lefevere (1992), who defined anthologies and translations as forms of rewriting and demonstrated their representational value. By considering translation anthologies as a form of representation, I highlight the role played by discourse in shaping translations, which is especially pertinent in contexts of asymmetrical power relations – in the context of my study, the hierarchy between Chinese literature and the Sinophone becomes evident. Anthologizing involves selection, structuring, and presentation, while the translation of the different works put together by the editor offers evidence of the "prejudice of perception," which means that choices made by translators reflect how a culture construes its sense of Self in relation to others as well as its sense of the Other (Hermans, 1999, p. 95). Translation anthologies therefore reflect a double mechanism of rewriting. As such, anthologies "gain interest for the study of both the formation of cultural identity and of intercultural relations, the creation, development and circulation of national and international canons, and the process of canonization of texts, authors, genres" (Seruya et al., 2013, p. 4). The distinctive context of Hong Kong literature anthologies allows us to study not only representations of the Other – which is the most common form of transfer – but also representations of the Self. This is something characteristic of Hong Kong and other marginalized and postcolonial literatures, since some translators choose to translate from their mother tongue into their second language. In fact, the line between mother tongue and second language often becomes blurred in these contexts in which bilingualism is common. I will later discuss, for example, how Hong Kong translator and anthologizer Martha Cheung aims at countering the grand narratives imposed on Hong Kong from the outside with narratives chosen by the people of Hong Kong.

In the field of comparative literature, literary history, and cultural theory, the number of monographs on the study of anthologies – and not specifically on translation anthologies – is more important. Some of the publications from the last decade include the following: Odber de Baubeta's (2007), Di Leo (2004), Ferry (2001), Price (2000), and Korte et al. (2000). Despite the publication of these monographs, works on anthology studies are "scattered and piecemeal" (Di Leo, 2004, p. 7). Anthologies are often only mentioned in passing as part of another topic, such as book publishing, college teaching, canonization, and the nature of discourse (Di Leo, 2004, p. 7). More importantly, a review of the literature shows that translation anthologies are generally either underrepresented or examined without paying attention to the fact that they include translated literature. The main difference between this study and anthology studies in general is that, as D'Hulst (2013, p. 34) has argued, translation anthologies should be studied "from a due intercultural transfer approach," which means that I pay attention to how a culture is presented to readers from another culture.

One of the main purposes of anthologies is to preserve and recover texts (Mair, 1995; Kilcup, 2004; Essmann & Frank, 1991). This function is significant in the context of Hong Kong literature, with the growing interest in building up an identity since the 1980s, and the increased feelings of self-representation since the 2019 unrest.

Regarding the study of Hong Kong literature anthologies, research carried out until now has been descriptive and bibliographic, paving the way for more critical studies. Two main publications must be mentioned in this context: Chan's (2008) article offers a detailed historical description of Hong Kong fiction anthologies published in Chinese, and Hsu's (2011) bibliography collects Hong Kong literature translations in several languages and is an important source of information for cataloguing anthologies.

The study of Hong Kong literature translations, in general, has received very little scholarly attention. Scattered academic works treat issues as varied as the translation strategies adopted in a particular translation (Yang, 2000); the lack of translations of Hong Kong popular fiction (Raine, 2008); the reception of martial arts fiction in English (Liu, 1997); and linguistic hybridity in translation (Chong, 2007).

4. Sources for This Study

This chapter is based on the close reading of the paratexts of 24 translation anthologies in English and 6 in French; 12 out of the 24 English anthologies are exclusively dedicated to Hong Kong literature, while 12 include authors from Hong

Kong, China, Taiwan, and the diaspora. In the case of the French anthologies, only two are exclusively dedicated to Hong Kong literature, while the remaining four include works by one or two Hong Kong authors. The criteria for inclusion in this study has been that they include at least two stories written originally in Chinese by different authors described as "Hong Kong authors" in the anthology. I have included four issues of *Renditions* in the study because, although it is a literary magazine, it serves the purpose of collecting a selection of works, and the editors themselves consider it an anthology ("in 1988 we brought to readers of *Renditions* the first ever anthology of Hong Kong writings in the form of a special double issue" [Hung, 1997, p. 7]).[4]

The earliest anthology, edited by Soong and Minford, dates from 1984 and includes works by Yu Kwang-chung, Xi Xi, and Laurence Wong Kwok-pun, in addition to other writers from Taiwan, China, and the diaspora. Four years later, *Renditions* published special issues 29 and 30 dedicated to Hong Kong. This publication was also initiated by Stephen Soong and finalized by Eva Hung,[5] who has penned seven of the anthologies. In the first half of the 1990s, various anthologies of Chinese and Sinophone literature saw the light and included some Hong Kong authors (such as Hung, 1990; Duke, 1991; Wang & Tai, 1994; Curien, 1994). Several anthologies exclusively dedicated to Hong Kong sprung up before and after the Handover, as Hong Kong was facing a huge change, and its inhabitants wanted to share their views on the city (such as Parkin, 1995; Hung, 1997, 1999; Cheung, 1998), and anthologies of Chinese and Sinophone literature continued to include more than two authors of Hong Kong literature (see Lau & Goldblatt, 1995; Cheung & Lai, 1997; Tam et al., 1999). In the 2000s, the publication of Hong Kong literature anthologies continued (see Xu & Ingham, 2003; McKirdy & Gordon, 2005; Hung, 2006, 2008; Kelen et al., 2013; Hung, 2001), and Chinese and Sinophone literature anthologies that included Hong Kong authors became more numerous (Curien & Jin, 2001; Cheung & Lai, 2001; Chan, 2001; Curien, 2004, 2006; Curien & Mizio, 2004; Huang, 2005; Mu et al., 2006). Hung's (2008) is still to date the most comprehensive Hong Kong literature anthology, published in two volumes, including poetry, fiction, and essay. The most recent anthology was published in English and Chinese in two separate volumes by PEN Hong Kong in 2017. Five anthologies include works translated from Chinese and works originally written in English (Parkin, 1995; Lam, 1998; Xu & Ingham, 2003; McKirdy & Gordon, 2005; PEN, 2017). The chronological account of the publication of the anthologies gives us an overall picture of the object of discussion and presents the necessary historical context.

Most of these anthologies are widely available in university libraries in the US, Canada, Europe, Australia and New Zealand, other parts of Asia, such as Singapore and sometimes Macau, Mainland China, and some Southeast Asian universities. Only two of them have had a more limited circulation and can only be found in Hong Kong (these are Lam, 1998; McKirdy & Gordon, 2005). They are both poetry anthologies, and despite their limited circulation, I have included them in the study because they have attracted international readers in Hong Kong.

5. Findings

5.1 Self-representations Versus Voices From the Outside

Various Hong Kong anthologizers react to images of Hong Kong imposed from the outside – not just from the West, but also from China, as we will see in the examples later – and wish to make Hong Kong voices heard. Cheung (1998, p. xi) reflects on the politics of representation in the introduction to *Hong Kong Collage* and explains that "we have to stand back and look at the representations for what they are – not truths, but just representations, attempts to speak on behalf of something or someone." She also insists that although this might be obvious, it is a reaction against imposed representations and voices from the outside.

> [T]o counter the grand narratives, the master images, and the controlling identities – imposed on Hong Kong from the outside – with narratives, images, and identities chosen by the people of Hong Kong for themselves.
> (Cheung, 1998, p. xii)

Hung, when publishing the 47 and 48 *Renditions* issues in 1997, specifically refers to anthologies done in the Mainland and criticizes their outdated nature.

> Hong Kong literary histories and Hong Kong authors' series have sprung up in China in the last few years. The quality of the books is variable, but one limitation is common: they have not taken into consideration the most up-to-date works. This would not have been a handicap if the literary scene were stagnant, but that is far from the case for Hong Kong of the 1990s.
> (Hung, 1997, p. 7)

Some other anthologizers claim that their anthology is done by and speaks of Hong Kong people, reflecting the varied origins of "Hong Kong people," which shows that "the Self" in the Hong Kong context is actually a heterogenous group of people. For example, in *Poetry Lives!*, McKirdy and Gordon have lived in Hong Kong for most of their lives and have participated in literary circles for a long time, whereas in *Hong Kong 20/20*, the editors and authors are a mixed group of various origins.

The aim of all anthologies exclusively devoted to Hong Kong literature is to present it as a distinct category. However, there is one exception to this. In the introduction to *From the Bluest Part of Harbour: Poems from Hong Kong*, Parkin and Wong (in Parkin, 1995, p. xiii) do not refer to Hong Kong literature or poetry and instead use the term "Hong Kong Chinese poets" and "Chinese poetry written in Hong Kong." This "Chinese" could be understood in opposition to "English" or other language and nationalities. According to Parkin and Wong, what "Hong Kong Chinese poets" have in common is that they want to "make a significant contribution to Chinese culture" (p. xiv). When describing the poets' background, they clearly align themselves with a nationalist rhetoric.

The poet's education and professional lives seem very modern and Western in outlook (and this is especially true of two of the women poets, Louise Ho and Juliette Chen); but their sensibility and temperament tell us that each of them reserves in the chambers of the heart a special décor, atmosphere, and a sense of proportion that is of China and Asia.

(Parkin, 1995, p. xiv)

This reference to a special "sensibility and temperament" that is Chinese and Asian and that is understood in opposition to modern and Western attitudes reveals a self-orientalizing reductionism and puts this introduction in the same group as the imposed images from the outside that other anthologizers are trying to contradict. Published in Hong Kong right before the Handover, it follows a Chinese nationalist logic.

Not all anthologizers necessarily react to voices from the outside; some are inspired by them. In the introduction to *City Voices*, Xu Xi tells us that her first encounter with Hong Kong writing was through "Western residents and visitors for whom English was a native tongue, both linguistically and culturally" (Xu & Ingham, 2003, pp. 18–19). She acknowledges that their perspective was often orientalized and romanticized but, contrary to other anthologizers, does not criticize it. For example, she mentions *The World of Suzie Wong* by Richard Mason, published in 1957, as a source of inspiration, while Cheung (1998) refers to that same work as responsible for disseminating stereotyped images that should be rectified and compensated with local voices.

In the case of the French anthologies, Curien (2006, p. 11) highlights how through these stories readers can learn about the images of Hong Kong, the themes and the forms that local writers want to explore. In *Hong Kong: approaches littéraires*, Curien (2004) thanks Leung Ping-kwan for introducing her to the writers, which suggests that he was partly involved in the editorial process. It is worth highlighting Leung's role in disseminating Hong Kong literature internationally. Based on Hsu's *A Bibliography of Hong Kong Literature in Foreign Languages*, as for 2011, over 50 out of around 500 English translations were done by Leung Ping-kwan, including individual poems and stories in journal and book-length publications. With 17 exceptions, all these publications were issued by Hong Kong publishers (Mattison, 2017, p. 151). Of course, the situation differs in French, in which case most translations were done by Curien and published in France.

5.2 The Fragility of Representation: Avoiding Definitions

I have mentioned that the origins of Hong Kong authors have been a source of debate in the study of Hong Kong literature. Hung (2008, p. 8) reminds readers about this debate by summarizing it as the "long debated question of whether to consider only writers who were born and bred in Hong Kong or include works in which the events of Hong Kong feature prominently." However, when looking at the prefaces and the selection of authors, there seems to be no disagreement, and such debate is nonexistent or invisible. All anthologizers have included authors who engage with Hong Kong and have lived in the city but were not necessarily born in Hong Kong. Only two of the introductions include a reflection on the writers' origins. Cheung (1998, p. ix) highlights that most of the authors included in her anthology were born and bred in Hong Kong; only three of them were born in Mainland China (Yan Chungou, Liu Yichang, and Xi Xi). Wong Shuk-han (in Kelen et al., 2013, pp. 8–9) claims that South-bound writers from the 1950s and 1960s included in their anthology have been much neglected by the English reading public, which is why they have selected a few of them (Liu Yichang, Evan Yang, Li Kuang, and Ronald Mar) as well as local writers of the same period (Li Wai-ling, Quanan).

On the other hand, most anthologizers describe their compilations as partial representations and claim that they do not intend to be definitive. They often refer to the subjectivity of their selection and insist on the fact that they do not offer a comprehensive definition of Hong Kong literature. Nevertheless, their introductions contribute to defining Hong Kong and its literature and are therefore unsuccessful in escaping their representative power. By denying (or lightening the burden of) their responsibility, they also attract the readers' attention to the fact that they are indeed offering one possible definition. The following quotations show a few examples of the humble tone of anthologizers when referring to their selection.

> We hope this collection will serve as a road sign for further exploration; it is certainly not meant as a final summing up.
>
> (Hung, 1997, p. 7)

> It makes no pretence to being the definitive anthology of Hong Kong fictional works that many say Hong Kong lacks. . . . It is an attempt, on the part of the editor, to tell her own story of Hong Kong through the mouths of other writers, almost all of whom were born and bred in Hong Kong. It is an unashamedly subjective, defiantly, idiosyncratic collection – a collage, rather than a representational painting.
>
> (Cheung, 1998, p. ix)

> A literary anthology that looks back at an era is in many ways a re-creation of that era's literary landscape, and therefore inevitably just as partial.
>
> (Hung, 2008, p. 1)

> The intention of this Anthology is not to try (it is impossible) to represent the whole Hong Kong poetry scene – however it does serve as an 'indicator' of Hong Kong poetry.
>
> (Chan, 2001, p. 8)

As all anthologies are representative and partial in nature, what is meaningful here is the fact that anthologisers feel the need to highlight this fact. Interestingly, Chinese literature anthologizers that include a small selection of Hong Kong literature together with other Chinese and Sinophone authors do not feel the need to mention the subjectivity of their selection or the fact that their anthologies are only partial representations. We have found no such claims in the introductions we have analyzed. This suggests that many Hong Kong literature anthologizers feel uncomfortable with the idea of fully representing Hong Kong literature or suggesting a possible definition of this literature.

In the earliest attempt at anthologizing Hong Kong literature in English, Hung (1988, p. 8) claims that a definitive anthology will have to wait until the definition of Hong Kong literature becomes clearer.

> In publishing a special *Renditions* issue on Hong Kong, our intention is to reflect this richness and diversity rather than to produce a definitive volume on Hong Kong literature. The latter task will have to wait until clearer ideas about the territory's literary output emerge from the continuing debates. And even then the controversy will not be easily avoided.

However, even if there was a clearer definition of Hong Kong literature or a better formed critical mass, there is no such thing as a definitive anthology. In addition, the trend to present anthologies as partial representations has continued over the years in subsequent publications. Even in Hung's *To Pierce the Material Screen*, which can be considered a rather comprehensive anthology that compiles over 100 pieces of fiction, poetry, and essays in two volumes, Hung (2008) claims:

> [My] choices are influenced by personal preferences or beliefs. . . . This, then, is my excuse and apology for producing an anthology which may be representative in certain ways, but is by no means comprehensively so.
> (Hung, 2008, p. 2)

All literatures are in the making, as the definition of any literary history evolves, and all representation can only be partial, but it seems that anthologizers of Hong Kong literature need to justify their selections, and sometimes they even go as far as apologizing. A silent marginalization of Hong Kong literature is palpable in the apologetic and humble attitude of anthologizers.

A second possible reason why anthologizers insist on the fact that they are offering a partial representation of Hong Kong literature would be that they are aware of the politics of representation and are reacting against assertive and imposed images from the outside, as discussed in the previous section. Weary as they are of reading stereotypical "truths" about their city, they adopt a cautious and humble tone.

There are a few exceptions to this partial representation trend, such as Xu Xi and Lo Wai Luen's prefaces in English, and Annie Curien's prefaces in French anthologies. In the introduction to *City voices*, Xu Xi claims that "[i]n compiling this anthology, the goal was to provide as *representative* – if not as comprehensive – a selection as possible to reflect the voices over time" (Xu & Ingham, 2003, p. 17).

Lo Wai Luen, in the introduction to *Hong Kong Stories: Old Themes New Voices*, explains, "I have decided to focus on this historical perspective which, I think, will present a clearer picture of Hong Kong literature as it is today" (Hung, 1999, p. 7). In the case of the French anthologies, Curien (2006; Curien & Mizio, 2004) does not say anything about the (lack of) representativeness of her selection. In this sense, the French anthologizer probably does not feel the need to be cautious to avoid criticism, as very little has been written about Hong Kong literature in French.

5.3 On Hong Kong Literature's Marginality and Its Relationship with Chinese and Western Literature

Hong Kong literature is not presented as a marginal literature. In anthologies of literature from China, Taiwan, Hong Kong, and the Chinese diaspora, anthologizers refer to the cohesive force of *wen* (Soong & Minford, 1984, p. 3) and an overlapping common culture (Wang & Tai, 1994, p. 238). They present the various literatures as being in dialogue and creating a heterogonous Chinese literature. Wang (1994, p. 241) claims that Mainland literature is being decentralized and that "literature from Hong Kong, Taiwan, and overseas – the 'marginal' Chinese communities – is to be taken seriously because its readers are already living, economically and culturally, inside modernity." He also argues that the center versus margin map is fictive and does not reflect the reality, as dialogues between many Chinas are possible. Tam et al. (1999, p. xvii) do not posit a homology between state, nation, and culture and believe that innovative writers break out of these boundaries. They also claim that each of the four communities represented in their anthology has taken a different path toward modernity and globalization. Power differences and hierarchies are omitted in the introductions, suggesting that there is a harmonious coexistence of various Sinitic-language literatures and that resistance to the hegemonic call of Chineseness (which is the *raison d'être* of Sinophone studies) is unnecessary.

Very few anthologies refer specifically to Hong Kong literature's relationship with that of the Mainland and with Western literature, and when they do, they do not necessarily praise the various qualities of Hong Kong literature. Lo Wai Luen (in Hung, 1999, pp. 9–13) describes early Hong Kong writing from the 1920s and 1930s as "immature" and "imitative" with no personal style, always looking to China to follow mainland Chinese writers' creative approach. She explains that writers from the 1990s have however managed to break away from that practice and have their own style. Hung (1988, p. 7) also describes the quality of Hong Kong writing as "uneven" and considers that it "does not merit unmitigated approval." She further reveals the marginal status of Hong Kong literature by defining it as "an area relatively unknown to both sinologists and translators" (1988, p. 8). In a later anthology, Hung clarifies that she considers creative writing of the 1940s as "second-tier" (2008, p. 3) but praises the local voices of the 1960s and the strong Hong Kong identity that emerged in the 1990s, around the time of the Handover.

Mary Stephen, in the anthology devoted to the *First Hong Kong Poetry Festival*, describes Hong Kong as an un-poetic place, noisy, polluted, materialistic, and overpopulated (Lam, 1998, p. v). Although a degree of sarcasm can be perceived in this part of the introduction, Stephen also tends to self-marginalize Hong Kong culture and literature by transmitting stereotypes about its people. She describes Hong Kong people as loud, exaggerated, impatient, susceptible, vindictive, vulgar, etc.

We see a completely different stance in the introduction to *City Poetry*, published three years later, where Chan Chi Tak insists that "Hong Kong poetry shines with true colors alongside the contemporary poetry of China and Taiwan, and deserves a comparable rival status" (2001, p. 6). Curien (2006, p. 9; Curien & Mizio, 2004, p. 14) adds a different perspective by referring to the marginality of literature in Hong Kong society. The French anthologizer points out that literature plays a minor role in the economy-driven city in comparison to literature's status in mainland China and Taiwan. Lo Wai Luen (in Hung, 1999) is the only one to refer to the relationship of Hong Kong literature to Western literature. She explains that writers of the 1990s "draw sustenance from Western literary theories and creative approaches" and are inspired by Western literary forms (p. 10). At the same time, they are interested in sharing a Hong Kong perspective and delve into Hong Kong issues and way of life.

The marginalization of Hong Kong literature is also palpable in the way the introductions to the anthologies that are not exclusively devoted to Hong Kong literature disregard its singular development and fail to mention its relationship to other Chinese and Sinophone literatures. They usually simply refer to the fact that they include works from China, Taiwan, Hong Kong, and the diaspora. These anthologies that include works by more than three Hong Kong authors do not explain any complexities or differences in the identity and cultural production of the various Chinese and Sinophone regions. Hong Kong and its literature are therefore invisible in these anthologies (see for example, Soong & Minford, 1984; Hung, 1990; Wang & Tai, 1994; Lau & Goldblatt, 1995; Huang, 2005). The same thing happens in French anthologies that include a few works by Hong Kong authors (see Curien, 1994, 2004, 2010; Curien & Jin, 2001).

Duke (1991) does not say much about Hong Kong literature either but mentions that "the problems of Hong Kong and Taiwan society today will be the problems of Chinese society tomorrow, and these stories both realistically and ironically delineate some of the dilemma facing modern urban Chinese characters" (p. xii). He also repeats some of the images mentioned in Hong Kong literature anthologies such as its hyper-commercialism, the diverse origins of the authors, and the fact that it was a cultural wasteland while it was a British colony.

On other hand, two anthologies describe the importance of drama and short-short stories in Hong Kong. Cheung and Lai (1997), on their anthology on drama, devote a section to each region (mainland China, Taiwan, and Hong Kong), describing their distinct features and historical development, and explain how events in China influenced Hong Kong writers. Mu and Chiu (in Mu et al., 2006) in their short-short story anthology highlight the importance and superiority of this genre in Hong Kong and describe the development of this genre in some detail. In addition, Tam et al.'s (1999) introduction describes Hong Kong as distinctively different and repeat some of the images mentioned in Hong Kong anthologies such as the rapidly changing society, its colonial past, free-market capitalism and the importance of economy, and anxieties around the time of the Handover.

The anthologizers of *City Voices*, which also includes Hong Kong literature written in English, remind us that anglophone Hong Kong literature is even more marginal (Ingham, in Xu & Ingham, 2003, p. 3). We could say that Hong Kong literature written in English is in a triple marginal position: against Chinese literature, English literature, and Hong Kong literature written in Chinese. This situation suggests that language is not the only determining factor in deciding the position of a literature in the global literary field; although written in English, a dominant language, Anglophone Hong Kong literature remains highly marginalized.

5.4 Language and Translation

Overall, the English introductions overlook translation and the various languages used in Hong Kong literature, while the French anthologies pay attention to these two matters. The anthologizers of *Hong Kong 20/20* are the only ones praising the "dual heritage" of Hong Kong literature written in two languages. This is also the only anthology that, in addition to including works written in both languages, publishes a twin volume in Chinese, with the same works, translating those that originated in English. This brings as to the question of language and translation. If Hong Kong literature is both written in English and Chinese, what do the anthologizers have to say about language and translation? What about bilingual writing and self-translation?

In the anthologies that we have analyzed, the anthologizers have made a choice of including only Hong Kong literature written in Chinese and translated in English or in French (in most cases) or both works originally written in English and translated from Chinese (in five cases). However, language and translation are topics that are either completely omitted or only mentioned in passing.

Lo Wai Luen (in Hung, 1999), Chan Chi Tak (2001), and McKirdy and Gordon (2005) do not refer to language or translation at all in their introductions. The only subtle reference to translation in Lo's foreword is the fact that the foreword itself has been translated. Hung (1988, 1997, 2008) thanks the translators for their work but does not say anything about the language in which Hong Kong literature is written, and other translation issues remain unmentioned. Wong Shuk-han (in Kelen et al., 2013, pp. 8, 10, 11) refers to the anthology as a "translation project" and English titles are followed by Chinese original titles written in Chinese characters, implicitly suggesting that the stories have been translated from Chinese. She also refers to the fact that the selection was made based on the well-known two-volume Chinese anthology, *An Anthology of Contemporary Hong Kong Short Stories* (香港當代作家作品合集選: 小說卷), published in 2011). All these anthologizers assume that Hong Kong literature is written in Chinese and is not necessary to remind the readers about this, which reveals both the invisibility of translation and the marginality of English language writing in Hong Kong. Hung (1988, 1997, 2008) adds a note on romanization. It is interesting to see that from 1997 she translates real people and place names using the official English names or romanized names that follow Cantonese pronunciation, and uses *pinyin* for pennames and fictional characters. Before that, *Renditions* used *pinyin* for all names. This reflects the increased local identity and the willingness to use local linguistic standards instead of following a centralized system from the Mainland.

There are two introductions in which Hung does, however, refer to translation in more detail. In the 66th special issue of *Renditions*, dedicated to the Chinese essay (which includes a section on Hong Kong essays), she briefly refers to the challenges of translating this genre and in the 56th issue, dedicated to new Hong Kong poetry, she explains that the collection emerges from a bilingual event in which "the participating poets write either in Chinese or in English, and the translated versions of their poems were projected on to the stage as they read" (Hung, 2001, p. 5). These are the only two instances in which Hung mentions English writing. Cheung (1998, pp. xiii–xiv) refers to the fact that most inhabitants of Hong Kong express themselves in Chinese and their thoughts have remained inaccessible to those who do not speak the language. She thus highlights the importance of Chinese language and reminds readers that the pieces that she chose were originally written in Chinese, although she does not say anything about translation.

In the five anthologies that in addition to translations also include Hong Kong literature written in English, although the bilingual linguistic reality is sometimes mentioned, there is no mention of the fact that some of the texts were originally written in Chinese and have therefore been translated for the present volume. In the two introductory essays of *City Voices*, Xu Xi and Ingham (2003) refer to the central role of Chinese language writing in Hong Kong and the marginality of English in this context. They also refer to the "bilingual poets" Leung Ping-kwan (although Leung being a bilingual writer is debatable) and Laurence Wong Kwok-pun but do not say much about other Chinese-language writers included in the anthology or about how or by whom they were translated. Xu Xi explains, "We did include a few local Chinese poets – meaning those who are not bilingual but publish primarily in Chinese – whose selected poems *originate in English* or are *self-translated*" (p. 18). This is the only vague allusion to translation in the introduction. All the works are presented as if they were written in English. The only reference to co-translation appears in the reference list, where we can see that some of Leung Ping-kwan's poems were co-translated and appeared previously.

Hong Kong 20/20 is more transparent and refers to Chinese and English writing as well as to translation in a straightforward way. This is the only English anthology that explicitly refers to Hong Kong literature being written in the two languages and includes both types of writings, with a predominance of English language works.

Curien (2006; Curien & Mizio, 2004), in her two French anthologies, explains the linguistic reality of Hong Kong in more detail, whereas the anthologizers of the English compilations seem to take for granted that readers are aware of this information. This could suggest that the target readership of the English language anthologies are readers who are familiar with Hong Kong. A search of the Worldcat database shows that these anthologies are, however, widely available in university libraries around the world.

Curien (2006; Curien & Mizio, 2004) explains Hong Kong's colonial background and bilingual artistic environment. She describes specific linguistic features such as the use of some old characters, classical idioms, and some syntactic elements and sentence structures influenced by the English language. She also highlights the fact that the knowledge of classical language and literature has continued and was not interrupted as in Mainland China.

In the anthologies that include Chinese and Sinophone literature in their selection, we have already seen that Hong Kong literature is often invisible; thus, the issue of language (i.e., Cantonese and English) is not mentioned at all. Cheung and Lai (1997, p. xxiii), in their drama anthology, are the only ones that mention Cantonese performances. Huang (2005, p. III) is the only one who delves a bit more into the topic of translation, perhaps because he is the only translator of the anthology and can therefore discuss the challenges he has faced. He explains he conducted surveys to understand readers' preferences and that he prioritized readability. He adds that sometimes the story was heavily edited by either the author or the translator (with the author's permission).

6. Conclusion

I have shown that the analysis of multiauthored translation anthologies can shed light on anthologizers' efforts to make their voice heard and react against imposed images of the city and its culture. My findings are based on the close reading of the prefaces, and it is important to acknowledge that the features I have chosen to focus on and the criteria that I have applied influence the representations and definition of Hong Kong and its literature that I am revealing. In a sense, my analysis involves selection and is thus similar to the role of anthologizers. For example, by focusing on anthologies that include translations, I am not looking at representations of Hong Kong literature written in English.

Through their selections and introductions, anthologizers share their own views on Hong Kong and its literature with a global readership. Unexpectedly, my analysis shows that they rarely mention Hong Kong literature's marginal position nor its relationship to Mainland Chinese literature or other world literatures, thus reducing the relevance of power differences and historical context. This lack of interest in defining Hong Kong literature and underscoring its specificity distinguishes these anthologies from local debates. In an interview with Dung Kai-cheung, the writer mentioned that when asked to define Hong Kong literature, most authors and scholars would refer to its marginality, and that, instead, he was interested in contextualising Hong Kong literature and its historical development as part of world literature.[6] I have shown that in most of these anthologies we find little evidence of these two trends, which is contrary to local debates on Hong Kong literature.

In addition, anthologizers' apologetic and humble attitude when referring to their selections suggests that they do not claim the importance of Hong Kong literature in the global literary scene. The fast-changing pace of the city and the fact that it is a literature in the making are used as justifications for providing provisional definitions of Hong Kong literature, highlighting its volatility, while all anthologies are provisional in essence and all literatures are in the making. Thus, insisting on this paradoxically highlights the instability of Hong Kong literature.

Translation anthologies of Chinese and Sinophone literature that include some Hong Kong works do not mention any specificities of Hong Kong literature, making them invisible. One of the most important specificities of Hong Kong literature, that is, its linguistic features, are invisible in most anthologies. The invisibility of language entails the invisibility of translation: these anthologies do not problematize the role played by translation in their own making. Translation is a crucial process in the compilation of these anthologies, as important as selection; it has, however, no place in the introductions and is denied its importance.

Through the study of Hong Kong literature translation anthologies, this chapter has contributed to the debate on the definition of Hong Kong literature and has shown how the representations of Hong Kong and its literature in these anthologies differ from images imposed from the outside and from local scholarly debates. These translation anthologies are globally circulated and are available in university libraries worldwide, which is why this study is indispensable to understand representations of Hong Kong and its literature. Looking at marginal literatures through the lens of translation anthologies can lead to expanding our understanding of their definitions and their global literary circulation. Further studies that examine other parts of the paratexts, the selection of authors and works included in the anthologies, as well as translation strategies are necessary to deepen our understanding of the global circulation of translated Hong Kong literature.

Notes

1 I would like to thank Lucas Klein and Carles Prado-Fonts for their feedback on previous drafts of this chapter. The research for this study was funded by the University Grants Committee of Hong Kong (Early Career Scheme, HKBU22610218) under the project *Hong Kong and Its Literature through a Double Lens: English and French Anthologies of Translated Literature*.
2 All the introductions are available in the HKKH Database of the project website: https://digital.lib.hkbu.edu.hk/hkkh/home
3 Some scholars, such as Liu Denghan (2000) and Lo Kwai-cheung (1990), proved that during the 1970s the debate was mainly on whether or not Hong Kong had literature; they argued that studies on Hong Kong literature did not start until the mid-1980s.
4 Following the criteria set previously, I excluded, for example, Rabut and Pino's (1996) *Le fox-trot de Shanghai*, which includes stories by Ye Lingfeng and Xu, who, although they are considered Hong Kong authors in some anthologies in Chinese (see, for example, Liu Yichang, 1997), are presented as Shanghai authors in the French anthology. I also excluded book series dedicated to Hong Kong, as they do not usually have a unifying preface; such as Hong Kong Atlas, with ten titles by various publishers translated from Chinese (Mattison, 2017), and the Penguin Hong Kong series, with ten books among which only one was translated from Chinese.

5 Interview with Eva Hung, available at the project website: https://digital.lib.hkbu.edu.hk/hkkh/interviews.php#skeletabsPanel4
6 The interview is available on the project website: https://digital.lib.hkbu.edu.hk/hkkh/interviews.php#skeletabsPanel3

References

Primary Sources (Anthologies)

Chan, C. (2001). *CityPoetry 2001: Poetry, Documentation, Essays*. Hong Kong: CityPoetry Project.

Cheung, M. P. Y. (1998). *Hong Kong Collage: Contemporary Stories and Writing*. Hong Kong, Oxford and New York: Oxford University Press.

Cheung, M. P. Y., & Lai, J. C. C. (1997). *An Oxford Anthology of Contemporary Chinese Drama*. Hong Kong: Oxford University Press.

Cheung, M. P. Y., & Lai, J. C. C. (2001). *Dialogue among Civilizations Through Poetry: 240 Poetry Readings in 200 Countries*. Hong Kong: Chinese University of Hong Kong.

Curien, A. (1994). *Écrire au présent: débats littéraires franco-chinois*. Paris: Éditions de la Maison des sciences de l'homme.

Curien, A. (2004). *Alibis: dialogues littéraires franco-chinois*. Paris: Éditions de la Maison des sciences de l'homme.

Curien, A. (2006). *L'horloge et le dragon: 12 auteurs et 14 nouvelles contemporaines de Hong Kong*. Paris: Éditions Caractères.

Curien, A. (2010). *ALIBI 2: dialogues littéraires franco-chinois*. Paris: Éditions de la Maison des sciences de l'homme.

Curien, A., & Jin, S. (2001). *Littérature Chinoise: Le passé et l'écriture contemporaine*. Paris: Éditions de la Maison des sciences de l'homme.

Curien, A., & Mizio, F. (2004). *Hong Kong, Approches Littéraires*. Paris: You-Feng.

Duke, M. (1991). *Worlds of modern Chinese fiction: Short stories and Novellas from the People's Republic, Taiwan and Hong Kong*. New York: M.E. Sharpe.

Huang, H. J. (2005). *An Anthology of Chinese Short Stories*. Beijing: Foreign Language Press.

Hung, E. (1988). *Renditions 29 and 30 (Spring and Autumn): Special issue on Hong Kong*. Hong Kong: The Research Centre for Translation, The Chinese University of Hong Kong.

Hung, E. (1990). *Contemporary Women Writers: Hong Kong and Taiwan*. Hong Kong: The Research Centre for Translation, The Chinese University of Hong Kong.

Hung, E. (1997). *Renditions, 47 and 48 (Spring and Autumn): Special Issue on Hong Kong Nineties*. Hong Kong: The Research Centre for Translation, The Chinese University of Hong Kong.

Hung, E. (1999). *Hong Kong Stories: Old Themes New Voices*. Hong Kong: The Research Centre for Translation, The Chinese University of Hong Kong.

Hung, E. (2001). *Renditions 56 (Autumn), Special Section: New Hong Kong Poetry*. Hong Kong: The Research Centre for Translation, The Chinese University of Hong Kong.

Hung, E. (2006). *Renditions 66 (Autumn), Hong Kong Essays*. Hong Kong: The Research Centre for Translation, The Chinese University of Hong Kong.

Hung, E. (2008). *To Pierce the Material Screen: An Anthology of 20th-Century Hong Kong Literature*, vol. 1 and 2. Hong Kong: Research Centre for Translation, the Chinese University of Hong Kong.

Kelen, C. (Kit), Wong, S., & Song, Z. (2013). *In Search of a Flat: An Anthology of Hong Kong Urban Short Stories*. Hong Kong and Macao: Association of Stories in Macao; Centre for Humanities Research, Lingnan University.

Lam, F. (1998). *First Hong Kong International Poetry Festival – A Collection of Essays: The Kiss of Poetry*. Hong Kong: Hong Kong Arts Centre & Provisional Regional Council.

Lau, J., & Goldblatt, H. (1995). *Running Wild: New Chinese Writers*. New York: Columbia University Press.

McKirdy, D., & Gordon, P. (2005). *Poetry Lives!: An Anthology of Hong Kong Poetry for Teens*. Hong Kong: Chameleon Press.

Mu, A., Chiu, J., & Goldblatt, H. (2006). *Loud Sparrows: Contemporary Chinese Short Shorts*. New York: Columbia University Press.

Parkin, A. (1995). *From the Bluest Part of the Harbour: Poems from Hong Kong*. Hong Kong: Oxford University Press.

PEN Hong Kong Anthology Editorial Committee. (2017). *Hong Kong 20/20: Reflections on a Borrowed Place*. Hong Kong: Blacksmith Books.

Soong, S. C., & Minford, J. (1984). *Trees on the Mountain: An Anthology of New Chinese Writing*. Hong Kong: Chinese University Press.

Tam, K., Yip, T. S., & Dissanayake, W. (1999). *A Place of One's Own: Stories of Self in Mainland China, Taiwan, Hong Kong and Singapore*. Hong Kong: Oxford University Press.

Wang, D. D., & Tai, J. (1994). *Running Wild: New Chinese Writers*. New York: Columbia University Press.

Xu, X., & Ingham, M. (2003). *City Voices: Hong Kong Writing in English, 1945 to the Present*. Hong Kong: Hong Kong University Press.

Secondary Sources

Abbas, A. (1997). *Hong Kong: Culture and the Politics of Disappearance*. Minneapolis, MN and London: University of Minnesota Press.

Chan, L. K. K. 陳國球. (2008). "'「選學」與「香港」–香港小說選本初探' (Anthologizing Hong Kong – A Study of Hong Kong Fiction Anthologies). In Special Issue: The Identity, Issues and Development of Hong Kong Literature." 現代中文文學學報 *Journal of Modern Literature in Chinese (JMLC)* 8 (2) – 9 (1): 81–111.

Chong, C. S. 莊清花. (2007). "從香港文學及其譯本看香港的混雜性 (The Hybridity of Hong Kong: A Perspective from Hong Kong Literature and Its Translation)." MPhil diss. Chinese University of Hong Kong.

Chow, R. (1993). "The Politics and Pedagogy of Asian Literatures in American Universities." In *Writing Diaspora: Tactics of Intervention in Contemporary Cultural Studies*, Chow, R. ed., 120–143. Bloomington, IN: Indiana University Press.

Chow, R. (1998). *Ethics after Idealism: Theory – Culture – Ethnicity – Reading*. Bloomington, IN: Indiana University Press.

Chow, R. (2011). "Thinking with Food, Writing Off Center: Notes on Two Hong Kong Authors." In *Global Chinese Literature*, Jing, T. & Wang, D. Der-Wei, eds., 133–155. Leiden: Brill.

Chu, Y. (2013). *Lost in Transition: Hong Kong Culture in the Age of China*. Albany, NY: Suny Press.

Chu, Y. (2018). *Found in Transition: Hong Kong Studies in the Age of China*. Albany, NY: Suny Press.

de Baubeta, P. A. O. (2007). *The Anthology in Portugal: A New Approach to the History of Portuguese Literature in the Twentieth Century*. Oxford, Bern, Berlin, Brussels, Frankfurt am Main, New York and Wien: Peter Lang.

D'Hulst, L. (2013). "Forms and Functions of Anthologies of Translations into French in the Nineteenth Century." In *Translation in Anthologies and Collections (19th and 20th Centuries)*, Seruya, T. et al. eds., 17–34. Lincoln, NE and London: University of Nebraska Press.

Di Leo, J. R., ed. (2004). *On Anthologies: Politics and Pedagogy*. Lincoln, NE and London: University of Nebraska Press.

Essmann, H., & Frank, A. P. (1991). "Translation Anthologies: An Invitation to the Curious and a Case Study." *Target* 3 (1): 65–90.

Ferry, A. (2001). *Tradition and the Individual Poem: An Inquiry into Anthologies*. Stanford, CA: Stanford University Press.

Frank, A. P. (1998). "Anthologies of Translation." In *Encyclopedia of Translation Studies*, Baker, M. ed., 13–16. London: Routledge.

Hermans, T. (1999). *Translation in Systems: Descriptive and System-oriented Approaches Explained*. Manchester: St. Jerome.

Hsu, A. (2011). *A Bibliography of Hong Kong Literature in Foreign Languages*. Hong Kong: The Centre for Humanities Research, Lingnan University.

Kilcup, K. L. (2004). "The Poetry and Prose of Recovery Work." In *On Anthologies: Politics and Pedagogy*, Di Leo, J. R., ed., 112–138. Lincoln, NE and London: University of Nebraska Press.

Kittel, H., ed. (1995). *International Anthologies of Literature in Translation*. Berlin: Erich Schmidt.

Korte, B., Schneider, R., & Lethbridge, S., eds. (2000). *Anthologies of British Poetry: Critical Perspectives from Literary and Cultural Studies*. Amsterdam; Atlanta, GA: Rodopi.

Lefevere, A. (1992). *Translation, Rewriting and the Manipulation of Literary Fame*. London and New York: Routledge.

Leung, P. K. 梁秉鈞. (1989). "都市文化與香港文學" (Urban Culture and Hong Kong Literature). 《當代》 *Contemporary* 38: 14–23.

Leung, P. K. 梁秉鈞. (1995). 香港文化 *(Hong Kong Culture)*. Hong Kong: Hong Kong Arts Centre.

Leung, P. K. 梁秉鈞, ed. (2008). "「香港文學的定位、論題及發展」專號 Special Issue: The Identity, Issues and Development of Hong Kong Literature." *JMLC* 8 (2) – 9 (1).

Liu, C. C., ed. (1997). *The Question of Reception: Martial Arts Fiction in English Translation*. Hong Kong: Centre for Literature and Translation, Lingnan College.

Liu, D. H. 刘登翰. (2000). "香港文學的文化身份 – 試論香港文學的「本土性」、民族性和世界性" (Cultural Identity of Hong Kong Literature: Nativity, Nationality, and Cosmopolitanity). In 活潑紛繁的香港文學：一九九九年香港文學國際研討會論文集 *(Hong Kong Literature Dynamic and Diversified: Proceedings of the 1999 International Conference on Hong Kong Literature)*, vol. 2, Wong, W. L. ed., 3–16. Hong Kong: The Chinese University of Hong Kong.

Liu, Y. C. (1997). 香港短篇小說選 (五十年代) *(An Anthology of Hong Kong Short Stories [1950s])*. Hong Kong: Cosmos Book.

Lo, K. C. (1990). "Crossing Boundaries: A Study of Modern Hong Kong Fiction from the Fifties to the Eighties." MPhil diss. Hong Kong University.

Lo, K. C. (2005). *Chinese Face/Off: The Transnational Popular Culture of Hong Kong*. Urbana, IL and Chicago, IL: University of Illinois Press.

Mair, V. H. (1995). "Anthologizing and Anthropologizing: The Place of Nonelite and Nonstandard Culture in the Chinese Literary Tradition." In *Translating Chinese Literature*,

Eoyang, E. & Lin, Y. F. eds., 231–261. Bloomington, IN and Indianapolis, IN: Indiana University Press.

Mattison, C. (2017). "Mapping Hong Kong's Atlas." *JMLC* 14 (2) – 15 (1): 147–160.

Price, L. (2000). *The Anthology and the Rise of the Novel: From Richardson to George Eliot*. Cambridge: Cambridge University Press.

Rabut, I., & Pino, A. (1996). *Le fox-trot de Shanghai et autres nouvelles chinoises*. Paris: Albin Michel.

Raine, R. (2008). "Overcoming Prejudice: On Translating Hong Kong Popular Fiction." 翻譯學報 *Journal of Translation Studies* 11 (2): 13–30.

Seruya, T., D'hulst, L., Assis Rosa, A., & Lin Moniz, M., eds. (2013). *Translation in Anthologies and Collections (19th and 20th Centuries)*. Amsterdam and Philadelphia, PA: John Benjamins.

Shih, S. M. (2008). "Hong Kong Literature as Sinophone Literature." *JMLC* 8 (2) – 9 (1): 12–18.

Shih, S. M. (2011). "The Concept of the Sinophone." *PMLA* 126 (3): 709–718.

van Crevel, M. (2008). *Chinese Poetry in Times of Mind, Mayhem and Money*. Leiden: Brill.

Wong, W. C. 王宏志. (2008). "'怎樣去界定香港文學：香港文學史書寫的一個最基本問題' (How to Define Hong Kong Literature: A Primary Question for the Writing of Hong Kong Literary History)." *JMLC* 8 (2)–9 (1): 21–39.

Wong, W. L. 黃維樑. (2000). "'香港文學的研究和推廣' (The Research and Dissemination of Hong Kong Literature)". In 活潑紛繁的香港文學：一九九九年香港文學國際研討會論文集 *(Hong Kong Literature Dynamic and Diversified: Proceedings of the 1999 International Conference on Hong Kong Literature)*, vol. 2, Wong, W. L. ed., 934–936. Hong Kong: The Chinese University of Hong Kong.

Yang, Y. S. 楊昱昇. (2000). "'混雜的狂城，變幻的亂馬 – 試論《紅玫瑰與雜種馬》英譯困難與策略' (On the Translation of 'Red Horse and Bastard Horse')." *Translation Quarterly* 18–19: 151–176.

Yeh, M. (1992). *Anthology of Modern Chinese Poetry*. New Haven, CT: Yale University Press.

9 Cultural Untranslatability of Heteroglossia

Hong Kong Poetry in Colonial Time

Chris Song

Introduction

Heteroglossia, the simultaneous coexistence of a variety of languages in a single language, is a widespread phenomenon in world literature, especially in the literature of the culture that enjoys or suffers from a multilingual environment for social, historical, or cultural reasons. However, the translation of heteroglossic literature has largely remained an under-researched topic. This chapter explores the (un-)translatability of heteroglossic literature with the examples of heteroglossic poems written by ethnically Chinese poets in colonial Hong Kong. Primarily written in the colonized's language (a Sinitic language, be it Chinese, Cantonese, or their combination), the verses of these poems are embedded with phrases in the colonizer's language (English). This chapter takes a historical approach to examine the poetic influences Hong Kong's heteroglossic poetry received in different times and discusses a variety of forms of the untranslatability of heteroglossia knotted into the colonial context in Hong Kong.

Previous studies on the intersection of heteroglossia, translation, and (post-)colonialism are scarce. Paul Bandia's (2012) article "Postcolonial Literary Heteroglossia: A Challenge for Homogenizing Translation" provides an informative fount and comparative angle for this chapter, as historicizing Hong Kong heteroglossic poetry inevitably engages the chapter with the city's colonial and cultural contexts. In his study on postcolonial literary heteroglossia, Bandia (2012) emphasizes the heterogeneity of language practice in the postcolony and how such heteroglossic practice challenges homogenic translation (p. 419–431), which "has an objective the effacement of differences in an act of linguistic homogenization . . . transforming one language into another . . . enabling monolingual readers to grasp the text in their own language while remaining monolingual" (p. 423). In contrast,

> Heterogenizing translation considers the plurilingual source text as already "in translation," as it represents the linguistic rift that translation is called upon to overcome. Translation is present in the source text by virtue of the fact that reading a heterogenous text is akin to translating.
>
> (p. 424)

DOI: 10.4324/9781003368168-10

Along these lines, his definition of heterogenizing translation naturally begets the question as to whether it is then necessary to translate such heteroglossic source text since it is "already in translation." Bandia does not deal with this question directly but specifies two modes of "reading or translating a heterogenous text": "centrifugal in its quest for full representation or in its refusal to reduce the text for expression in a homogenizing language"; "centripetal when it seeks to retrieve or synthesize the heterogeneous identity or hybridity expressed in the linguistic rift or schism found in the source text" (p. 424). He admits that heteroglossic text is "somewhat untranslatable" (p. 424). However, reading and translating are still two sets of very different linguistic activities. In reading heteroglossic text, readers may translate one language into another in their minds, but it is still a far cry from a translator rendering it through monolingual or plurilingual translation on paper or the digital screen.

Bandia asks a series of questions regarding the translating, translator, and target readership of the translation of heteroglossic text, but understandably he does not provide any definite answers. He points out, "Heterogenization raises the question of the translatability of cultures of hybridity and heterogeneity. For effective communication, a parallel must be drawn between the author, the translator, and the reader, who are linked by the heterogeneity of their experience" (p. 425). While this scenario may sound too ideal to realize, it also harbors doubts as to whether the same heterogeneous culture might become both the original and the receiving culture of the translation of its own literature and whether, paradoxically, such setup risks cultivating a conservative cultural ideology albeit unintended.

Although doubts may be raised about some of its assumptions, Bandia's article is an insightful point of departure for discussion of the translation of heteroglossic literature in (post-)colonial context. This chapter continues Bandia's exploration with examples of the heteroglossic poetry in the colonial period of Hong Kong and proposes a general hypothesis that the more deeply heteroglossia is tied to its (post-)colonial context, the less translatable it becomes. In his seminal *A Linguistic Theory of Translation*, J. C. Catford (1965) proposes a differentiation between linguistic untranslatability – "failure to find a TL equivalent is due entirely to differences between the source language and the target language" – and cultural untranslatability – "a situational feature, functionally relevant for the SL text, is completely absent from the culture of which the TL is a part" (p. 98–99). While the chapter does not draw heavily on Catford's theory, its argument nonetheless is made in light of his helpful differentiation. In the following, the chapter will provide a chronological review of the heteroglossic poetry of Hong Kong from the 1930s to the 1960s and argues it is often the cultural untranslatability, rather than the linguistic untranslatability, that makes heteroglossic literature appear untranslatable.

Hong Kong first saw its heteroglossic poems in the mid-1930s. Geopolitically, it was a time when the relatively peaceful city's British colonial authority was on the lookout for Japan's imperial and military aggressions up north. Cultural-politically, the colonial government was collaborating with various forces of traditional Chinese culture to resist the influence of the Mainland's New Culture Movement that sought to abolish traditional practices (Law, 2009, pp. 106–111). However, New Culture Movement passed down south, albeit slowly, through many forms of print matters, among which the most influential Chinese literary magazine at the time, titled *Xiandai* 現代 (Fr. *Les Contemporaines*), became one of the most important reading materials for many Chinese poets in Hong Kong and the works published there their sources of inspiration and objects of imitation. At the time, *Les Contemporaines*' editor-in-chief Shi Zhecun's 施蟄存 borrowed some features of Imagism to formulate his *à la mode* image-lyric poetry 意象抒情詩. Though without much depth or explanation, Shi Zhecun's image-lyric poetry rode on the expansive impact of *Les Contemporaines*, and this most popular style of new poetry on the Mainland reached Hong Kong eventually.

One of the most important features of image-lyric poetry was, as summarized by Shi himself, "mix in foreign or archaic words" 混入古字或外語 (Shi, 1981, p. 217). Instead of tracing this influence back to the 1920s Chinese symbolist Li Jinfa 李金髮 (Cheng, 2012, pp. 58–91), I argue the symptom of heteroglossia in Hong Kong poetry of the mid-1930s can also be attributed to Shi Zhecun's image-lyric poetry as they share certain observable similarities. The way in which Wu Tianlai 吳天籟 embeds foreign words into his rather sensual poems "雨" (Rain) and "SENSUALISM" is similar to how Shi Zhecun does his trick in his image-lyric poem about an experience in a café called "沙利文" (Sullivan).

雨

瀟瀟的雨是恨人的
淒冷的長街悄無人行
燈台的燭搖搖垂淚
顛簸的征魂是甚麼顏色呢
無邊的落葉
馱着灰闇的人世
擊筑落月的豪俠
今夜已是白髮三千丈
Trochaic 的調子
心上簷溜的滴答呵
輕輕地把簾子捲上
窗外的雨是恨人的
   (Wu, 1935/2014b, pp. 88–89,
    in Chan, 2014)

SENSUALISM

色士風飄起
Allegro 女人誘惑的股顫啊
霓虹 瘋魔的眼 強烈地
染透了少年紳士的心
少年久感髀肉復生了
掌上遂胴體的舞
九月蠢斯的雄舉
說不定殉情於雌的腋撫下
則勝利者遂闊步而舞
Neo-Sensualism 的胴體的舞哪
   (Wu, 1935/2014a, p. 89,
    in Chan, 2014)

*****

沙利文

我說, 沙利文是很熱的,
連它底刨冰的雪花上的
那個少女的大黑眼,
在我不知道的時候以前,
都使我的 Fancy Suudaes 融化了。
我說, 沙利文是很熱的。
  (Shi, 1932, p. 230)

While the European-language words are overwhelmed by Chinese verses in numbers, they stand out to beseech extra efforts in reading them. At the time, the cosmopolitan environments of Shanghai and Britain's colonial export to Hong Kong groomed omnipresent simulacra of European culture that projected an outlook of modernity that was both concrete and symbolic. Both poets withdraw available foreign words from their urban life with European cultural import and insert them into their largely Chinese poems. Wu Tianlai uses "Trochaic" and "Allegro" to describe the speaker's acoustic experience. Similarly, the melting of "Fancy Suudaes" (sic) in Shi Zhecun's poem signifies the rising physical temperature sensation as well as the heating-up feelings. Such imported paraphernalia as "Trochaic," "Allegro," and "Fancy Suudaes" (sic) adorn the speakers' sensuality differently. While Wu Tianlai's speakers are hollowed out by urban decadence's rhythm in Hong Kong, Shi Zhecun's speaker is disappointed by the superficial change of emotion in the recently modernized Shanghai.

As the embedded foreign words in the poems cited in the previous section are only slightly contextualized, translating the heteroglossic lines into English does not seem to yield a great degree of untranslatability at the surface level. From "Trochaic 的調子" to "trochaic pattern," from "Allegro 女人誘惑的股顫啊" to "women's sexy butts tremble allegro," or "都使我的 Fancy Suudaes 融化了" (sic) to "melt my Fancy Sundaes," maintaining the foreign words while translating Chinese into English causes neither obvious loss of meaning nor a great deal of oddities. However, the loss of heteroglossia, along with the cosmopolitanism in the 1930s Shanghai and Hong Kong it suggests, is inevitable in such translations. If they were to be translated into a reverse heteroglossic version, such as from "Trochaic 的調子" to "揚抑格 pattern," from "Allegro 女人誘惑的股顫啊" to "women's sexy butts tremble 快板," or from "都使我的 Fancy Suudaes 融化了" (sic) to "melt my 聖代雪糕," the readership of translation would have been limited to the Chinese-English bilinguals. Even though the strategy of reverse heteroglossia seems possible, the translations read as poems in their own rights would have rendered eccentric. After all, for the poems cited previously, the untranslatability lies outside of the text itself. While homogenic translation is still possible through the simple strategy of code-switching or transliteration, such translation erases the markers of the original culture's plurilingual characteristics. In other words, the untranslatability is cultural rather than linguistic.

The untranslatability also presents itself sometimes as the lack of the Chinese equivalent. For example, 聖代 or 新地 as Chinese transliterations of "sundae" are clear markers of the contemporary and might not refer to the ice cream desert in 1930s Shanghai. In other words, 聖代 and 新地 have not been established as conventional. Using "Fancy Suudaes" (sic) in his poem might have been the poet's most straightforward choice because its communicable Chinese equivalents had not become available yet. Such lack can only provide a partial explanation. More often than not, the poets might have deliberated on inserting words in European languages into his predominantly Chinese poems. For example, in 1933, Outer Out 鷗外鷗, a poet known for his peculiar heteroglossic writings and concrete poetry, published a poem titled "愛情乘了 Bus" (1933), which has been widely collected in Chinese modernist anthologies. By 1933, 公共汽車 had already been established as a standard translation of "bus." The same could be said of some of the English words thrust into the following two poems: Zhang Gong's 張弓 "都會特寫" (An urban sketch) and Xi Yun's 西湄 "香港是夜的世界" (Hong Kong belongs to the world of the night).

都會特寫

虹似的：PRINCE; DUKE; KNIGHT;
虹似的。（長胖的 BUSES 底肉底之徵逐喲）
1934, 流線樣的車, 撒下
"HONEY MOON NIGHT"
"ALL BUSES STOP HERE"
冰島上的 PENQUIN 群。
STEAM 底熱, 炙乾了瀝青上腳走之汗汁囉,
SEARCH LIGHT, SEARCH LIGHT
　射穿雲底濃層。
匿在黑角落上的女人, 漢子：
「當心, 今晚月亮太亮了喲」
(Zhang, 1934/2014, p. 100, in Chan 2014)

香港是夜的世界

夜的街是不寂寞的,
Neon 燈照耀著行人的臉,
Alhambra
Rido
堂皇的百貨世界,
從那兒,
縱情跳他妖冶的狐步,
從那兒,
換取舶來的貨品。
(Xi Yun, 1939, p. 608)

In addition to "bus," the English words "PRINCE; DUKE; KNIGHT," "STEAM," "PENGUIN," and "SEARCH LIGHT" in Zhang's, as well as "Neon" in Xi Yun's, had already secured their accepted Chinese translations by the time they wrote the poems. However, their heteroglossia bears conspicuous untranslatability. In Zhang's, "HONEY MOON NIGHT" could be the name of a melody; "ALL BUSES STOP HERE" are obviously words on a traffic sign. In Xi Yun's, "Alhambra" is the name of a theater, "Rido" of a dance club (see Cheng, 2012, pp. 85–91). These European-language words directly represent the speakers' acoustic and visual perceptions of their immediate surroundings. Zhang's speaker hears "HONEY MOON NIGHT" melody and sees the "ALL BUSES STOP HERE" sign. The neon signs of "Alhambra" and "Rido" are precisely what show up in Xi Yun's speaker's sight. If these two poems were to be translated into English, keeping the European-language words as they are in the original might have been the most sensible strategy. The local audio and visual culture that the English phrases carry appears untranslatable, although linguistically speaking, they could be translated. Reverse heteroglossia would have been superfluous as it would mean straightforward translations for "HONEY MOON NIGHT" 蜜月之夜 and "ALL BUSES STOP HERE" 巴士停泊區 and transliterations for "Alhambra" 阿爾罕布拉 (or its Chinese name 平安戲院) and "Rido" 利多, which would misrepresent what the speakers perceive. In such cases, the untranslatability renders itself an unnecessity of translation.

Some scholars have simplistically attributed the heteroglossia in Zhang's poem to Hong Kong's age-old stereotype of a colony where Chinese tradition and Western culture coexist (e.g., Zhao, 2003, pp. 148–150). Perhaps they would have made such oversimplified assumptions about any work of Hong Kong literature that shows even the slightest Chinese-Western cultural hybridity. While this may be partially true, the change of context also presented an opportunity for some poets to deepen their writing of heteroglossic poetry. The second Sino-Japanese War that broke out in 1937 outlined a pervading context to the writing of modern Chinese poetry, not least heteroglossic poetry in Hong Kong and Mainland China. By 1937, Outer Out's poetry obviously became less lyrical than "愛情乘了 Bus" and started to engage with the war. His exemplary "第二回世界訃聞" (The second obituary of the world) written in Hong Kong right after the war's outbreak starts and ends with the same six lines of "WAR!" with increasingly larger types, acoustically resembling newspaper boys' urgent yells getting closer and closer to the speaker:

WAR!
WAR!
WAR!
WAR!
WAR!
WAR! WAR!

This first stanza is followed by an alarming outcry of inflation and opportunistic investments that seek to profit from the war:

銅鐵市場閉市, 進口斷絕！
金屬器具昂起！
出口商深入我國腹地
收買犁鋤鑊廢銅廢鐵！
禁運輸出口令頒佈！
    (Outer Out, 1937/1985,
        pp. 23–28)

The heteroglossic pattern recurs throughout the poem. Andrea Bachner (2014) points out that, in this poem, Outer Out's "juxtaposition of different scripts as a reaction to an impending intercultural conflict in the concrete medium of the newspaper" (p. 85). When the poem was first published in 1937, the poet could only use Chinese "戰爭呵！" to replace "WAR!" possibly due to the poetry magazine's typographical restriction but also with the intention to cater the poem to the general Chinese readership:

戰爭呵！
戰爭呵！
戰爭呵！
戰爭呵！
戰爭呵！
戰爭呵！戰爭呵！
  (Outer Out, 1937,
      p. 2–7)

He notes,

> The "戰爭呵!" in this poem can be more suitably read aloud in such intonation as newspaper boys' selling extras "喎呵!" or can be read as its rather coincidental synophone "WAR!." As the publication is tailored for general readers' [language] capacity, [this poem] is printed with "戰爭呵!" 此詩之「戰爭呵！」爲更適宜於叫賣號外的「喎呵！」那樣口調亦可改讀作「WAR！」這一諧音亦甚巧合吧。但在此次揭載時爲了普及讀衆的閱讀力故，仍以「戰爭呵！」付印了
>
> (Outer Out, 1937, p. 2).

Outer Out's "第二回世界訃聞" was intended to be written with the alternation of English and Chinese stanzas, as he restored the heteroglossic and typographical features to his poem in his book, *Poems of Outer Out* 鷗外鷗之詩, published in 1985. In addition to the interlingual synophonous relationship between "喎呵!" and "WAR!," the former also sounds like an interjection in Cantonese that expresses an exclamation of surprise, regret, and/or horror. In commenting on this poem, Leung (2005) draws on the concept of "defamiliarization" from Russian formalism to explain Outer Out's special typographical arrangements for "WAR!," which is "embedded among Chinese texts to exaggerate its effect as an onomatopoeic sign," and by using this defamiliarized sign, the poet "hopes to surprise the people who are numbed" by normal Chinese news headlines (p. 171–172). Thus, in terms of its war context and linguistic complexity, this poem is significantly enriched by heteroglossia.

If "WAR!" were to be translated into "戰爭呵!" just like its first, monolingual version, the poetic richness that depends on the bilingual echoes within the poem would have been lost. Worse if it were to be translated entirely into a monolingual English poem by keeping "WAR!" while translating all other Chinese verses into English. However, the reverse heteroglossia, meaning translating either language into the other, seems to be working relatively well in terms of keeping the context and the bilinguality. The English readership would probably figure out what the translated heteroglossic poem is about (the war), although they would have to work out what the defamiliarized "戰爭呵!" means, which could be an easy fix by providing a note, as the poet himself also relied on notes, even his comics, for his readers to read the poem as he had designed it. In this case, heteroglossia is not entirely untranslatable but could be translated in a specific way in which the context is kept, but the interlingual phonetic and semantic paronomasia is lost inevitably. Simply put, for the translation of this poem, it is not the text itself that is untranslatable but the heteroglossic complexity tied to its context. From "愛情乘了 Bus" to "第二回世界訃聞," Outer Out had come out of the influence of Shi Zhecun's image-lyric poetry as the war context observably lent a certain level of depth to the heteroglossia in his work. Outer Out's "第二回世界訃聞" marks the maturity of heteroglossic poetics of modern Chines poetry in the sense that it surpasses the superficial embedment of foreign-language words that only (mis-)leads readers to a simplistic, impressionistic manifestation of multicultural cosmopolitanism.

Furthermore, Outer Out applies his heteroglossic poetics to a poem titled "和平的礎石" (The cornerstone of peace) about former Governor of Hong Kong Francis Henry May's bronze statue that symbolizes the colonial government's rather sluggish, unmoving coastal defense against Japanese aggression. The "cornerstone" in the title is meant to be ironic.

和平的礎石

東方國境的最前線的交界碑！
太平山的巔上樹立了最初歐羅巴的旗。

SIR. FRANCE HENRY MAY

從此以手支住了腮了。
香港總督的一人。
思慮着什麼呢？
憂愁着什麼的樣子。
向住了遠方
不允說出他的名字，

金屬了的總督。
是否懷疑巍巍高聳在亞洲風雲下的
休戰紀念坊呢。
奠和平的礎石於此地嗎？
那樣想着而不瞑目的總督，
日夕踞坐在花崗石上永久地支着腮
腮與指之間
生上了銅綠的苔蘚了──。

在他的面前的港內，
下碇着大不列顛的鷹號母艦和潛艇母艦美德威號
生了根的樹一樣的。
肺病的海空上
夜夜交錯着探照燈的X光
縱橫着假想敵的飛行機
銀的翅膀
白金的翅膀。

手永遠支住了腮的總督，
何時可把手放下來呢？
那隻金屬了的手。

(Outer Out, 1939, p. 29)

In the original version of the poem published in 1939, the name of Francis Henry May is misspelled as "SIR FRANCE HENRY MAY." One could say the poet made a simple mistake. However, setting aside the poet's intention could yield meaningful postcolonial readings of this heterography. In her seminal "Can the Subaltern Speak?" Gayatri Chakravorty Spivak (1994) critiques the ways in which colonial authors "pathetically" misspelled names of colonized subjects, "transposing proper names into common nouns, translating them, and using them as sociological evidence" (p. 101–102). In reverse, in Outer Out's "和平的礎石," the colonized subject's misspelling of a colonial administrator's name in the colonizer's language clearly evinces a calmed subversive feeling against the colonizer's linguistic authority. Although it does not amount to an overt satire, the misspelling could be interpreted as an echo of the poem's generally placid anti-colonial sentiment. Thus, the colonized's literary heteroglossia bears a possibility of subversive heterography in an anti- or even postcolonial context. Had the poet simply used a Chinese translation, "梅含理爵士," the poem would not have carried the tension between the colonizer's and the colonized's language.

To translate this poem into English, one would have to consider three options regarding how to handle the difficulty this misspelled name presents: (1) to keep it, (2) to correct it, (3) to translate it into Chinese. Keeping it with a note would be a sensible solution as the poem's anti-colonial language politics could be preserved. Correcting it implicates abiding by the colony's language hierarchy, which would disrupt and reverse its language politics. Translating it into Chinese would mean embedding "梅含理爵士" to the English translation of the Chinese poem. Not only does such reverse-heteroglossic monster misrepresent the speaker's visual perception (no Chinese ideograph is engraved on this bronze statue), but it also makes the Chinese characters appear alien to the majority of English readership and thereby weakens the interaction between the two languages. Thus, in such a complex (anti-)colonial context, the heterography resists to be translated, and heteroglossia again renders untranslatable, not for a linguistic reason but for a cultural reason.

Two years after Outer Out wrote "和平的礎石," Hong Kong fell into Japanese occupation during the war. The bronze statue of Sir Francis Henry May mentioned by the poem was shipped to Japan and melted down along with many other statues on Statue Square. After three years and eight months under the rule of Japan, Hong Kong returned to its status as a Crown colony of the UK in 1945 and enjoyed an economic boom during the Cold War, though not without ideological battles and large-scale social movements. Again, its poetry was deeply connected to its cold-war colonial context and in the meantime coincided with an introduction of Western modernism in the 1950s and 1960s. In terms of heteroglossic poetry of this period, Quanan's 崑南 (1935? –) works are exemplary. While he received education in an English-language school and thereby became interested in Western culture in general. Like the works of many Hong Kong modernists, Quanan's poetry was also heavily influenced by T. S. Eliot (1888–1965), one of the most important figures in English modernist poetry in the twentieth century. Quanan even had Eliot's famous line "I have measured out my life with coffee spoons" as an ornamental quote to introduce his heteroglossic poem "布爾喬亞之歌" (Song of a bourgeois), a representative work of the mid-century literary modernism in Hong Kong.

Similar to Eliot's poetry that depicts the general spiritual hollowness and internal wasteland of barren modern life in the West, Quanan's "布爾喬亞之歌" presents a bourgeois' mental reality filled with sensual decadence, degenerating despair, and complete loss of aspiration in the capitalist commercialized society of Hong Kong. The difference lies in the former's intellectualism with erudite allusions and the latter's forthright representation of the poet's wearisome urban experience (Cheng, 2012, p. 96). The English phrases and lines embedded in Quanan's poem suggest how bourgeois life is subdued by various mundane minutiae of modern capitalist society. The poet also projects his sense of being defeated by commercialized society and disappointed by social relationships to the speaker of the poem, who has lost his literary aspiration and therefore seeks comfort from bodily sensations that numb and suppress his cultural consciousness. The poem opens with an office typist's day-to-day boredom in life:

> 桌上那灰色打字機是一副呆鈍的模樣
> 拼出生活不變的母音：A, E, I, O, U
> 我穿上汗味的夏威夷匆匆下樓，一邊唱
> "If I give my heart to you . . ."
> (Quanan, 1956/2020, p. 262,
> in Chan, 2020)

The five basic vowels of the English language have defined the Chinese typist's life within the typewriter's monotonous repetitions. Next are two lines that tell us the office clerk seeks excitement after work. The speaker hums the lyric of an English pop song, supposedly with a euphoric melody, contrasting the mechanical clattering of typing. Entering the night, he is immersed in the world of sensations triggered by audio and visual technologies that are recently combined for the cinema:

> 一個光管之夜
> 華爾滋的夜
> 茄士啡的夜
> 我走進夜
> CINEMASCOPE 55
> EASTMANCOLOR
> STEREOPHONIC SOUND
> (Quanan, 1956/2020,
> p. 262, in Chan, 2020)

His desire is routinely patterned by the rhythms of dances at an accelerating excitement that eventually prompts him to seek satisfaction from prostitutes:

> 黑暗中，世界靜止，每個人窒息，醉倒⋯⋯
> RUMBA SLOW
> MODERATO MAMBO

TEMPO DI CHA CHA
習慣了的音階和步法
可是慾望製造機會碰觸舞女的胸脯
                (Quanan, 1956/2020, p. 262,
                                in Chan, 2020)

After a few stanzas of fierce sensations, the speaker's inner world sinks into the stream of consciousness where he finds himself a yellow-skinned Nobel laureate that shocks the white-skinned races in the future:

我是一九七六年諾貝爾文學獎金獲選人
美麗的富商千金愛上我說要和我結婚
「是中國的天才震撼白色的種族！」
「是肉體和靈魂結合在象牙的白屋！」
Lord I am not worthy
Lord I am not worthy
But speak the words only
                (Quanan, 1956/2020, p. 265,
                                in Chan, 2020)

The self-deprecation in these lines cannot be more obvious as the inner dream are the exact opposite of outer reality. The speaker then cites Matthew 8:8 to confess painfully that "I am not worthy." These three lines taken from the King James Bible are not any prayer but suggest the speaker's painful feeling that no religion can provide spiritual comfort to alleviate the ordeal he feels.

To translate this heteroglossic poem, all English lines, phrases, and words the poet has inserted in the original poem would have to be left untranslated. In other words, reverse-heteroglossia would not be an option. "A, E, I, O, U" are simply untranslatable. The rest, if translated, would not have been recognizable to the majority of the English readership. In addition, the poem is so tied up to its colonial context through such cultural items mentioned in English that even transliteration would seem a risky option. Drawing on Theodore Adorno and Max Horkheimer's theory on cultural industry, Wai-lim Yip acutely points out that the popular culture in colonial Hong Kong contributes to the reification and commodification effects on the colonized subject who can but resort to sensual excitements as a way of denial and resistance (see Yip, 2016, pp. 485–519). Yip deepens his argument with the example of Quanan's "布爾喬亞之歌" and identifies what the words and phrases (including those in English) signify as elements of "instrumentalized life under colonial culture" 殖民文化下的工具化生活 (Yip, 2016, p. 506) and therefore, following this logic, constitute the cultural industry of colonial Hong Kong. In translating the poem into English, even the English lines are left as they are in the original poem, it is indeed doubtful whether a homogenic translation would be able to preserve the colonial context in Hong Kong from which the original poem derives its critique.

Cultural Untranslatability of Heteroglossia 163

The racial tension and suppressed cultural consciousness eventually prompted Quanan to explore the complex issue of cultural identity through the bewildering hybridization of languages in the ideologically polarized colony during the Cold War, such as in his most famous heteroglossic poem "旗向" (The direction of the flag):

旗向
之故

起來（不願做奴隸的人們）
噫 花天兮 花天兮

TO WHOM IT MAY CONCERN
This is to certify that
閣下誠咭片者 股票者
畢生擲毫於忘寢之文字
與氣候寒暄（公曆年月日星期）
「詰旦 Luckie 參與賽事」
電話器之近安與咖啡或茶
成閣下之材料 – 飛黃騰達之材料

敬啓者 閣下夢夢中國否
汝之肌革黃乎 眼瞳黑乎

之故

起來（不願做奴隸的人們）
噫 花天兮 花天兮

"Dear God of Beat, Elvis Sweet
It's me: Connie Teddy Girl"
提廣告彩燈 美哉
亮 Limbo 眉角 夜未央
姑娘樂直直乎山水
Let Me take a ticket date
粲然若輪船公司之招貼
曝于倡側而空破之朝代中

敬啓者 姑娘夢夢中國否
伊之肌革黃乎 眼瞳黑乎
之故

起來（不願做奴隸的人們）

噫 花天兮 花天兮

「蓋文章經國之大業」
「文質彬彬 有君子之致」
公子拋貯獻誦（瓦耶釜耶）
其詩鳴靡靡以結繁
天機高 爬格子更籌蒙露
策縱橫 終吾身而已矣
行之乎色事之空
盡得風流 風流盡得

敬啓者 公子夢夢中國否
君之肌革黃乎 眼瞳黑乎

之故

起來（不願做奴隸的人們）

噫 花天兮 花天兮
之故

(Quanan, 1963/2020,
pp. 102–103, in
Cheng, 2020)

Similar to Quanan's other heteroglossic poems, a few lines in English are interpolated into lines written in various types of Sinitic languages: *wenyan wen* 文言文 (classical Chinese) and *baihua wen* 白話文 (vernacular Chinese), business Chinese and literary Chinese, as well as Cantonese. The solemn first line of PRC's national anthem, "起來（不願做奴隸的人們）," is juxtaposed with a classical Chinese line that indicates the speaker's urge to solicit a prostitute, 花天, which also further suggests alcoholism 酒地, introducing the sharp contrast between the Mainland's socialist revolutionary ideology and the colony's capitalist numbing decadence. The speaker of the poem, a colonized subject, is trapped in between and pulled by the two opposing ideological forces and is lost in a labyrinthine collage of lines and phrases in English and Chinese taken from formal letters, stock market, horse race, sensual pleasure, advertisements, journalism, popular songs, and the *Analects* 論語, which constitute an absurd colonial reality the speaker has to face. Each section ends with a question (in classical Chinese) to the readers about whether they still dream about China, their skins still yellow, and eyes still dark. The poem is clearly intended for ethnically Chinese readers in colonial Hong Kong, and the question is asked to engage them with the complex issue of cultural identity. Citing this poem, Leung (1996) argues, "a Chinese national identity and a Western identity are both being questioned and rendered absurd" (p. 244). Just as Leung (1996) points out, translation "cannot do justice" to such hybrid poetic language and the identity issue it implies (p. 244). In other words, for this poem, the untranslatability of the poetics of heteroglossia lies in its hybridization of languages entwined with the colonized subject's confused identity in the colony. Suppose the poem was to be translated into English, the question about cultural identity in the colony would have to be directed to English readers, who would probably figure out it is not for them to answer. The translation into English would risk reducing the poem's most important theme and language hybridity to insignificance.

Leung's (2012) comment on Quanan's "旗向" becomes the most cogent when he remarked on its heteroglossia, which has gone beyond the coexistence of different languages in one work to emphasize the interactions among these coexisting languages: "Beneath pleasantries and absurdities, these different scripts interrogate and subvert one another in this modernized urban culture" 在諧謔與怪異底下，這些不同的文字從這現代化的都市文化裡面彼此互相質詢與顛覆 (p. 39). Leung's remark echoes Mikhail M. Bakhtin's idea of heteroglossia, which not only refers to the multilanguagedness of a work in any apparently unitary language, but also encapsulates the basic condition of communication that governs "the operation of meaning in any utterance" of the coexisting languages in its unique social, historical, psychological, and physical condition. For Bakhtin (1981), the utterances of the competing languages "functions of a matrix of forces practically impossible to recoup, and therefore impossible to resolve" (p. 428). In light of such Bakhtinian heteroglossia, each utterance of each language in Quanan's "旗向" participates in a complex dialogue from its own perspective constituted by its condition. No translation of individual words or phrases, no matter in what language, can be thought of as independent or self-sufficient. The dialogic relations among all utterances in its resolvable web of meanings may well overwhelm any attempt to treat the translation of each language separately. This heteroglossic poem is untranslatable because, in Bakhtin's (1981) words, its heteroglossia ensures "the primacy of context over text" (p. 428). Furthermore, while he underscores that dialogized heteroglossia does not mean linguistic anarchism, Bakhtin's theory clearly indicates the order of languages is always subject to change (see Holloway & Kneale, 2009). Therefore, heteroglossic literature with an unstable ordering of languages implies disruption of the hierarchy of languages in social reality. In Quanan's "旗向," English (the colonizer's language) does not enjoy any higher status than Chinese (the colonized's language), as both are collaged into the heteroglossic dialogue of the poem that derives meanings from its anti-colonial context on the one hand and feeds a sense of dissension into such context on the other. Thus, heteroglossia begets dissent. The anti-colonial poem seems to resist being translated into English because the translation would have subjected the original and target language to the colony's linguistic hierarchy, which is what the poem seeks to revolt against.

This chapter has reviewed the heteroglossic poetry of Hong Kong poets, including Zhang Gong, Xi Yun, Outer Out, and Quanan. From the 1930s to the 1960s, Hong Kong's heteroglossic poetry had been increasingly tied to its colonial context. The stronger the tie, the more culturally untranslatable the heteroglossia became, regardless of how linguistically translatable it is. The untranslatability of its heteroglossia can assume linguistic or cultural forms, such as the lack of equivalent in another language, unnecessity of translation, anti-colonial contextuality, and dialogism. The untranslatability often appears to be cultural more than linguistic. While this chapter does not provide all the answers to the questions regarding the translating, translator, and readership of heteroglossic poetry, it nonetheless continues the scholarly efforts to understand the relationship between heteroglossia and translation in a (post-)colonial context. This pursuit is believed to be meaningful for postcolonial translation studies.

With examples from contemporary African postcolonial literature, Bandia (2012) illustrates the ways in which literary heteroglossia that registers concrete plurilingual experience in postcolony may transcend the conventional critical paradigm in postcolonial translation studies built on a series of interconnected binary oppositions between "Western oppression and Third World resistance, autonomy and subjugation, and colonizer and the colonized" (p. 420). It can be easily observed in Bandia's article that the paradigm shift is caused by the change of the object of postcolonial critique in contemporary postcolony. Whereas postcolonial elites incorporate this critical paradigm into a neo-colonial discourse to justify their regimes, literature of the mass steps out of anti-colonial and enters anti-neo-colonial discourse (Bandia, 2012, p. 421).

Each colony or postcolony generates its unique context, in which heteroglossia is brought to engage with translation in a different way and therefore establishes a different relationship between heteroglossia and translation. While this chapter concerns itself with Hong Kong's heteroglossic poetry in the colonial period, its dialogized heteroglossia, as in Quanan's "旗向" in this period, still seems to go beyond the colonizer-colonized paradigm, as the critique is meant for both the colonial power and the original cultural traditions. This chapter also paves the way for the studies of Hong Kong's heteroglossic poetry in its postcolonial, even neo-colonial, context, similar to the neo-colonial situation of postcolonies in Africa that Bandia describes. Since the sovereignty of Hong Kong was handed over to the People's Republic of China (PRC) in 1997, the postcolonial elites appointed by the PRC central government have become the ruling circle of the postcolony through the implementation of "Hong Kong People Administering Hong Kong" 港人治港 and more recently "Patriots Administering Hong Kong" 愛國者治港 policy.

The masses struggle for social, economic, and linguistic justice and a certain level of autonomy through various peaceful or violent means. Contemporary Hong Kong's heteroglossic poetry, such as those written by Yam Gong 飲江, is often composed of modern Chinese, literary Chinese, English, and most of all, the language of the masses, Cantonese, not so different from Quanan's "旗向" back in the 1960s. His volume *Moving a Stone* (2022) in English translation by James Shea and Dorothy Tse must contribute to the discussion of the translation of heteroglossic poetry. Florence Ng's 吳智欣 poetry volume *Wild Boar in Victoria Harbor* 維多利亞港的野豬 (2019) collects her poems in the composite of English, Chinese, Cantonese, and Cantonglish. Her heteroglossic poetry affirms the status of Cantonese as the masses' mother tongue, which is faced with perceived belittling, oppression, and marginalization. In the neo-colonial context, contemporary Hong Kong's heteroglossic poetry may represent a heterogeneous force that maintains language equality in the text where these languages may coexist dialogically, although the dialogues are not always amiable. The picture is further complicated by poets who are from or grew up in Hong Kong, such as Sarah Howe, Mary Jean Chan, Jennifer Wong, etc., whose works, primarily written in English, contain Cantonese or Chinese phrases that are meant to problematize the tension among languages associated with the issue of identity. Such complex context must establish new relationships between heteroglossia and translation, which may be the endeavor of future research.

References

Bachner, A. (2014). *Beyond Sinology: Chinese Writing and the Script of Culture*. New York: Columbia University Press.
Bakhtin, M. M. (1981). *The Dialogic Imagination: Four Essays* (Caryl Emerson & Michael Holquist, Trans.). Austin, TX: University of Texas Press.
Bandia, P. (2012). Postcolonial Literary Heteroglossia: A Challenge for Homogenizing Translation. *Perspectives: Studies in Translatology* 20 (4), 419–431.
Catford, J. C. (1965). *A Linguistic Theory of Translation*. London: Oxford University Press.
Chan, C. T. 陳智德. (Ed.). (2014). *Xianggang wenxue daxi Yijiuyijiu – Yijiusijiu · Xinshi juan* 香港文學大系一九一九－一九四九·新詩卷. Hong Kong: The Commercial Press. Abbreviation: *NPV 1919–1949*.
Chan, C. T. 陳智德. (Ed.). (2020). *Xianggang wenxue daxi Yijiuwuling – Yijiuliujiu · Xinshi juan yi* 香港文學大系一九五〇－一九六九·新詩卷一. Hong Kong: The Commercial Press. Abbreviation: *NPV 1950–1969 1*.
Cheng, C. H. 鄭政恆. (2012). Xianggang shige yu ban Tang Fan yuyan 香港詩歌與半唐番語言. *Xiandai Zhongwen xuekan* 現代中文學刊 (2), 85–91.
Cheng, C. H. 鄭政恆. (Ed.). (2020). *Xianggang wenxue daxi Yijiuwuling – Yijiuliujiu · Xinshi juan er* 香港文學大系一九五〇－－一九六九·新詩卷二. Hong Kong: The Commercial Press. Abbreviation: *NPV 1950–1969 2*.
Holloway, J., and J. Kneale. 2009. Dialogism (After Bakhtin). In R. Kitchin & N. Thrift (eds.), *International Encyclopedia of Human Geography*, 143–149. Amsterdam: Elsevier.
Law, W. S. (2009). *Collaborative Colonial Power: The Making of the Hong Kong Chinese*. Hong Kong: Hong Kong University Press.
Leung, P. K. 梁秉鈞. (1996). Modern Hong Kong Poetry: Negotiation of Cultures and the Search for Identity. *Modern Chinese Literature* 9 (2), 221–245.
Leung, P. K. 梁秉鈞. (2005). Zhongguo san, siling niandai kangzhanshi yu xiandaixing 中國三、四〇年代抗戰詩與現代性. *Journal of Modern Chinese Literature* 6 (2)–7 (1), 159–175.
Leung, P. K. 梁秉鈞. (2012). Dushi wenhua · Xianggang wenxue · wenhua pinglun 都市文化·香港文學·文化評論. In *Xianggang wenhua shi lun* 香港文化十論, 32–64. Hangzhou: Zhejiang daxue chubanshe.
Ng, F. 吳智欣. (2019). *Wild Boar in Victoria Harbor* 維多利亞港的野豬. Hong Kong: Kubrick.
Outer Out 鷗外鷗. (1933). Aiqing cheng le Bus 愛情乘了Bus. *Xin shidai* 新時代 5 (5), 7.
Outer Out 鷗外鷗. (1937). Di'er hui fuwen 第二回訃聞. *Shi chang* 詩場 (2), 2–7.

Outer Out 鷗外鷗. (1939). Heping de chushi 和平的礎石. *Tati* 大地 3 (2), 29.
Outer Out 鷗外鷗. (1985). Di'er hui shijie fuwen 第二回世界訃聞. In *Ouwai ou zhi shi* 鷗外鷗之詩, 23–28. Guangzhou: Huacheng chubanshe. (Original work published 1937)
Quanan 崑南. (2020a). Bu'erqiaoya zhi ge 布爾喬亞之歌. In *NPV 1950–1969 1*, 262–266. (Original work published 1956). Hong Kong: The Commercial Press.
Quanan 崑南. (2020b). Qi xiang 旗向. In *NPV 1950–1969 2*, 102–103. (Original work published 1963). Hong Kong: The Commercial Press.
Shi, Z. 施蟄存. (1932). Shaliwen 沙利文. *Xiandai* 現代 1 (2), 230.
Shi, Z. 施蟄存. (1981). *Xiandai* zayi (yi)《現代》雜憶（一）. *Xinwenxue shiliao* 新文學史料 4 (1), 213–220.
Spivak, G. C. (1994). Can the Subaltern Speak? In P. Williams & L. Chrisman (eds.), *Colonial Discourse and Post-Colonial Theory*, 66–111. New York: Columbia University Press.
Wu, T. 吳天籟. (2014a). SENSUALISM. In *NPV 1919–1949*, 89. (Original work published 1935). Hong Kong: The Commercial Press.
Wu, T. 吳天籟. (2014b). Yu 雨. In *NPV 1919–1949*, 89. (Original work published 1935). Hong Kong: The Commercial Press.
Xi Yun 西溟. (1939). Xianggang shi ye de shijie 香港是夜的世界. *Wenyi zhendi* 2 (7), 608.
Yam Gong 飲江. (2022). *Moving a Stone*. Translated by J. Shea and D. Tse. Brookline, MA: Zephyr Press.
Yip, W. L. 葉維廉. (2016). Zijue zhi lü: You luoling dao si – Chulun Kunnan 自覺之旅：由裸靈到死 – 初論崑南. In *Jingshi ban de huoyan: Liang'an sandi xiandai shilun 晶石般的火焰：兩岸三地現代詩論*, 2 vols., 485–519. Taipei: National Taiwan University Press.
Zhang, G. 張弓. (2014). Duhui texie 都會特寫. In *NPV 1919–1949*, 100. (Original work published 1934). Hong Kong: The Commercial Press.
Zhao, X. 趙稀方. (2003). *Xiaoshuo Xianggang* 小說香港. Hong Kong: Joint Publishing.

Biographical Note

Chris Song is an assistant professor at the Department of Language Studies (UTSC) with a cross-appointment at the Department of East Asian Studies (UTSG) of the University of Toronto. His research falls at the intersection of translation studies, modern literature in Chinese, and Hong Kong culture. He is appointed by the International Federation of Translators as the managing editor of *Babel: International Journal of Translation* (John Benjamins). His co-edited volume, *The Bloomsbury Handbook of Modern Chinese Literature in Translation*, is forthcoming in 2023.

10 Translating Hybrid Texts in Hong Kong

A Case Study of the English Translation of Chan Koon Chung's *Kamdu cha canting*

Dechao Li

1. The Concept of "Hybrid" and "Hybridity" in Literary Criticism and Postcolonial Studies

Borrowed from biology, the concept of "hybrid" originally refers to "the offspring of two animals or plants of different species, or (less strictly) varieties; a half-breed, cross-breed, or mongrel" (*Oxford English Dictionary*). Etymologically speaking, the term carries itself with negative association when its Latin etymon "*hybridia*" was used as "an insult, to refer to someone of mixed racial origin" (Schäffner & Adab, 2001, p. 168). In fact, the term is still used disapprovingly in biology and genetics to refer to the selection of animals, where purebreds are much valued over mix-bred or hybrid ones. In some East Asian (such as Chinese and Korean) cultures, the Chinese term "杂种," or the Korean equivalent "잡종," which are literal translations for "hybrid," is one of the strongest and most offensive words used to humiliate someone in these two cultures.

Luckily, this strong derogatory connotation indicated in the ordinary usage of the nomenclature is absent in some humanities disciplines, especially in literary criticism or postcolonial studies, which have used the term extensively to describe the benefits or extra values brought about by a mixed state of entities and/or a blending or mixing process of literary themes, heterogeneous discourse, cultural traits, and codes.

Mikhail Bakhtin, the twentieth-century Russian philosopher and literary theorist, is among the first scholars to use the concept of hybridization to explore the nature, structure, and features of novelistic prose. Hybridization, which he believes to be one of the three basic categories of language in the novel (the other two being "the dialogized interrelation of languages" and "pure dialogues"), refers to the use of "two social language within the limits of a single utterance" (Bakhtin, 1981, p. 358). The mixing of "two different linguistic consciousnesses, separated from one another by an epoch" (Bakhtin, 1981, p. 358) is no better shown in Cathy's father's teasing remarks in the following dialogue taken from the novel *Wuthering Heights* by Emily Brontë:

> I remember the master, before he fell into a doze, stroking her bonny hair – it pleased him rarely to see her gentle – and saying, "Why canst thou not always

be a good lass, Cathy?" And she turned her face up to his, and laughed, and answered, "Why cannot you always be a good man, father?"

(Brontë, 1976, p. 37)

In this description of a warm and humorous exchange, the father, Mr. Earnshaw, pokes fun at his daughter by deliberately using some archaic English forms such as "canst" and "thou" in his question for her, "Why canst thou not always be a good lass, Cathy?" By using two socially and chronologically distant terms that are different from the rest of this question, Mr. Earnshaw is presenting two "linguistic consciousnesses" – to use Bakhtin's parlance – as well as two different systems of language. According to Bakhtin, this intentional hybrid, in which "a mixture of two individualized language consciousnesses" (Bakhtin, 1981, p. 359) inspires and illuminates each other, is one of the effective devices to create the artistic image of a literary language. In this example, the artistic tension that has been caused by the combination of the two distinct social languages in this question is obviously sensed by Cathy, who reacts by laughing and turning her face up to his father with a funny and provocative rejoinder, "Why cannot you always be a good man, father?"

Bakhtin further elaborates that mixing two linguistic forms can also be represented through two language intensions in a novel: one by the character and the other by the author. Both of them lend to the novel two voices or two accents in the hybrid, which results in polyphony, that is, a multiplicity of views and voices, in a literary work. In other words, hybridity is an essential element that enables narratives to be interpreted with "a plurality of independent and unmerged voices and consciousnesses" (Bakhtin, 1984, p. 7).

Whereas Bakhtin approaches hybridity from the perspective of literary and artistic effects, a group of scholars in postcolonial studies, such as Homi Bhabha, Néstor García Canclini, and Gayatri Spivak, largely applies this concept either as a tool to describe the special linguistic and cultural features of literary works produced in former colonies or to elaborate how the special cultural mixedness portrayed in these works impacts the formation and awareness of identity of the people in these ex-colonial states. Starting from the early 1990s, the concept of hybridity, which was often associated with the multicultural awareness in postcolonial discourse, has been frequently seen as a positive resistance to cultural imperialism or any forms or works that might lead to the reinforcement of cultural hegemony.

In his classic work *The Location of Culture* (1994) in which the effects of hybridity on identity and culture are examined, Homi Bhabha scrutinizes the shaping cultural force on the colonial masters and the colonized exerted by the hybridity of colonial identity. On the one hand, this hybridity, which results from "the processes of iteration and translation" (Bhabha, 1994, p. 58), confuses or even dismays the colonial authority; on the other hand, it also forces the colonial subject to have its identity formed in a place defined by the colonizer. However, this cultural hybridity status also "opens up a space of translation" for a political identity "that is new, *neither the one nor the other*" (Bhabha, 1994, p. 25) (emphasis in original). In addition to the cultural and political interpretations of hybridity in postcolonial discourse, Bhabha also investigates how the colonial hybrid could be utilized as a form of subversion to destabilize "the mimetic or narcissistic demands of colonial power" (Bhabha, 1994, p. 126) by presenting the cultures concerned in an ambivalent space. Faced with the hybridity in various objects, the colonial authority could not easily return to its familiar discourse that projects a discriminatory gaze at its subjects but have to rethink what this hybridity brings to its power as it reveals "something other than what its rules of recognition assert" (Bhabha, 1994, p. 112). Since hybridity also obscures the sources of traditional discourses on authority, the colonial power also finds it in an ambivalent state as it loses its dominant control of discursive conditions and interpretations.

If literary critics such as Bakhtin uses the concept of hybridity primarily for the sake of expounding the artistic or aesthetic effects brought about by the polyphony it helps to create in the narratives, postcolonial scholars, including Bhabha, mainly value its cultural subversive function, which defies the political expectations from the colonial power or to the extent of undermines it.

Similar to the disciplines of literary criticism and postcolonial studies, translation studies has also witnessed an increasing use of the terms "hybrid" and "hybridity" in its theoretical discourse or the application of these concepts in translation practice. The following section is a brief survey of how this concept is interpreted from different approaches in translational studies.

2. Hybridity in Translation Studies

2.1 Hybridity as Represented by Special Linguistic Features in the Target Text and Produced Under Certain Conditions

Following a language contact perspective on the use of language by human beings, some translation scholars regard translational language as hybrid in nature, in which a blended usage of different registers or forms is frequently seen in the target text. In a recent study on linguistic hybridity and translation from the perspective of narratology, Klinger (2015) discusses how the translation of the hybrid features in the source text might "trigger TT shifts in perspective, cultural identity and allegiance" (p. 38).

In an early programmatic article on the hybrid text in translation, Schäffner and Adab (2001) argue that the hybrid linguistic features are the natural corollary of any interlingual translation process, which entails intercultural exchanges and the face-off of two linguistic conventions and rules. As a result of the interaction and contact of the two cultures (one being the source and the other target) involved in these bilingual transfer processes, some of the target texts inevitably reveal hybrid linguistic features, which "somehow seem 'out of place'/'strange'/'unusual' for the receiving culture, i.e., the target culture" (Schäffner & Adab, 2001, p. 169). These hybrid features of the translation should be differentiated from translationese or even mistranslation in the target text: the former being the result of the intentional and motivated decisions made by the translator, whereas the latter being the consequence of the lack of translation competence of the translator. Schäffner and Adab's view of regarding a hybrid translation as a translator's deliberate translation decision is in stark contrast to the opinion of Robinson (2016), who equates hybrids in the translation to clumsy expressions that are usually resulted from the translator's overreliance on his or her unwitting and automatic reaction to certain translation tasks.

Schäffner and Adab (2001) also argue that hybrid translations are most likely to appear in the following three contexts (pp. 171–172): (1) when there are no established genres or linguistic models in the target culture for the translator to follow when producing the target text; (2) the translator does not want to produce the translation in accordance with the target text genre conventions, even though the same genre exists both in the source and the target culture; (3) the translator produces either a homogeneous or heterogeneous translation under the influence of globalization.

However, Schäffner and Adab's definition of hybrid translation from a purely linguistic perspective and the description of the different scenarios they tend to occur actually raise more questions than answers. Firstly, they have never made clear what kinds of linguistic features constitute the hybrid features in the translation. Their characterization of hybridity in translation as language features that are "out of place'/'strange'/'unusual'" sounds too subjective to be used in the actual description of translational language, as every reader has his or her own standards or expectations regarding what constitutes the so-called unnatural linguistic features in the target text, ranging from the small units such as vocabulary, syntax, to larger types, including textual organization and genre. Other reader-related factors like educational background, reading norms and habits, as well as horizon of expectation as argued by Jauss, all play a part in determining whether certain features of a translational language strike a reader as "out of place" or not. What makes this hybridity-identifying procedure more complicated is the fact that some of these factors (such as reading norms and habits) are not static: they are constantly changing in accordance with the time. All these factors make any attempt to objectively evaluate the hybridity features in the target text sound like an unreachable goal. Secondly, Schäffner and Adab's definition of hybridity is solely based on linguistic representations in translation, namely, the more out-out-tune these linguistic codes with the conventions of the spontaneously written language in the target culture, the more probable that these codes will be regarded as hybrid language. But as it is often true with many translation readers, it is often the exotic cultures described in the translation, rather than the translational language alone, that decide the degree of hybridity in the target text. Frequently, a translation written in fluent target language will still be considered a hybrid text simply because of the foreign cultural objects, events, or traditions it describes. Put it differently, hybridity is not only a linguistic concept but also a cultural one, as convincingly argued by scholars in postcolonial studies. Thirdly, the demarcation line between a hybrid form of translation and a translationese or mistranslation is not as clear-cut as we tend to believe. The borderline between what constitutes a hybrid translation and an unacceptable translation can be fuzzy or even subjective. For example, the English sentence "I couldn't agree more," which is frequently used to express a speaker's total agreement, can be either translated into version 1: "我不能够同意得更多了" (literally, "I couldn't agree more") and version 2: "我完全同意" (literally, "I completely agree") in Chinese. Comparatively speaking, version 2 is much more idiomatic than version 1, although the first version is more literal in reproducing the original meaning. Unlike English in which a negative sentence can be used to express approval as long as it is modified with comparative forms such as "more" or "less," traditional Chinese lacks such a linguistic device to express the same meaning. Thus version 1 might sound ungrammatical or like a translationese to Chinese language purists. However, the first version, as well as other similar expressions of using negative forms to express agreement, are increasingly gaining ground, especially among younger generations in China who are more receptive to Europeanized Chinese in their daily communications. For these young Chinese readers, version 1 is perfectly acceptable or even more preferred over version 2 because of its hybrid grammatical features, the use of which might distinguish them from other ordinary Chinese speakers. Lastly, the fact that translation activity, which is essentially a social practice, cannot take place in a vacuum indicates there are multiple scenarios in which hybrid texts might occur. In addition to Schäffner and Adab's three conditions, which are concerned mainly with the literary translations or linguistic conventions between the source and target languages, other non-linguistic factors might play an important role in the translator's decision to produce hybrid target texts. As mentioned previously, the considerations of human entities involved in the translation process, including the reader's expectations and reading habits, the purpose of the translation from the publisher, commissioner, or translator, as well as those factors from non-human entities, such as translation policy, the concrete situation in which translation takes place (i.e., with or without the use of translation aid), the reception norms for hybrid translations in the target culture, etc. All these show that a study of hybridity from a solely linguistic perspective in translation studies might not be enough.

2.2 Hybridity as a Combination of Text Types

The early 1980s has witnessed the use of the concept of hybridity to describe the multiple functions that coexisted in a genre or text-type in linguistics and discourse analysis. In the first systematic study of text linguistics, De Beaugrande and Dressler (1981) describe the concept of text types as the "global frameworks controlling the range of options likely to be utilized" (p. 141). According to them, readers usually have expectations about the linguistic traits for particular text types during the reading process. While acknowledging the distinctive linguistic features with which a text type is usually associated, they also add that some general and well-accepted classifications of text typology, such as description, narration, and argumentation, will be found in various combinations with the other text types. Literary texts are one of the typical representative examples of such a hybrid text type, as they "contain various constellations of description, narration, and argumentation" (De Beaugrande & Dressler, 1981, p. 173). The concept of multifunctional text types is later picked up by Hatim and Mason (1990), who define hybridity or hybridization as "the multifunctionality of texts, i.e., the fact that texts always serve more than one rhetorical purpose" (p. 241). To them, it is crucial to identify all specific rhetorical purposes in a hybrid text so that those communicative functions, together with the language registers that are associated with them, could be properly reproduced in the target text. Given the fact that "hybrid texts are by definition dynamic/marked" (Hatim & Mason, 1997, p. 154), considering the heterogeneous or even extreme nature in the use of different registers, the best way for the translator to translate this multifunctional text type is to achieve "an approximation to the reality of textual practice" (Hatim & Mason, 1997, p. 107), rather than given an exact reproduction of all these hybrid features in the target text.

Hatim and Mason's use of the notion of hybridity to describe different textual functions of a target text does not gain much ground in translation studies, in which a finer text typology proposed by Reiss (1971/1989) is more frequently used instead. In Reiss's discussion on the translation of text types and genres, she proposed a translation model in which she argued that the predominant function of the source text decides not only the "specific translation methods according to text type" (Reiss, 1976, p. 20) during the translation process as well as determines how the target text should be judged or evaluated. Reiss's linking three language functions (i.e., informative, expressive, and appellative) with text types provides a neat solution for the classification of a myriad of possible genres in reality, which makes it possible for her to further connect all these text types to translation strategies and assessment criteria. To sum up, compared with Hatim and Mason's brief discussion on hybridity, Reiss's framework offers a more detailed explanation of how multifunctional texts work in a communicative situation and how they should be translated accordingly.

2.3 Hybridity in Postcolonial Translation Studies

Inspired by the postcolonial discourse on hybridity aiming at exposing and resisting cultural imperialism imposed on the world by the West, some translation scholars explore the linguistic features as well as the literary and cultural significance of hybrid texts produced in ex-colonial regions or countries and discuss how the special space of in-betweenness in the language, literary tradition, and identity in the source colonial culture could be duly recognized and adequately reproduced in the target text.

Different from Schäffner and Adab (2001) and Hatim and Mason (1990, 1997), who adopt either a micro or a macro linguistic perspective to the study of hybridity in the target text, Snell-Hornby (2001) focuses on both the linguistic and cultural values of hybrid discourse and define them as texts "written by the ex-colonised in the language of the excoloniser, hence creating a 'new language' and occupying a space 'in between'" (p. 207). Instead of regarding hybrid texts as the results of any form of interlingual translation process, just as Schäffner and Adab do, Snell-Hornby believes that hybridity primarily comes from the constant intercultural interaction between nations or the trend of globalization, where powers, cultures, and people are in constant contact and under mutual influence. In essence, her definition is mainly based on Samia Mehrez's (1992) definition from the perspective of postcolonial studies, who argues that hybridity is especially found in postcolonial texts in which "culturo-linguistic layering" exists (Mehrez, 1992, p. 121). By examining the German version of Salman Rushdie's novel *The Moor's Last Sigh* as an example, Snell-Hornby explains in detail how the original linguistic and literary hybridity have been reduced in the target text and how these features could be more holistically and effectively translated by drawing on themes and frames theories.

Other scholars adopt a similar line to the study of hybridity, including Lu (2003) and Han (2002, 2005), who discuss how this concept could shed light on literary translation in a Chinese context, especially from the perspective of translation strategies. Both Lu and Han regard hybrid features as the natural consequence of foreignized translation, which presents original foreign elements in ways that do not conform to the literary traditions, linguistic conventions, or cultural practices of the target culture. The sometimes unnatural or influent versions out of the strategy of foreignization, according to them, are however, "very important in the development of language, culture and literature of the target end" (Han, 2002, p. 57) by supplying it with new forms and contents. Culturally, although hybrid translations might lead to "the colonization of Chinese culture to some extent" (Han, 2005, p. 200), they would neither affect the autonomy nor result in too much heterogeneity of Chinese culture, if "proper screening and handling procedures have been conducted" (Han, 2005, p. 200). However, Han falls short of explaining in what forms and aspects his "colonization of Chinese culture" are represented and what the so-called proper procedures refer to.

2.4 Defining Postcolonial Hybrid Literature in the Study

Similar to Snell-Hornby, the current study also adopts a postcolonial approach to studying hybridity in literary translation. In this study, the term hybrid postcolonial literature is used to describe the following two types of literary works: the first are the literary texts that are written in the language of the ex-colonizer by "postcolonial bilingual subjects" (Mehrez, 1992, p. 121), whose use of the language exhibiting linguistic features that conform neither to the language conventions of the ex-colonizer nor to the habitual language use of the former colony. The second type of hybrid literary texts is very similar to the first category, except that the texts are by the ex-colonized in their own language, showing features that somehow seem linguistically "unusual" in their own culture. Different from Schäffner and Adab's view that hybridity is the result of interlingual process, it is argued here that hybrid literary texts can exist without translation and are the proper objects of study of their own right.

Inspired by Snell-Hornby's analysis of Salman Rushdie's hybrid text *Midnight's Children* and *The Moor's Last Sigh*, a checklist for identifying the macro and micro hybridity features, ranging from lexical and grammatical items, syntactic structures, coinage, jargon, metaphors, puns, allusions, language varieties to idiolects, will be used in analyzing the linguistic features of postcolonial hybrid literary works. Same as Snell-Hornby, the scenes and frames theoretical model will be used to decide general translation strategies in a top-down manner, "proceeding from basic decisions as regards language varieties, rhetoric and style in the text as a whole to the individual grammatical and lexical items which will then depend on them" (Snell-Hornby, 2001, p. 215).

3. Translating Hybrid Postcolonial Literature in Hong Kong: A Case Study of the English Translation of Chan Koon Chung's *Kamdu cha canting*

Given the special language and the unique cultural and literary in-betweenness of hybrid literature, it will be interesting to see how the hybridity features and their embodied cultural identity have been duly represented in the target text. Such an exploration is especially of cultural significance for a place such as Hong Kong, which has been a colony under British rule since 1841. With a colonial history of 156 years, Hong Kong, which is close to the mainland, China, has always been a place where Western languages, cultures, and Chinese ones intersect. Even though Hong Kong was handed over to China in 1997, a lot of Hong Kong residents still have ambivalence about their discourse and cultural identity, which is made even more complicated as a consequence of the increasing influence of the culture from the Chinese mainland (Fung & Pun, 2021). The clashes and the reconciliation between the Western and Eastern values, the cultural conflict that is resulted from Hong Kong's unique place as the gateway for Western culture for more than a century, and Hong Kong people's dilemma about national and local identity are described and documented in some of the literary works written by Hong Kong writers after 1997, all of which provide fertile ground for the study of hybridity, which creates a space in between in the postcolonial Hong Kong society. In the current study, the short story *Kamdu cha canting* written by Chan Koon Chung – a Hong Kong indigenous writer – is selected as an example to probe into the linguistic diversity and cultural dynamic and struggle of collective identities of Hong Kongese.

3.1 Introducing Chan Koon Chung and His Short Story *Kamdu cha canting*

Born in Shanghai in 1952, Chan Koon Chung moved to Hong Kong with his family in 1956. After graduating from the University of Hong Kong with a bachelor's degree in sociology in 1974, he has worked in various capacities, such as a journalist, editor, publisher, and writer. He proves himself to be quite an able and versatile author as he can produce quality works in many genres, ranging from screenplays, prose, novel, and short stories, whose popularity among Hong Kong readers earned him the title of "'Annual Writer' (年度作家)" by the Hong Kong Book Fair in 2013.

With few exceptions, his fiction draws fodder from the kaleidoscopic city life of Hong Kong and delineates the "petty" stories of all walks of people he had observed so closely since he was a boy. Written in a language mixture of Mandarin, Cantonese, and English, his stories are often fusions of different cultures in Hong Kong (including the predominant British and Chinese cultures as well as some minor ones, such as Indian, Pakistan, and Nepalese cultures, etc.), for which he was hailed as "a pioneering critic for metropolitan life and culture" (Chinanews, 2011, November 08). His fictions, which often embody particular colonial historical and linguistic features of Hong Kong, are particularly revealing of the unique position of Hong Kong modern literature as a special "subsystem" in the polysystem of modern Chinese literature (Even-Zohar, 1978). To use Samia Mehrez's term, Chan's stories are "hybrid" or "métisses" texts due to "the culture-linguistic layering which exists within them" (Mehrez, 1992, p. 121) (1992, p. 121).

Chan's short story *Kamdu cha canting* is one of the three stories collected in his book *Hong Kong Trilogy*, which was first published in 2004. An expanded and revised edition of the book was published by Oxford University Press in 2013. According to Chan, all three stories depict the lives of the baby boomer generations who are deeply "influenced by hybrid cultures in Hong Kong" (Chan, 2004b, p. 229). The story of *Kamdu cha canting* is narrated from the perspective of a Gweilo – who is half British and half Chinese, showing his observations at an eponymous tea restaurant he frequents in Hong Kong. Due to the 1997 Asian financial crisis, he loses his job as an automobile salesperson and has to eat a barbecue dish at the restaurant every night. This gives him plenty of opportunities to get to know well other restaurant-goers who come from all walks of life in Hong Kong. Later on, the financial crisis also affects other sectors, including the restaurant owner, who decides to fold the business soon. Seeing this, these regular customers invite him to take over the shop to keep it running. This invitation puts him in a difficult situation as it forces him to decide whether he should stay or leave Hong Kong.

3.2 Hybridity in Kamdu cha canting: An Analysis

The hybridity of Chan's *Kamdu cha canting* can be analyzed from literary, cultural, and linguistic aspects.

Literary aspects here broadly refer to the components (theme, protagonist, narrative point of view, structure, plot, etc.) that constitute a work of literature in whatever forms, such as fiction, poetry, prose, or drama. In Chan's postcolonial story, the hybrid literary feature can be immediately felt when the story is narrated from the start by an unnamed protagonist, who is a half-Chinese and half-Briton young man. He can understand and speak the local dialect Cantonese fluently but with very little knowledge of written Chinese. Indeed, the image of this main character reminds Chinese readers, especially those in Hong Kong, of the typical type of mixed-race people in this former colony. Due to the long history of British occupation, interracial marriage, which was not uncommon in pre-colonial Hong Kong, is most frequently seen between British expatriates and women of Chinese ethnicity. Their children, born in Hong Kong and raised under the influence of both English and Chinese cultures, were often torn between using Chinese and not using Chinese as their native language. Before 1997, given the colonial status of Hong Kong, English is often considered a language of a higher status because it is the language of the colonizer. Thus, most biracial people, such as the main character, would most likely choose English as their mother tongue. However, their upbringing in Hong Kong, where Chinese is still the dominant language spoken by a majority of the population, makes their interaction with Chinese-speaking people unavoidable. To communicate with Chinese-speaking citizens in this multicultural city, many mixed-race people have learned to speak Cantonese, the daily language used in Hong Kong, just as the main character here did. However, their reluctance to fully master the oral and written forms of this colonizer's language betrays their hidden sense of linguistic superiority. Through this subtle description of the hybrid linguistic choice of the protagonist, Chan vividly presents to his reader the liminality of the character's identity.

Furthermore, through the eyes of this hybrid protagonist, things or objects that are originally so familiar to local Hong Kongers, such as his previous working experience, car brands, etc., are now portrayed with parodic effects and interpreted in a defamiliarizing manner, all of which further reinforce the liminal spaces the author tries to create in the story.

The story ends with the protagonist's dilemma of whether to stay in Hong Kong to take over the tea restaurant or to begin a new business in Shanghai. This ending is symbolic of the character's struggle between a choice of hybridity versus non-hybridity. Whereas his choice of Hong Kong would suggest he ends up coming to terms with the hybridity identity he has now, his option to go to Shanghai to start all over again would mean his forsaking of the previous colonial identity by embracing the one that has been newly imposed on him after the handover of Hong Kong to China in1997.

The hybridity of the text is also evident in the multiple cultures portrayed in the story. The story happens in the setting of a "cha canting" (literally, a tea restaurant) with the name of Kamdu. In Hong Kong, a lot of employees have to be on the job for long working hours, which makes them hardly have time to prepare dinners by themselves at home after work. So most of them choose to eat out, especially in "cha canting," or tea restaurants that provide not only Cantonese cuisine but also adapted Western dishes. "Cha canting" probably gets its name from the cup of tea, either Chinese tea or milk tea in English style, which the restaurant serves its customers when they first sit down at a table. With its amalgamation of both Chinese and Western cuisine it serves and the intimate and essential role it plays in most people's lives in Hong Kong, "cha canting," this Hong Kong–styled café "has become a symbol of the Hong Kong local food culture since the late twentieth century" (Leung, 2006, p. 68) as well as a perfect allegory for the cultural hybridity in this city. Indeed, most of the story's content can also be interpreted as the narrator's contemplation at the tea restaurant. His thoughts, which are represented in the form of a free flow of associations with whatever comes to his mind, highlight the banalities of social exchange between ordinary people and the "metisses" of Hong Kong local culture as a result of over 150 years of colonial history and the increasing globalization in recent decades.

The literary and cultural hybridity aspects mentioned previously all find their way in various linguistic features, which range from macro linguistic features such as "language varieties, idiolects, jargon, metaphors, puns, coinage and an infinite abundance of allusions" (Snell-Hornby, 2001, p. 209), as well as micro textual features, including vocabulary, syntax, style, etc. How these literary and cultural hybrid features "shape concepts and texts differently" (Jakobsen, 1993, p. 158) and how these linguistic hybrid innovative usages are exploited creatively to forge a new language, which is not necessarily transferable to other languages or target cultures, will be the topic of the next section.

4. A Textual Analysis of *Kamdu cha canting* and Its English Translation

In this part, a textual analysis will be conducted on the linguistic hybrid features of *Kamdu cha canting* and its existing English translation to examine whether the original linguistic hybridity, along with its literary and cultural symbolic meanings, have been duly reproduced in the translation.

This hybrid postcolonial short story, co-translated by Poon Ka-Man and Robert Neather as *Kamdu Tea Restaurant*, was published in *The Literary Review* in 2004.

The hybrid cultural significance can be felt immediately when Chinese readers begin to read the first paragraph of the story:

> ST (1): 金都茶餐厅，英文叫 Can Do, 正门向美丽都大厦横门, 后门傍仙乐都夜总会(最近一直内部装修暂停营业), 左边维多利亚时钟酒店(前伊顿英文补习夜校), 右转角马会(前皇家赛马会)场外投注站 (underlined parts added).
>
> TT (1): Kamdu Tea Restaurant, English name Can Do. Front door facing the side door of the Mirador Building; back door beside Xanadu Night Club (recently under interior renovation, business temporarily suspended). On the left is the Victoria hourly-rated Love Hotel (former Eton English Tutorial Night School); round the right corner is an off-course betting branch of the Jockey Club (former Royal Jockey Club).
>
> (Chan, 2004a, p. 138)

In ST (1), Chan presents an immediate linguistic plurality to his readers by implying the "in-between" cultural space in which the narrator is situated. This is revealed by the intentional use in the first sentence of the three bracketed parts employed to contrast the current and the previous status of the recreational venues mentioned. The change of names or status of these places explicitly indicates the great extent of transformation that Hong Kong has undergone before and after the colonial periods.

In the original text, it is indicated that the English name for the restaurant is Can Do, the English pronunciation of which is similar to the Cantonese pronunciation of the Chinese name *Kamdu*. However, in addition to the acoustic similarity between these two terms, the English name Can Do is rich in local cultural connotation, as it reminds local readers of the "can do spirit" originating in the early 1970s in Hong Kong and is still popular today. This "can do" attitude that defines Hong Kong has at least the following cultural implications for Hongkongers: first, it indicates a person's hardworking mentality by suggesting "anything you can do, I can do better," which reminds us of the notoriously well-known workaholic culture in this city; second, it also represents a core value of being willing to take up whatever challenges come with the job and overcome these difficulties in the end. Another term for this intangible cultural quality in which Hong Kong people take pride is the "lion rock spirit," which describes Hong Kong people's motto of "never giving up" in the face of adversity. The English name Can Do also echoes the ending of the story, in which the English words of "can," "can do," and "do" are used several times to describe the narrator's dilemma of whether he "can do" a business in Shanghai or Hong Kong. With its multiple layers of symbolic meaning, the name of the restaurant name is a rich, hybrid cultural image.

In TT (1), the translators made their first attempt to reproduce the hybridity of this hybrid postcolonial text by trying to imitate the paratactic Chinese structure in the first sentence. Instead of translating the original Chinese "金都茶餐厅, 英文叫Can Do" into a more fluent and idiomatic English version, such as "The English name for Kamdu Tea Restaurant is Can Do," they chose to use two seemingly independent phrases "Kamdu Tea Restaurant, English name Can Do," which can be roughly regarded as "block language" (Quirk et al., 1985, p. 845), which are not complete and grammatical sentences, in English. According to Quirk et al. (1985), block language messages, which "are most often non-sentences, consisting of a noun or noun phrase or nominal clause in isolation; no verb is needed" (p. 845), are most often used in newspaper headlines, advertisements, and other notices. But here, the superimposition of these two language segments, which are not logically linked to each other with cohesive links, as most common English sentences do, is largely used to highlight the syntactic features of original Chinese by imitating their information structures. Thus, with the unconventional use of the block language in TT (1), the linguistic hybridity of the translational language can be immediately appreciated by English readers. However, the cultural significance and allusion of "can do spirit," which the original Chinese name of the restaurant strongly suggests, is lost in the English translation "Kamdu Tea Restaurant," as few English readers will be evoked of any Hong Kong cultural core values that are associated with this term when reading this translation.

The linguistic hybridity of the story is further enhanced by defamiliarizing syntactic structures used to describe cultural banalities of Hong Kong. Note later how

Chan manages to create an in-between literary language that is neither in line with Chinese nor English grammar in ST (2):

> ST (2): 如无意外, 样样顺风顺水, 老板阿杜过几年大可以返东莞乡下买幢西班牙式洋楼, 养只番狗, (如果发展商悟烂尾)屋前小型人工湖, 屋后迷你十八洞高球场, <u>左邻劳工子弟出身香港现任高官个阿妈, 右里来历不明樟木头新发财位阿二, 行行企企叹世界听谭咏麟李克勤锄大弟食野味睇无线拍蚊过世</u>。 (underlined parts added)

In the underlined sentence of this example, long lists of pre-modifiers are used before such noun phrases as "阿妈" (with a pre-modifier of 15 characters) and "阿二" (with a pre-modifier of 13 characters), which forms a strong contrast with Chinese normal noun phrases in which fewer than five pre-modifiers are generally used. Similarly, peculiar syntactic features are also found in the last part of the final sentence of ST (2), in which six verb phrases (e.g., "行行企企叹世界," "听谭咏麟李克勤," "锄大弟," "食野味," "睇无线," and "拍蚊过世"), each indicating a typical way of living in Hong Kong, are connected with each other without using any punctuation, thus forming an extremely long paratactic structure that is rarely seen in a normal Chinese sentence. Stylistically, the abundant use of local colloquial registers to describe these leisure activities also makes this hybrid postcolonial text sound remarkably like the spoken words from the mouths of grassroots people in the city.

The cultural hybridity revealed from the linguistic hybridity in ST (2) is equally impressive. In this linguistically defamiliarizing paragraph, the narrator makes liberal use of banal cultural references, such as "purchasing a villa with a Spanish air about it," "keeping a dog of foreign breed," "playing golf," which are lifestyles usually associated with the so-called higher-class, more Westernized Hongkongers, to contrast with other activities such as "listening to Cantonese pop songs," "playing the popular Cantonese poker game of big two," "watching local TV channel Jade," which are common leisure hobbies of the grassroots Hong Kong people. These two different lifestyles, which in essence represent the cultural imaginations of both the East and the West, conceive Hong Kong citizens' lives as a hybrid mixture of Eastern and Western traditions, again testifying to the in-between nature of culture in Hong Kong.

However, the cultural and linguistic hybridity implied by the underlined sentence in ST (2) is lost to some extent in Poon and Neather's translation:

> TT (2): Neighbour on the left will be the mother of a current Hong Kong government senior official from a worker's family. Neighbour on the right will be the mistress of a Zhangmutou nouveau riche of unknown origin. He'll loaf around enjoying life listening to songs by Alan Tam and Hacken Lee playing Big Two gorging on game-meat watching channel Jade killing flies to live a life.
> (Chan, 2004a, p. 138)

In TT (2), the original clumsy, lengthy pre-modifiers were rephrased into grammatical and fluent English structures: "Neighbour on the left will be the mother of a current Hong Kong government senior official from a worker's family. Neighbour on the right will be the mistress of a Zhangmutou nouveau riche of unknown origin." These two English sentences, both grammatical and idiomatic, cannot remind target readers of the original hybrid Chinese sentence, which, in the context of the story, is fittingly spoken by a half-Chinese and half-Briton narrator who has only a limited knowledge of written Chinese. In contrast, the hybrid linguistic features represented by the unbroken, unpunctuated flow of information displayed by the superimposition of six verb phrases in the final clause of ST (2) were retained intact in TT (2). The English translation "He'll loaf around enjoying life listening to songs by Alan Tam and Hacken Lee playing Big Two gorging on game-meat watching channel Jade killing flies to live a life," which is a highly long English sentence that has been converted from the original Chinese clause, is used here to try to represent the narrator's stream of consciousness as the original does. Target readers can immediately sense the syntactic hybridity of this sentence as they struggle to understand the units of meaning and the cultural metaphors or allusions embodied by this convoluted sentence, just as the source readers do when reading the original Chinese sentence. It is worth noting that the translators do not come to terms with this syntactic and cultural hybridity by "bending back" all the original phrases into rational codes, that is, by making them easier to understand with more fluent structures and idiomatic phrases. Instead, they also resort to a highly estranging English structure, which helps to highlight or even heighten the original syntactic and cultural hybridity. From the perspective of the use of vocabulary, it should also be noted that typically Cantonese colloquial terms (e.g., 行行企企叹世界, 锄大弟) and cultural references (e.g., "拍蚊过世") are used in the final clause of ST (2), which add to the linguistic hybridity of the paragraph concerned. In the translation, the spoken phrase "行行企企叹世界" (literally, "walking and standing to enjoy the world") was translated as "loaf around enjoying life," a more literary and idiomatic expression in English. The culture-loaded slang verb "锄"[1] used in describing the poker game "锄大弟" (literally, "dig Big Two") was replaced with a more generic term of "play" that is mostly used to describe a poker game in English. Finally, the original phrase "拍蚊过世" (literally, "killing mosquitoes to lead a life") refers to the humid weather all year-round that favors mosquito activities in Hong Kong. However, the cultural allusion of "mosquitos" was replaced with "flies," a different kind of insect in the translation, thus completely losing one of the cultural references most familiar to Hong Kong people.

To sum up, despite the translators' successful attempt to retain the syntactic hybridity of ST (2) in their translation, they fail to reproduce the typical Cantonese cultural locality, which is represented by a wide range of colloquial expressions and typical cultural references. As we see in TT (2), some of these expressions have been neutralized into standard literary language in English, and some references have been replaced with images that read more natural or logical to English readers. Since cultural locality forms an essential part of Hong Kong's hybridity, such modifications cannot do sufficient justice to the heterogeneous ways employed by the author to represent the particular in-between position that Hong Kong culture and people are occupying during the postcolonial period.

5. Translating the Hybridity of *Kamdu cha canting*: A Scenes-and-Frames Approach

From the textual analysis of the STs described in the previous section, hybridity in the postcolonial short story of *Kamdu cha canting* can be represented through linguistic, cultural, or literary features in the text, which are often intertwined with each other. The unusual linguistic features, ranging from syntax, vocabulary, and register, are frequently reminiscent of the popular values and social practices that are portrayed as mixed or adapted versions of Western and Chinese cultures in Hong Kong. A reader's experience of hybridity is reinforced each time he or she reads, interprets, and empathizes with the description. However, this hybrid reading experience, due to a totality of interpretation of all these features, also poses problems for translators working with hybrid texts in a postcolonial context. As the previous analysis of the TTs shows, the retention of one particular feature (such as the syntactic one) at the expense of others (such as the cultural and literary ones) inevitably undermines the overall representation of hybridity in the translation. To fully account for the language features of hybrid postcolonial literary texts, Snell-Hornby (2001) argued that the scenes-and-frames approach is the best theoretical model to analyze the linguistic "complexity and profusion" (p. 213) that abound in these texts. With its emphasis on both macro linguistic frames and the micro linguistic units that lead to such scenes, the scenes-and-frames approach can help translators appreciate the overall effect of hybridity and understand how this effect is realized by linguistic markedness or stiltedness in the text. In the current research, the same scenes-and-frames model is adopted to examine the combined effect of hybridity of Chan's *Kamdu cha canting* from both macro and micro perspectives, aiming at reproducing its hybrid effects in the translation in a holistic manner.

The scenes-and-frames framework is first based on the semantics developed by Fillmore (1977, 1985) in his case grammar and further expounded by Lakoff (1977, 1982) later. Arguing for "an integrated view of language structure, language behavior, language comprehension, language change and language acquisition" (Fillmore, 1977, p. 55), Fillmore rejected an atomistic or pure formalistic view of language that has dominated linguistics research in America at the time. Instead, he favors an experiential and holistic view of language in which users associate words or other grammatical categories "with prototypical instances of scenes" (Fillmore, 1977, p. 63). Here, scenes are not only referring to visual images but also "any kind of coherent segment, large or small, of human beliefs, actions, experiences, or imaginings" (Fillmore, 1977, p. 63) that might be evoked in the language users' mind. Scenes are induced or prompted by frames, which are made up of concrete linguistic choices. For instance, a verbal action introduces a particular perspective to the world, which is in turn connected with a particular scene. In the case of hybrid literary texts, this approach means examining special linguistic items and finding out how these linguistic means are used to form particular scenes of hybridity in the text. A general understanding of the cultural and literary background and significance of the text helps translators develop translation strategies in a top-down manner, proceeding from general options such as motifs, genres, themes, and choices of characters, to "from basic decisions as regards language varieties, rhetoric and style in the text as a whole to the individual grammatical and lexical items which will then depend on them" (Snell-Hornby, 2001, p. 215).

Thus, a scenes-and-frames approach to the translation of *Kamdu cha canting* will start from a holistic understanding of the cultural, historical, and literary hybridity as embodied by its linguistic choices in the text, which is exemplified by the analysis of the language in ST (1) and (2) in section four. After having the overall scene of the hybridity in mind, the translator could approach the text from each type of hybridity observed by analyzing the frames prescribed by the system of linguistic choices in the text. Among all these language options, the translator should pay extra attention to retaining the linguistic frames (such as references, allusions, concepts, forms of address, etc.) that can evoke scenes of source cultural hybridity in the target reader's mind. The original frames that are too culture-bound to be translated literally could be best explained by adding a gloss so that the resulting scenes that the English-speaking readers activate will be more or less the same as the Cantonese readers.

To achieve an optimal degree of hybridity in the translation, the translator does not need to deliberately bend the original frames that are couched in normal, grammatical Chinese in the story, as this deliberately made-up foreignizing language more often than not leads to artificial translationese that results in an over-representation of the original hybrid effects. In contrast, for the frames expressed in linguistically hybrid forms, the translator needs to try his or her best to preserve the special grammatical and lexical items in the translation to evoke the scene of hybrid Hong Kong in the target reader.

Bearing the thrust of scenes-and-frames approach to the translation of *Kamdu cha canting* in mind, we have come up with revised translations for the underlined parts in ST (1) and ST (2) in the previous section.

> Underlined part (1):金都茶餐厅, 英文叫 Can Do,
> Revised TT (1): Can Do tea restaurant, its Chinese name Kamdu.
> Underlined part (2):左邻劳工子弟出身香港现任高官个阿妈, 右里来历不明樟木头新发财位阿二,
> Revised TT (2): Neighbour on the left will be a from-the – grassroots current Hong Kong government senior official's mother. Neighbour on the right will an unknown-origin Zhangmutou the-new-rich's Second Mrs.
> Underlined part (3): 行行企企叹世界听谭咏麟李克勤锄大弟食野味睇无线拍蚊过世。
> Revised TT (3): He'll walk and stand around to enjoy the world and listen to Alan Tam and Hacken Lee music and dig Big Two and eat game-meat and watch channel Jade and chase and swat mosquitoes to live a life.

Compared with TT (1) and (2), hybrid cultural elements that are expressed via estranging and mixed linguistic forms are more accentuated in the revised translations to evoke similar scenes in the mind of the English reader. In revised TT (1), the original information structure is modified in such a way as to present the English name of the restaurant first, followed by the transliteration of its Chinese name Kamdu. The aim is to set the English name "Can Do" as well as its cultural connotations, which are more familiar to the target reader, against the scene evoked by the foreign linguistic frame of Kamdu, thus forming a contrast between familiarity and strangeness. This opening line, with its new focus on the English name of the restaurant, "Can Do tea restaurant," rather than its Chinese one, also functions as a cultural metaphor for the spirit so closely associated with Hong Kong people in a postcolonial era. Additionally, it immediately conveys a sense of hybridity, which is the theme of the story, to the reader when he or she starts reading the text.

In revised TT (2), Poon and Neather's version, in which the more grammatical and fluent English structure was used to render the long list of pre-modifiers, is replaced with a literal rendition of the original sequencing of these modifiers as well as their meaning. The noun phrases in the revision, such as "a from-the-grass-roots current Hong Kong government senior official's mother" and "Neighbour on the right will a unknown-origin Zhangmutou the-new-rich's Second Mrs." create linguistic frames that lead to the imagination of hybrid cultural scenes in Hong Kong and in Zhangmutou, a town nicknamed "little Hong Kong" in the mainland, China, due to its proximity to and cultural resemblance with the metropolis.

Similarly, the longwinded, unpunctuated syntax of underlined part (3) was retained faithfully in the revised TT (3). In addition, the abundant verb phrases used in the example are also translated as literally as possible. For example, the Chinese phrase that contains five verbs "行行企企嘆世界" is translated into "walk and stand around to enjoy the world," a more foreignizing version than Poon and Neather's fluent rendition of "loaf around enjoying life." The connective "and" is also used profusely in the revision to recreate a syntactic structure that sounds dull and repetitive, a rhythm that alludes to the mundane and monotonous life most ordinary Hongkongers live. Altogether, the estranging grammar, the unfamiliar diction, and the unusual use of diction that have been deliberately exploited in the revised TT (3) all help to activate scenes of hybridity in the postcolonial Hong Kong among the target reader.

6. Conclusion

The importance of the concept of hybridity in providing a unique prism through which lives, thoughts, behaviors, communications, and traditions of the people in the postcolonial period can be better examined has long been acknowledged by scholars of cultural studies such as Homi Bhabha, Néstor García Canclini, Stuart Hall, Gayatri Spivak, and Paul Gilroy. Abundant literary works have also been written on this topic to express the linguistic and cultural in-betweenness of the people from ex-colonized lands. There is no exception with Hong Kong, a former British colony. Due to its long colonial history, Hong Kong is one of the frequent subjects in Chinese postcolonial literature. However, the discussions on translating the hybridity, as revealed in these literary works, are relatively few and far between. Based on a scenes-and-frames approach to the translation of hybrid literary texts as proposed by Snell-Hornby (2001), the current study illustrates how the macro (i.e., scenes) and micro perspectives (i.e., frames) offered by the model can shed light on the translation of cultural, literary, and linguistic hybridity of Chan Koon Chung's short story *Kamdu cha canting*. It is argued that the approach enables the translator to adopt a holistic view of the hybrid postcolonial literature and develop translation strategies to deal with different types of hybridity in the text accordingly. Additionally, the "in-between" space created by the hybridity also allows the translator to search for creative means to fully tap on the artistic and innovative potential of hybrid literature in the translation.

Note

1 In Cantonese slangs, "锄" means "kill" or "beat," whereas "大弟" refers to the number 2 on a poker card. Thus the expression "锄大弟" means "killing or beating number 2" in a poker game in the local language of Hong Kong. This expression is used only in Cantonese-speaking regions.

References

Bakhtin, M. (1981). *The dialogic imagination: Four essays* (C. Emerson & M. Hosquist, Trans.). University of Texas Press.
Bakhtin, M. (1984). *Problems of Dostoevsky's poetics*. University of Minnesota Press.
Bhabha, H. K. (1994). *The location of culture*. Routledge.
Brontë, E. (1976). *Wuthering heights*. Oxford University Press.
Chan, K. C. (2004a). Kamdu tea restaurant (K. M. Poon & R. J. Neather, Trans.). *The Literary Review*, *47*(4), 138–153.
Chan, K. C. (2004b). *Xianggang sanbuqu* 香港三部曲. Oxford University Press.
Chinanews. (2011, November 8). Xianggangwenhua "duomianshou" Chan Koon Chung jiang jixu shuxiezhongguo 香港文化"多面手"陈冠中将继续书写中国. *Zhongguo xinwen wang* 中国新闻网. www.chinanews.com.cn/hb/2011/11-08/3445365.shtml
De Beaugrande, R., & Dressler, W. (1981). *Introduction to text linguistics*. Longman.
Even-Zohar, I. (1978). *Papers in historical poetics* (Vol. 15). Porter Institute for Poetics and Semiotics, Tel Aviv University.
Fillmore, C. J. (1977). The need for a frame semantics in linguistics. In H. Karlgren (Ed.), *Statistical methods in linguistics* (pp. 5–29). Skriptor.
Fillmore, C. J. (1985). Frames and the semantics of understanding. *Quaderni di semantica*, *6*(2), 222–254.
Fung, A. Y. H., & Pun, B. L. F. (2021). The transforming Hong Kong polarized cultural identities: The cultural dynamic and relocation of Hong Kong cultural production. *Social Identities*, *27*(3), 292–306.
Han, Z. -M. 韩子满. (2002). Wenxuefanyi yu zahe 文学翻译与杂合. *Chinese Translators Journal* 中国翻译, *23*(2), 54–58.
Han, Z. -M., 韩子满. (2005). *Wenxuefanyi zaheyanjiu* 文学翻译杂合研究. Shanghai Translation Publishing House.
Hatim, B., & Mason, I. (1990). *Discourse and the translator*. Routledge.
Hatim, B., & Mason, I. (1997). *The translator as communicator*. Routledge.

Jakobsen, A. L. (1993). Translation as textual (re) production. *Perspectives*, *1*(2), 155–165.
Klinger, S. (2015). *Translation and linguistic hybridity: Constructing world-view*. Routledge.
Lakoff, G. (1977). Linguistic gestalts. Proceedings of the Thirteenth Regional Meeting of the Chicago Linguistic Society, Chicago.
Lakoff, G. (1982). *Categories and cognitive models*. LAUT.
Leung, S.-W. (2006). Hong Kong-styled cafe and the identity of Hong Kongese. In T.-L. Lui, E. K.-W. Ma, & C.-H. Ng (Eds.), *Hong Kong cultural studies*. Hong Kong University Press.
Lu, H.-M., 卢红梅. (2003). Fanyi yu hunzawenben 翻译与混杂文本. *Modern Foreign Languages* 现代外语, *26*(3), 275–282.
Mehrez, S. (1992). Translation and the postcolonial experience: The francophone North African text. In L. Venuti (Ed.), *Rethinking translation* (pp. 120–138). Routledge.
"hybrid." Oxford English Dictionary. Retrieved August 10, 2022, from www.oed.com/view/Entry/89809
Quirk, R., Greenbaum, S., Leech, G., & Svartoik, J. (1985). *A comprehensive grammar of the English language*. Longman.
Reiss, K. (1976). *Texttyp und übersetzungsmethode: Der operative text*. Scriptor Verlag.
Reiss, K. (1989). Text type, translation types and translation assessment (A. Chesterman, Trans.). In A. Chesterman (Ed.), *Readings in translation theory*. Oy Finn Lectura Ab. (Original work published 1971)
Robinson, D. (2016). *Translation and empire: Postcolonial approaches explained*. Routledge.
Schäffner, C., & Adab, B. (2001). The idea of the hybrid text in translation: Contact as conflict. *Across Languages and Cultures*, *2*(2), 167–180.
Snell-Hornby, M. (2001). The space 'in between': What is a hybrid text? *Across Languages and Cultures*, *2*(2), 207–216.

11 "Big Translation" and Cultural Memory

The Construction and Transmission of National Images[1]

Xuanmin Luo

Translation plays a particularly important role in the cultural transformation of a nation; this function can never be replaced by other disciplines. More importantly, it is closely relevant to the modernity and rejuvenation of a nation (Luo, 2012, p. 5). Nowadays, translation and translation studies in China are attracting increasing attention than ever before. Numerous translations of Chinese academic works have been produced, more and more translation projects have been funded by the government, and there is great enthusiasm among scholars for translating Chinese classics into foreign languages. "As China has ushered in a new round of translation boom, the workload of translating Chinese works into foreign languages has long exceeded that of foreign ones into Chinese" (Huang, 2015, p. 5). Due to the national emphasis on translation studies and practice, a large number of translation research projects have been launched in recent years at both the national and provincial levels, such as the five major projects in foreign language literature supported by the National Social Science Fund of China in 2015. In addition, new academic journals on translation studies have emerged, such as *East Journal of Translation, Translation Horizons, Translation World, Translation Forum*, etc. Moreover, the existing translation journals have set up special sections to explore new topics and phenomena in translation studies, such as "Translation and the Construction of National Image," "Chinese Literature Going Global," and "Translation Studies of Chinese Classics," etc. Despite the upsurge, translation studies in China "is still featured by a lack of self-consciousness" (Lv, 2014, p. 1), which is manifested as "theoretical aphasia" that blindly follows the Western translation studies without retrospection. Consequently, there remains much room for improvement in the construction of Chinese translation theory and national image.

1. The Dilemma of Current Translation Studies

There remains a gap between Chinese and Western scholars in terms of the breadth, depth, and degree of innovation of translation theory, or to put it positively, "there is still enormous room for development" (Tan, 2012, p. 8). The reason is that the influence of Chinese translation studies in today's world is still very limited, and we have hardly produced any recognized academic works that

DOI: 10.4324/9781003368168-12

converse on par with the West. Some scholars called this phenomenon "aphasia" (Cao, 1996, p. 51). In 1983, with two articles published in *Chinese Translators Journal*, Luo Xinzhang (1983) called for the establishment of systematic translation studies in China. Unfortunately, the situation is still such that although there are plenty of authoritative scholars, there are few original translation theories in China, which deserve our thorough reflection. Various reasons may account for this phenomenon – to name a few, the Western-dominated mentality, the inherent Western centralism, and China's long marginalized status in academic circles.

It is an indisputable fact that Chinese scholars always prefer foreign theories to native ones. Lu Xun's "yingyi" and Venuti's "foreignization" share great similarities. Lu put forward the concept of "yingyi" in 1909, while Venuti did not come up with a similar concept of "foreignization" until 1999. Although many Chinese scholars are familiar with "yingyi," their discussions on Venuti's "foreignization" have far outnumbered those on "yingyi" (Luo, 2016, p. 33). Strangely enough, the few subsequent studies on "yingyi" benefited from the introduction and dissemination of the concept of "foreignization" in China.

The bizarre phenomenon of Chinese scholars relying on foreign translation theories to advance the interpretation of Lu Xun's thoughts in Chinese translation studies requires closer examination. Whenever Western scholars put forward a certain "turn", Chinese scholars either follow blindly, without in-depth research or without a comprehensive grasp of their propositions or interpret the theory from Western philosophical and cultural perspectives, so that the learned knowledge can hardly benefit our own research on Chinese translation theories. If we only follow the footsteps of Western translation scholarship, we will eventually lose ourselves in various so-called "turns". The key to the dilemma, after all, is attributed to a lack of cultural confidence and cultural consciousness.

For one thing, some scholars have adopted Western theories and can hardly wait to apply them to translation studies before thoroughly understanding the new terms and concepts. Such researches are just like shooting stars and have no lasting academic vitality. For another, certain scholars seek to make a name for themselves with new branches of theories in translation studies, although the majority of them have neither in-depth knowledge in the relevant disciplines nor rigorous academic training. However, these facts never give rise to any hesitation or doubt while they enjoy their titles as "theorists" or "scholars". Consequently, the so-called "indigenous" translation theories would not be conducive to translation studies in China. Instead, they would become a laughingstock because of their emptiness, looseness, and lack of originality.

Recently, the "technical turn" in translation studies has caused great concern in the academic world. Literary translations and philosophical translations are measured against technical standards. Without technical parameters or corpus data, translation studies seem not to be translation studies, or at least cannot be considered reliable. Such a technical mentality denies the depth of theoretical thought, while the latter represents academic innovation and development. Academic work is synonymous with "technology", and "research" means "learning to use a technology" – such a situation makes translation studies "shapeless" and unimaginable. Even worse, some researchers who do not have qualified technical training get too involved in this technical trend by simply taking data from computers or corpus and concluding that translation A outperforms translation B or that translation A is manipulated to a greater extent than translation B, and so on. Moreover, in such studies, a majority of conclusions are more subjective than objective and cannot justify themselves. This phenomenon is reminiscent of Zhang Boran's claim two decades ago that "in pursuing the scientific aspects of translation studies, the humanistic nature of translation studies is ignored" (Zhang, 1997, p. 9). The technical turn, then, deserves our vigilance and reflection. We are firmly opposed to academic research based solely on subjective ideas, and we should not overestimate the role of technology. If all academic thoughts are shaped by technical means and all translation theories are replaced by technology, Chinese translation studies will never have a destination. However, we do not deny the role and importance of technical tools. As the old saying goes, "A handy tool makes a handyman." We should recognize that tools are employed in scientific research. Data together with technical diagrams can only explain phenomena, while the mechanisms and thoughts behind the research design are the real essence. Take as an example the ore exploited in a mine. Without proper processing and extraction, it would remain as ore and never have a chance to become a rare metal.

At present, we have reaped excellent fruits in translation studies, but they have not been coordinated into a joint force and have not developed into an influential school of thought. The cultural transmission of translations has not gained the attention it deserves in translation studies, and existing research is limited to textual analysis. This is understandable, but in any case, translations are meant to be read, appreciated, and disseminated, which presupposes the transcendence and intertextuality of translation. At a time when global instability, cultural conflict, and international exchange coexist, translation activities would never meet the multiple demands if its focus remained on "faithfulness". Instead, we should create a strong cultural awareness to deal with the dilemma in translation studies. In addition to the traditional approaches of translation analysis, we should also view translation from the perspective of historical development, theoretical innovation and discourse dominance, and broaden our academic horizons to conduct interdisciplinary translation studies. Therefore, we need to advance translation studies with a broader view, to reflect on the relationship between translation and cultural transmission, between translation and cultural heritage from various perspectives, taking a national standpoint.

To date, our academic research has focused heavily on individual cultural memory, that is, individual communicative memory, and ignored the importance of collective cultural memory. Traditional, monotonous research approaches have narrowed research so that only fragmented individual memories can be traced back (Luo, 2014). Literary translation works are no exception. Impressive translations can bring pleasure to readers. But such pleasure cannot promote the creation of classics. Translated classics will come into being only when the act of translating gives birth to collective cultural memory, which may trigger different cultural impacts at different levels, say, regional, national, or international. For example, the year 2016 marked the four hundredth anniversary of the deaths of Shakespeare and Tang Xianzu (汤显祖). The former was memorized through influential activities around the world, while the latter enjoyed nationwide commemorative activities only in China and, embarrassingly, did not even receive the same attention as the activities commemorating the former in China. We can import the film *Lion King*, an animal version of *Hamlet*; we can produce the film *The Banquet*, featuring a Chinese palace coup, to reproduce Shakespeare's *The Prince's*, not to mention various films, stage performances, and plays inspired by Shakespeare, and retranslation of his works in China. Tang Xianzu, a Chinese playwright, on the other hand, has not succeeded in building such a collective cultural memory. Although Bai Xianyong (白先勇) reinterpreted Tang's work *Peony Pavilion* in the form of Chinese Kun Opera and brought it to the stage, it is generally far from satisfactory to explore, reinterpret, or perform Tang's works. The immediate consequence of the lack of collective cultural memory is to hinder the construction of the grand Chinese academic discourse system; worse still, it negatively affects the transmission of Chinese culture abroad. In a nutshell, collective cultural memory is a key to the construction of national images.

As China becomes stronger in its comprehensive national power and right to international discourse, international academic exchanges have gradually deepened and our theoretical consciousness has been awakened. "As China opens its arms to embrace the world more tightly, the voice of Chinese culture going global is becoming louder" (Xu, 2014, p. 2). Against this background, the phenomenon of "academic discourse aphasia" in our academic circle has improved, but the fundamental problem of how to become "a strong force of translation studies" has yet to be solved.

2. Cultural Memory and Translation Studies

The concept of cultural memory, which originated in German, has been translated into English, and its current Chinese definitions are varied and inconsistent. Based on previous interpretations and the study of the Assmanns (2008), we define the term as follows: cultural memory is used repeatedly by social groups through a series of symbolic representations, media communication, institutional operations, and social practices, and in the process of its formation, the memory of the past has been constructed, which has a transmission function and is commonly recognized by the members of the social group. Cultural memory includes elements such as individuals, institutions, symbols, interactions, transmissions, and constructions.

At the end of the twentieth century, the Assmanns from Germany expanded previous research on memory by proposing the concept of "cultural memory" and attempting to establish a theory of cultural memory. According to this theory, memory can be divided into short-term communicative memory and long-term cultural memory. The former includes memory in the form of oral utterances or memories shared among contemporaries, also known as the recent past, but in any case, the length of memory can only be traced back to three generations.

"Collective cultural memory is based on experience and knowledge, which is transferred from active carriers to material data carriers. In this way, memory can remain stable while running through generations" (A. Assmann, 2012, p. 45). Maurice Halbwachs, a French scholar, furthered the theory by arguing that memory has social properties and that memory emerges from the collective group and, in turn, creates the collective group, and individual memory, belonging to collective memory, is an intersection of different social memory networks. "Individual memory is an overlook to the collective memory, which changes along with our position in the collective group and adjusts itself according to our relationship with the rest of the environment" (M. Halbwachs, 2012, p. 65).

Cultural memory theory, which has a 20-year history, has a highly interdisciplinary and integrative theoretical perspective. Nevertheless, it has been neglected for a long time, and only recently is it gradually becoming a hot topic in academia. Jan Assmann, the advocate of cultural memory, holds that culture is closely related to human memory. Cultural studies has two functions: collaboration and continuity, both of which embody the synchronic and diachronic dimensions of culture (A. Assmann & J. Assmann, 2012, pp. 20–21). The collaboration aims at establishing a symbolic system that provides participants with a technical and conceptual field of communication that is synchronous. It is also acquired through communicative memory inherited from cultural texts. Continuity, with the purpose of understanding cultural history, focuses on the emergence, disappearance, and transmission of cultural forms, contents, and media. In cultural studies, continuity requires a shift from a synchronic to a diachronic perspective because it cannot be realized without cultural memory. Numerous texts that sink in the ocean of cultural memory will not survive. Continuity of cultural memory can become attainable only by separating the speech act of a text from its original setting, by interpreting, rewriting, translating, and valorizing the text in a millennial time-space. Continuity gives new life to the text, allowing the depth and profoundness of culture to be highlighted in this creative activity. Both collaboration and continuity have contents, forms, codes, interactions, and functions. They are not absolute opposites but form complementary relationships. An audience can have both individual cultural memory and collective memory. With the lapse of time, culture accumulates and persists. Take the example of a national epic: the content is to sing highly of national heroes; the form is constructed, highly fixed, and even popularly worshiped; and the epic codes may exist in diverse forms, such as inscriptions, petroglyphs, words, and other relatively recognized symbols. It may come from oral literature with its encoding system covering a series of rituals, such as chants, dances, and even sacrifices. Thus, translation and collective memory form a symbiotic relationship. That is to say, to translate a national epic into mere words is far from satisfactorily effective – the cultural memory embedded in the epic can never be revitalized without field investigations, live chants of the indigenous ethnic people, or in a word, deeply rooted in its cultural soil. Translation is cultural transmission. Cultural memory, translation, and cultural transmission are closely connected to each other. In terms of cultural transmission of translations, cultural memory becomes a highly valuable topic.

The majority of the contemporary translation studies in China are featured as an individual, fragmented, and short-term. Although they share the characteristic of synchronicity, they all lack diachronic studies from the perspective of cultural memory. To establish self-justifying Chinese translation studies, we should renew our perspectives on cultural memory and focus on diachronic research. While giving full play to our research strengths, we should also make a concerted effort to overcome our shortcomings to push the frontier of translation studies. Severe demerits still restrain our research, for many current types of research are too superficial to form a systematic understanding by probing into the ideological and cultural thoughts. In other words, these studies neither focus on the formation of ideas or theories nor explore the cultural formation, development, inheritance, dissemination, variation, shrinkage, and extinction. We should move from the synchronic to the diachronic paradigm in translation research, overcome fragmentation and arbitrariness in research, and by shifting the focus from circulation of translated texts, dissemination of literature, and culture to the construction of national image, to promote translation as a great national cause.

Intertextuality has a close relationship with cultural memory. The transition from synchronic to diachronic research is a dynamic cycle because it is inseparable from the retrieval and interpretation of cultural memory, which in turn have to be realized via intertextuality. Intertextuality, as part of cultural memory study, rests on the theoretical assumption that since literary works are produced in the presence of other texts, the self-representation of each text also takes place in a memory space consisting of diverse texts (Luo, 2014, p. 42). Taking a critical eye to texts of the past is ultimately conducive to the framework where cultural memory and science is formed and practiced (J. Assmann, 2015, p. 327). Thanks to intertextuality, we can reinterpret the works and memories of the past, and we can ceaselessly create and disseminate new works. The recollection and interpretation of a text is not only an activity of the translational subject but also a process of accumulation and shaping of cultural memory. All in all, cultural memory is the most powerful engine to boost translation research and cultural transmission.

3. Cultural Memory and "Big Translation"

As mentioned previously, cultural memory is the memory of the past shared by members of a social group and constructed through the repeated use of a series of symbolic representations, media communication, organizational operations, and social practices. In the past, however, our translations focused on individual translators' behavior and produced a segmented and fragmented cultural memory. If a global vision is taken, the impact would be very limited. To generate collective cultural memory, it is necessary to move to a grand narrative and "big translation" to enhance the influence and attract more attention with translations taken as a whole. What is assured is that the powerful countries in translation must be those that excel in "big translation" or those whose individual and collective cultural memory is distinctive.

In terms of collective cultural memory of translation, foreign scholarship has a fairly good tradition. The "big translation" of Shakespeare's works is an illustrative example. In a sense, Shakespeare is not only collective cultural memory of the U.K. but also of the world. Shakespeare's works have been translated into many languages at different times, and they are also constantly being retranslated. Shakespeare's plays and musicals have been staged all over the world, and translations or adaptations of his works are still used by people from diverse professions. For example, the theme song of the opening ceremony of the London Olympics was inspired by *The Tempest*. Movies such as *Shakespeare in Love*, *Anonymous* were adapted from his life experience. Many revenge-themed films or cartoons take as their models *Hamlet*, such as *The Lion King* and *The Banquet*. Shakespeare's works have also been exploited as the source for various musical pieces, including Berlioz's *The Death of Orfeo*, an interpretation of the theme of *Hamlet*; Quilt's *Three Songs of Shakespeare* based on Shakespeare's *Twelfth Night*; and *Wedding March* by Mendelssohn, Liszt, and Horowitz, which originates from *A Midsummer Night's Dream*. The shared feature of these examples is to take a particular feature of the original and reinterpret or re-represent it in another form, creating a new translation. These incessant rewritings and re-representations make cultural memory more real, profound, and comprehensive. To achieve this goal, an enduring passion and sense of sustainable development are indispensable. Another example is the study of Bai Juyi (白居易), a renowned Chinese poet of the Tang Dynasty, who has been more deeply studied in Japan than in China. Bai's poems, favored by the Japanese, are often borrowed or imitated in Japan. Literary creative practice in Japan takes a line from Bai's poems (くだいわか or Kudaiwaka) and interprets or represents it continuously to create new poems. In a sense, the illustrative form of "Kudaiwaka" is a form of "big translation," for it plays an important role in promoting Bai Juyi to "go into" Japanese culture and become Japanese cultural memory.

What is "big translation"? It is a set of collective and coordinated translation activities, including the three types of translation proposed by Jacobson, namely, intralingual translation, interlingual translation, and intersemiotic translation (Jacobson, 2000, p. 113). With the ultimate goal of the effectiveness of textual and cultural transmission, "big translation" gives priority to the interaction and constructiveness among various translations to establish a far-reaching collective cultural memory, to accept literary works as global classics through imitation, adaptation, retranslation, and adaptation. Canonization and globalization are the dual touchstones of "big translation." Translation and cultural transmission are important research topics in the context of globalization. Since differences exist in culture, linguistic structure, and way of thinking, cultural transmission does not go smoothly as conflicts and misunderstandings always occur from time to time. Many earlier translations of Chinese classics were misunderstood and mistranslated to varying degrees due to the translators' inability to fully understand the Chinese language and culture. However, because of the limited conditions of those times, these translations were somehow accepted. But if these misunderstandings and mistranslations are not eliminated or corrected, Chinese cultural memory will be distorted, and China's national image construction and cultural transmission will be hindered. With the implementation of the Belt and Road Initiative, "big translation" will play an inestimable role in deepening cultural exchanges and promoting the transmission of Chinese culture. As "the Belt and Road Initiative" indicates, translation would undertake the mission to pave the way. However, the challenging tasks confronted by translators and translation researchers include how to promote Chinese culture and literature to the world, how to link Chinese literature with foreign literature via translations, and how to live together in peace, enjoying prosperity and development. It is extremely necessary to diversify the perspectives of translation studies – anthropology, folklore, religion, psychology, mythology, and narratology should all be incorporated to function in "big translation"; thus translation and cultural transmission can be closely linked, and significant breakthroughs can be made in terms of theory and methodology to gain insights into "big translation", big data, and big vision, all of which are key issues for us to think about.

"Big translation" must be based on a broad vision to create an ideal situation; for that, a broad vision presupposes an international, global, hypertextual, and interdisciplinary level to approach translation – it implies not only synchronic translation and research in various fields, such as politics, economics, technology, and culture, but also diachronic researches of translations of classics, moreover, via synchronic and diachronic translation researches, the collective cultural memory of national translation. A big vision indicates that translation resources should be searched geographically to overcome the insufficiency and improve the integrity of translation research. The American scholar Sandra Bermann also pointed out,

> The present (translation) research has been deepened and become burgeoning, interdisciplinary studies have been diverse, such as literary texts between languages and cultures, links between poetry and dance performance, movie and novel, photography and essay, academic expression and thinking mode, etc.
> (Bermann, 2009, p. 434)

A broad vision allows translation scholars to avoid the influence of "cultural centrism", to eliminate blind spots in translation studies, and shift our attention to those that have been considered trivial or even marginal "because it is only in such an expansive, non-homogeneous geography that some fundamental principles of cultural history become effective" (Apter, 2008, p. 592).

"Big translation" is about collective, collaborative, multi-semiotic translational activities within a broad vision, and it involves macroscopic lingual-semiotic translation to form a diachronic cultural memory. Elucidating and interpreting Chinese classics is particularly important in translation. "Big translation" repeatedly interprets and constantly illustrates the existing textual symbols so as to achieve recreation and gain a more profound understanding. "Global concern," an essential feature of "big translation," means translational activities are not specific or focused but are inclusive and scattering. "Lingual-semiotic" implies that translation is not only linguistic but also symbolic or, more precisely, a combination of both. The sensory effect of "big translation" is mosaic, so a panorama cannot be attained without a view from a distance. It is also symphonic. Only through coordination and collective efforts can the musical piece be played to its fullest extent. Such collaboration can eventually produce collective cultural memory. Therefore, in this sense, in order to increase the speed and effect of cultural transmission and nurture a collective cultural memory, we should construct lingual-semiotic translation in a global view to achieve multi-role, multimedia, and lasting effects. The cultural transmission requires cross-over participants, such as translators, writers, critics, artists, directors, etc., whose works can be translated works, literary creations, criticism, music, drama, film, etc. Cultural transmission of "big translation" depends on various carriers inclusive of books, audiovisual products stage, internet, etc. In a word, a multi-perspective and collaborative translation can have a tremendously powerful effect. "Big translation" is both interdisciplinary and inter-semiotic. The ultimate purpose of "big translation" determines that cultural transmission is not only our current research project but will always be an important one. The interpretation, translation, and cultural images of Chinese classics have needed unremitting efforts for generations to enhance the promptness and effect of cultural transmission and ultimately promote the formation of collective cultural memory.

4. Collective Cultural Memory Generated by "Big Translation"

Cultural memory, as a new engine of translation studies, will greatly promote translation and translation studies in China. Classics are excellent works that are repeatedly interpreted, read, appreciated by passionate souls, and inherited for generations. Cultural memory is built on classics, while classics depend on interpretations, and interpretations are due to the circulation of theory. The circular relationship between classics, interpretations, and theories gives rise to collective and national cultural memory. Writers (artists), translators, and critics work together on an original text; the diachronic and synchronic textual semiotics ferment in the new era; and a renewed life of the text is gained via "big translation".

Shanhai Jing (《山海經》), a Chinese classic full of myths and legends in the pre-Qin period (before 221 bc), is the oldest geographic book. It mainly describes ancient geography, natural resources, mythology, witchcraft, religion, as well as ancient history, medicine, folk customs, and ethnic groups. Many Chinese cultural memories, such as Jingwei Tianhai (精衛填海, bird Jingwei trying to fill up the sea with pebbles), Nüwa Butian (女媧補天, Goddess Nüwa Patches up the Sky), and Kuafu Zhuiri (夸父追日, Giant Kuafu Races with the Sun) can be traced back in this book. *Shanhai Jing* included originally both pictures and texts; at least some parts were illustrated with pictures. Later, the ancient pictures were lost. Fortunately, its texts survived and were circulated (Ma, 2000, p. 20). *Shanhai Jing* signals the starting point of cultural memory in Chinese mythologies. Since the stories are fragmented, lacking a temporal narrative line, and short of reasoning and evolution of discourses, *Shanhai Jing* is essentially a static spatial narrative work. Yuan Ke commented, "There are few myths with complete plots in *Shanhai Jing*. Upon checking, there are only seven or eight stories" (Yuan, 1988, p. 21). Due to the lack of a temporal narrative line, relocating the independent spatial narrative or changing the atmosphere will not hinder the acceptance of the narrative. However, under such circumstances, *Shanhai Jing may* present obstacles for Western readers accustomed to works in chronological order. Other specifications for impressive plots and transitional links in a translated work would not attract foreign readers; thus, a collective cultural memory can never be formed. Worse still, textual symbols, which are merely a medium for the inheritance and transmission of cultural memory, have their limitations. Readers need to know the cultural implications of *Shanhai Jing* by reading illustrated versions. Reading the translation of its textual version alone may diminish or distort the cultural connotations. Considering this, we should give priority to the collective cultural memory to build a grand narrative system of Chinese myths via "big translation."

In "big translation," temporal narration can be supplemented and elucidated by the interpretation of the textual symbols. "Big translation" can even offer ordinary readers and children the opportunity to become familiar with ancient myth from different perspectives and with different symbols. Continuous interpretations of classics are essential for the heritage and transmission of cultural memory. In addition to intralingual translations, *Shanhai Jing* also has interlingual and intersemiotic translations. For example, *The Legend of Mountains and Seas* (《山海經傳》), the play by Gao Xingjian (高行健) published in 1992 to outline a genealogy of ancient Chinese mythologies, is an innovation and development of the narrative system of Chinese mythology. At Hong Kong Arts Festival in 2012, director Lin Zhaohua (林兆華) presented Gao Xingjian's play to the audience and created a sensation in literary and art circles. In fact, *The Legend of Mountains and Seas* was staged by Hong Kong director Cai Xichang (蔡錫昌) in 2008, but Lin followed Gao's advice to incorporate traditional folk arts, such as Huayin Laoqiang (華陰老腔, the old tone of Huayin in Shaanxi Province) and the folk masks of Guizhou Province (Opera Culture Web 2012). As different media have their own merits and demerits, the vitality of cultural memory calls for comprehensive and multi-perspective cooperation to achieve mutual benefits. Therefore, different translation forms of *Shanhai Jing* are expected, including the illustrated version, the symphonic version, and even the TV series version. From intralingual, interlingual, to inter-semiotic translation, they fuse as a whole via diverse media to form "big translation." A work may become a classic, form a collective cultural memory, and enjoy global popularity once it is interpreted and re-represented by generations. In addition, *Shanhai Jing* also boasts songs, films, picture albums, etc. In her doctoral dissertation, Wang Min conducted a multimodal intertextuality study on the mythology of *Shanhai Jing*, which includes textual close reading, comparative analysis of multiple languages and profound thinking on the translation of Chinese mythologies. It is truly a significant study (Wang, 2019).

Haishanghua Liezhuan (《海上花列傳》, The Sing-song Girls of Shanghai) (Han, 2005) was a novel written by Han Bangqing (韓邦慶) in the late Qing Dynasty. It was first serialized in a magazine and then assembled into a book. Written in Wu dialect, the book is China's first dialectal novel. Han's panoramic view of brothels in Shanghai at the end of the Qing Dynasty involves contemporary officials and businessmen. Due to the Wu dialect, the distribution of the work is rather limited. It is said that this novel was obscure at first but gradually gained some popularity thanks to the recommendation of Lu Xun and Hu Shi. In the 1950s, Eileen Chang translated the book from the Wu dialect into Mandarin, thus completing the intralingual translation. Later many new editions of the book appeared, with diverse titles, such as *Haishang Hua* (海上花), *Haishang Huakai* (海上花開), and *Haishang Hualuo* (海上花落), etc. These intralingual translations are actually a process of developing, representing, and interpreting the cultural memory of the source. Later, Eileen Chang went to the United States and translated the novel into English in the 1980s. In 1998, Hou Hsiao-hsien (侯孝賢) and Zhang Fan (張凡) directed the film Haishang Hua (《海上花》, *Flowers of Shanghai*) with the novel as the source text, starred by Tony Leung (梁朝偉), Michelle Monique Reis (李嘉欣), Carina Lau (劉嘉玲), and other famous actors. Later, Kong Huiyi (孔慧怡) of the Chinese University of Hong Kong retranslated Eileen Chang's version with an English introduction. This retranslated *The Sing-Song Girls of Shanghai* published by Columbia University Press in 2005 became a sensation. *The Sing-Song Girls of Shanghai* was originally a novel in the Wu dialect describing Shanghai society and culture in a particular period. However, through the combined efforts of generations to re-represent it in various forms of lingual-semiotic translations and on different carriers, it has gained popularity throughout the country and even reached the outside world. This is what the author advocates as "big translation." Interpretation, reproduction, re-representation and recreation give fresh memory to the work, which is to be fully retained and become the collective cultural memory. As an old saying goes, "When things reach their extremes, change occurs; after change they evolve smoothly, and thus they are preserved for a long time." Both the vitality of works and the formation of cultural memory are inseparable from change and recreation – this is the potential effect in lingual-semiotic translation from a macroscopic perspective.

5. Conclusion

"Big translation" and cultural memory, with Chinese translation and culture as the background, are holistic, multi-perspective, and comprehensive strategic concepts. They are interdisciplinary, humanistic hereditary, and sustainable in development. It is especially important to strengthen cultural self-confidence and cultural self-consciousness in cultural transmission. Cultural self-consciousness "means that people living in a certain culture have a full knowledge of their culture, are familiar with its origin, formation process, features and tendency, but do not have any idea in blind 'cultural reclamation'" (Fei, 2016, p. 190). Cultural self-consciousness in translation involves a clear understanding of one's own culture and history, a thorough comprehension of the culture and mindset of the target languages, and the ability to conduct research and take up translation with a contrastive approach. However, translation studies cannot thrive if cultural self-confidence functions alone, for it is inseparable from cultural self-awareness. To build China's collective cultural memory, a group of scholars must work tirelessly with determination and passion to interpret, illustrate, and translate Chinese classics and literary works and pass them down from generation to generation.

Nowadays, China's economy is developing steadily, and national investment in humanistic research is on the increase. Scholars engaged in literary, cultural, and translation studies should seize the opportunity, harbor a big vision, collect big data, and create "big translation" to construct China's collective cultural memory, cultivate China's own translation studies, promote dialogue and cooperation between China and the West in translation research, and fulfill the mission of Chinese culture "going global" before being accepted and absorbed by foreign cultures to share Chinese wisdom with the world.

Note

1 Supported by "Research on the Transmission and Evaluation Mechanism of English Translations of Chinese Classics," Key Project of the National Social Science Fund of China, 2015 (Grant No. 15AYY001).

References

Apter, E. S. (2008). Untranslatables: A world system. *New Literary History*, *39*(3), 581–598. https://doi.org/10.1353/nlh.0.0055

Assmann, A. (2008). Cannon and archive. In A. Erll, A. Nünning, & S. B. Young (Eds.), *Cultural memory studies: An international and interdisciplinary handbook*. Walter de Gruyter.

Assmann, A. (2012). Jiyi de sange weidu: shenjing weidu, shehui weidu, wenhuaweidu 记忆的三个维度：神经维度、社会维度、文化维度. In A. Erll. & Feng Yalin (Eds.), *Materialbuch zur gedachtnisforschung* 文化记忆理论读本. Peking University Press.

Assmann, A. & J. Assmann. (2012). Zuori chongxian — meijie yu shehui jiyi昨日重现——媒介与社会记忆. In A. Erll. & Feng Yalin (Eds.), *Materialbuch zur gedachtnisforschung* 文化记忆理论读本. Peking University Press.

Assmann, J. (2015). Das kulturelle gedachtnis: schrift, erinnerung und politische identitat in fruhen hochkulturen 文化记忆：早期高级文化中的文字/回忆和政治身份. Jin Shoufu & Huang Xiaochen Trans. Peking University Press.

Assmann, J. (2008). Communicative and cultural memory. In A. Erll, A. Nünning, & S. B. Young (Eds.), *Cultural memory studies: An international and interdisciplinary handbook*. Walter de Gruyter.

Bermann, S. (2009). Working in the and zone: Comparative literature and translation. *Comparative Literature*, *61*(4), 432–446.

Cao, S. 曹顺庆. (1996). Wenlun shiyuzheng yu wenhua bingtai 文论失语症与文化病态. *Literary and Artistic Contention* 文艺争鸣, (2), 50–58.

Fei, X. 费孝通. (2016). *Culture and Cultural Self-Awareness*. Qunyan Press.

Halbwachs, M. (2012). Jiti jiyi yu geti jiyi 集体记忆与个体记忆. In A. Erll & Feng Yalin (Eds.), *Materialbuch zur gedachtnisforschung* 文化记忆理论读本. Peking University Press.

Han, B. (2005). *The sing-song girls of Shanghai*. Columbia University Press.
Huang, Y. 黄友义. (2015). Zhongguo zhandao le guoji wutai zhongyang women ruhe fanyi 中国站到了国际舞台中央，我们如何翻译. *Chinese Translators Journal* 中国翻译, (5), 5–7.
Jacobson, R. (2000). On linguistic aspects of translation. In L. Venuti (Ed.), *The translation studies reader*. Routledge.
Luo, X. 罗新璋. (1983). Woguo zicheng tixi de fanyi lilun 我国自成体系的翻译理论. *Chinese Translators Journal* 中国翻译, (7), 9–13.
Luo, X. 罗选民. (2012). Guanyu fany yu zhongguo xiandai xing de sikao 关于翻译与中国现代性的思考. *Foreign Languages in China* 中国外语, (2), 1–1.
Luo, X. 罗选民. (2014). Wenhua jiyi yu fanyi yanjiu 文化记忆与翻译研究. *Foreign Languages in China* 中国外语, (3), 1–1.
Luo, X. 罗选民. (2016). Cong yingyi dao yijie: Luxun de fany yu zhongguo xiandai xing 从"硬译"到"易解"：鲁迅的翻译与中国现代性. *Chinese Translators Journal* 中国翻译, (5), 32–37.
Luo, X. (2017). Cultural memory and big translation. *Asia Pacific Translation and Intercultural Studies*, 4(1), 1–2.
Lv, J. (2014). Current translation studies in China: Predicament and solution. *Shanghai Journal of Translators*, (3), 1–6.
Ma, C. (2000). Pictures in the classics of mountains and seas: Look for another part of the book. *Literary Heritage*, (6), 19–29.
Opera Culture Web. (2012, February 25). *Gao Xingjian's of Mountains and Seas directed by Lin Zhaohua*. Retrieved from www.xiquwenhua.net/xiqudaquan/xinwen/2012/26121.html
Tan, Z. (2012). Chinese translation studies: Retrospect, reflection and prospect. *Chinese Translators Journal*, (4), 7–9.
Wang, M. (2019). *A study on the translation of Chinese mythology in early Europe*. Beijing: Tsinghua University.
Xu, J. (2014). Face to history and reality: Two suggestions on translation studies in the new era. *Journal of Foreign Languages*, (3), 2–3.
Yuan, K. (1988). *History of Chinese mythology*. Shanghai: Shanghai Literature & Art Publishing House.
Zhang, B., & Jiang, Q. (1997). Reflections on the establishment of Chinese translation studies. *Chinese Translators Journal*, (2), 7–9.

12 The Function of Literary and Cultural Communication of English

Ning Wang

When we look at the issue of globalization from the perspective of culture, we cannot avoid dealing with an inevitable language problem, namely, the popularization of English and the spread and promotion of Western culture and humanities in the world through this lingua franca. As Chinese scholars, we all know that Chinese culture and literature are far from being known in the world, although it has a great heritage and a long history, because Chinese is very difficult to master and does not occupy a dominant position. Since we do not deny the fact that we live in an age of globalization, we should recognize that the impact of globalization on culture is largely achieved through the medium of language. English undoubtedly functions as a lingua franca in the age of globalization. The enormous impact of globalization on the mass media exerts tremendous pressure on those outside the English-speaking world: in the present and in the future, it would be extremely difficult for our survival and work efficiency not to know English, the language of the global age. In this chapter, I will mainly focus on the translation and dissemination of Chinese literature and culture in the English-speaking world after looking at the function of English in global communication.

Globalization and the Formation of Global Englishes

It is true that globalization has made such a strong impact on various national cultures that it is beyond one's expectations and resistance. Today when we see a Spanish girl who has settled down in Australia wearing an Italian suit with an American-made gum in her mouth and sitting in a Benz driven by a Vietnamese Australian come to eat in a well-decorated Chinese restaurant, we will by no means be astonished. For in such a vast "global village," the interpenetration of different cultures is no longer curious. Even in such English-speaking postcolonial countries as Canada and Australia characterized by cultural diversity with the majority of the population composed of immigrants, we can still easily find the influence made by other cultures and languages on the mainstream culture there. Thus, in those postcolonial countries, there is on the one hand large-scale aggression and deep-going penetration of strong cultures into weak cultures, but on the other hand, there is also the attempt of anti-penetration and resistance of weak cultures to strong cultures. The so-called "glocalization" is such an effective strategy that finds particular embodiment in constructing their national and cultural identity or identities. Language as a major means of cultural communication is more forcefully affected by the advent of globalization. Fortunately, to the English-speaking people, the influence of globalization on culture to a great extent is helpful to the popularization of English, which has in the past centuries "become a lingua franca":

> In virtually every country in the world, foreigners are learning English to enable them to speak across frontiers in a language most likely to be understood by others. In practice, however, such learners soon discover that learning of English is part of a process of putting out of mind their own language. As this is virtually impossible, the varieties of English spoken by Indians, Nigerians, Japanese, Russians, Germans, and so on, tend to be a remarkably different one from the other, however closely they are based on the two main learning models, American English and British English. Foreign sounds and unfamiliar constructions abound in any of these internationalized varieties of English.
>
> (Burchfield, 2002, & Kirkpatrick, 2007)

That is, using English for communication worldwide has also caused variations of the language, and by and by, these varieties of English will make and have probably already made it possible for a global English or global Englishes to come into being (Wang, 2010). When people of all countries are learning the English language, they, with it as their mother tongue, feel particularly proud. They do not have to spend much time mastering another language, nor do they have any difficulty communicating with people outside of their countries in their native language. Along with the popularization of English worldwide, however, another implied crisis is gradually emerging: confronted with the large-scale aggression of the American English in the age of globalization, the once-dominant "King's English" or "Queen's English" used by British people has now been more or less "marginalized." English, which used to be spoken by British people chiefly, has now been marked with so many indigenous characteristics that it can no longer be viewed as a national language only. The disappearance of the boundary of English on the one hand enabled it to become the most important lingua franca, but on the other hand, it has also caused the loss of its identity as a national language. This is probably a paradox with which we cannot but be confronted.

Obviously, any language, if intending to preserve its eternal vitality, should be in a dynamic state of development and evolution, always being able to absorb external elements. It is particularly true of the English language. When the Norman conquest took place in 1066, it enabled large numbers of French words to come into English, which enlarged and enriched the English vocabulary. From today's point of view, the strong life-force of English is partly due to the fact that the British Empire had been a hegemonic power where the sun never set before the end of the nineteenth century. Its citizens could communicate with local people in their mother tongue wherever they traveled or lived. They could even find the rise and fall of their national flag at any time in almost any place on the earth. This undoubtedly helped to establish the hegemonic position of English in the world. In the twentieth century, along with the gradual weakening of the British Empire and the independence of large numbers of its former colonies, the country was severely challenged by other hegemonies. In speaking of language, such popular languages as French, German, Spanish, Arabic, Chinese, and Russian have once attempted to expand their boundaries by moving among the major world languages. But their attempts were all shadowed by the hegemonic power of the United States and Great Britain. Instead of being shaken, the position of English has become all the more established. English, as the most widely used international language, actually functions as a lingua franca for people from different countries or regions to communicate, especially in the age of globalization. Compared with its forceful influence and wide popularization, the so-called Esperanto is nothing but an artificial language invented by a few cultural utopianists. Then there arises a question: why does this phenomenon appear? This is what we, as non-English-speaking scholars, should confront and analyze historically and theoretically.

First of all, cultural colonization is a rather long process. Having spent much time and energy in conquering a small and weak nation, the colonialists would immediately think of colonizing it culturally, which usually needs much longer time and greater energy, and sometimes even more efforts made by generations of people. Language, as a major means of conveying cultural conventions, is of great importance, and it is at once caught on the horizon of the colonialists. But it is always a hard task to totally change its fixed means of communication. In this aspect, English has succeeded in becoming the official language and even the mother tongue of quite a few colonies. Once a language became a nation's cultural convention and major means of expression, its function could hardly change. We can easily find the colonial signs of linguistic influence in such countries or regions as South Africa, Indonesia, India, Pakistan, and China's Hong Kong, Macau, and Taiwan. Therefore, even when colonies became independent one after another and the British Empire collapsed, the dominant position of English was still very steady. But on the other hand, it has largely been mixed up with those ethnic languages and dialects forming different varieties of English or "English(es)" of indigenous characteristics. We call these "world Englishes" or "global Englishes" (Singh et al., 2002). which has severely deconstructed the hegemonic position of "standard" English. And the advent of globalization has undoubtedly remapped the world language system with the originally popular languages even more popular and the weak languages either weaker or even extinguished. This fact just indicates the two poles of cultural globalization: cultural homogenization and cultural diversity. In this way, we should adopt a dialectical attitude toward cultural globalization: taking into consideration the possible cultural homogenization for the purpose of protecting our own national culture without neglecting the inevitable cultural plurality and diversity.

Second, some nation-states' "self-colonization" has also helped to form the hegemonic status of English. Just as Gayatri C. Spivak has pertinently pointed out, "There is often a certain loss of style in the descent or shift from the high culture of nationalism within territorial imperialism to that search for 'national identity' that confuses religion, culture, and ideology in the newly independent nation" (Spivak, 1999, p. 64). For a rising developing country to realize its own nation's modernization should, first of all, identify itself with those developed Western powers. The "overall Westernization" in modern China has proved the fact: in order to throw off the yoke of the feudal tradition and destroy the old culture and its communicating means, such May 4th leaders as Lu Xun, Hu Shi, and Liang Qichao once called for the large-scale translation of Western academic trends and literary works for the purpose of giving birth to a new modern Chinese language and its literary discourse. Obviously, the translation of most of the Western works into Chinese was, to a large extent, fulfilled by means of English, which inevitably led to the tendency of "Europeanization" or "Westernization" of both Chinese language and culture. Furthermore, these Chinese writers, in the process of promoting Chinese culture and literature toward the goal of modernity, gradually realized the importance of English, so quite a number of the writers and critics had a good knowledge or ability of English, at least in reading. Toward the end of World War II, the hegemony of English had already come into being. Although the major foreign language taught in China's institutions of higher learning was once Russian in the years following the founding of the People's Republic of China in 1949, immediately after the Cultural Revolution, this coexistence of Russian and English in China's university curriculum changed with English dominating in China's foreign language teaching. In the past decades when China wanted to apply for hosting the Olympic Games in 2008, it attached the greatest importance to the popularization of English, viewing it as one of the most inevitable abilities for university professors and government officials (Wang, 2000). Even taxi drivers in Beijing were also encouraged to learn some English so that they could directly communicate with athletes from different countries or regions. It is true that frantically promoting and popularizing English in a large country of 1.4 billion people has undoubtedly helped English to become the most frequently used lingua franca. Some people regard this practice as a sort of "self-colonization," but to me, its strong and weak points will be evaluated by future historians.

Third, and perhaps most importantly, due to the rise of the United States and its overall dominance in the world economy, politics, and culture, the popularization of English has once again been promoted. In China today, when we come to the counters of foreign languages in any book shops, we will easily come across textbooks published in the United States, which shadows those published in Britain and other English-speaking countries. Along with the prevalence of the typical American cultural phenomena like McDonald's and Hollywood, the young intellectuals are made to believe that globalization is nothing but Westernization, and Westernization means Americanization, as the United States stands at the forefront of the developed Western countries. To identify with the United States, the only effective means is to first learn English well so as to study in the United States.[1] The series of attempts have finally helped the American English to replace the "King's English" or "Queen's English," marginalizing the latter while largely expanding the boundary of the former. In this way, American English, as the newly rising linguistic power, starts to influence and penetrate into other "Englishes" or other minor languages.

At the present, the process of cultural globalization has been speeded up with the triumph of economic globalization, which finds particular embodiment in the popularization of Internet. Whether or not we recognize this fact it has already permeated in all aspects of our cultural and literary production as well as theory and criticism. In the process of cultural globalization, English is most benefited as it has been more popularized with the help of Internet. However, English, as the most popular language on the Internet, is now challenged by another emerging phenomenon: the rise of Chinese. As for this, I have already discussed it elsewhere (Wang, 2010).

The Function of Cultural Communication of English

As a Chinese humanities scholar, or more specifically, a scholar of English and comparative literature, I am more concerned about how Chinese literature and culture are translated and disseminated in the English-speaking world. Since academic research in China is becoming more and more international or global, the internationalization of China's humanities cannot be achieved without the intermediary of English. Similarly, English has been playing the role of the lingua franca, always in a dominant position in international academia and cultural communication. Chinese culture going global more or less means going to the English-speaking world first. Many scientists have long regarded English as the only means of communicating with the international academic community and promoting their research results. But on the other hand, a few people, especially some humanistic intellectuals who are engaged in the study of traditional Chinese culture, are very much worried about the spread and penetration of English in the era of globalization. They even worry that the influence of English may damage China's national and cultural identity and even make the Chinese discourse of literary and cultural studies "colonized." Several years ago, some conservatives even proposed removing English from China's national college entrance examination. Until now, such voices have still seemed to grow, leading to a direct consequence that China's college English graduates have encountered difficulties in employment. What is even worse is, some representatives of the National People's Congress and members of the Chinese People's Political Consultative Conference who have strong nationalistic sentiments have also advocated eliminating English from the national entrance examination, or at least reducing its share of the overall score.

It is true that Western culture has penetrated into China's literary and cultural critical discourse through the medium of English, making Chinese literary and cultural theory full of "Westernized" terms and concepts. But according to the Marxist view, the development of culture does not necessarily have to be in direct proportion to the development of the economy, and economically developed countries and regions may not necessarily produce excellent cultural and artistic works, so it is possible that immortal artworks will emerge in countries and regions with relatively backward economies but exceptionally developed imaginations of writers and artists, which has been borne out by the rise of Latin American "explosive literature" and the creative practices of some Third World or postcolonial diaspora writers who have won Nobel Prize in Literature during the past two decades. Therefore, in terms of cultural communication, our strategy of international integration does not necessarily mean the integration of Western theory but means equal dialogue Chinese scholars will have with the latter. At present, the phenomenon of the so-called "aphasia" in Chinese cultural and literary criticism is only temporary and relative. The phenomenon of "aphasia" is, to a large extent, due to the fact that those theorists know so little about the international frontiers of theoretical subjects that even with the intermediary of translation, it will still be difficult to have an equal dialogue with the Western and international counterparts. So how shall we overcome this difficulty?

Since English has become an international language used all over the world, and Chinese cannot be popularized among more countries and nations in a short period of time except for China and a few Chinese-speaking countries or regions, if we can make use of English as a powerful media to make our own voice heard and construct our own research discourse in international academia, it will certainly play a more positive role in the spread and promotion of Chinese cultural ideas around the world. At present, in the era of globalization, with the growing strength of China's comprehensive national power, the call for the construction or reconstruction of China's national image is growing louder and louder. Since the image of China that we construct or reconstruct in international academic circles is mainly for foreigners to see, it is imperative for us to use the world's common language to tell China's story well. That Chinese writer Mo Yan won Nobel Prize in Literature in 2012 is largely because his main English translator, Howard Goldblatt, used beautiful and idiomatic English to retell his stories and almost embellished Mo Yan's language, making his work more accessible to the English-speaking readers. However, many contemporary Chinese writers who are as well-known as Mo Yan have missed out on the Nobel Prize largely for lack of an excellent translator like Goldblatt although their domestic popularity is better than Mo Yan (Wang, 2014). We could even further affirm that without Goldblatt's superb English translation of Mo Yan's major novels, plus Anna Chen's equally superb Swedish translation of his major works, Mo Yan would not have won the prestigious Nobel Prize, or at least his prize-winning would have been postponed for years.

Thus, worries about English hegemony are not confined to Chinese culture. With the popularization of English, the study of culture and national identity has attracted more and more attention from scholars in the East and the West. As Homi Bhabha's hybrid theory shows, people's ethnic and cultural identities have become increasingly blurred with the advent of cultural travel and communication in the age of globalization, in which cultural translation plays an important role (Bhabha, 1994). Similarly, Chinese and Western scholars with dual identities and international visibility can also play a role in both Eastern and Western academic fields. Due to their frequent international intercourse and activities, their linguistic identity is naturally ambiguous. English is in fact the only means by which they could communicate with the outside world. They must write their most important academic works in English for publication in leading international journals or with prestigious publishing houses in order to gain recognition in the Western and international academic community. For this phenomenon, we should pay particular attention to the function of English in cultural communication because it also occupies an important position in the field of literary and cultural studies.

But on the other hand, the impact of globalization on culture is also reflected in its impact on the English language itself. The English we use today is not King's English or Queen's English as it once was, but rather, global English(es) with indigenous characteristics, which have taken on colonial and Third World slang and nonstandard pronunciation. The phenomenon of people all over the world learning English, in fact, to some extent, mercilessly dispels the hegemony of English, which leads to the promiscuity and variability of English, thus resulting in the multicultural development trend. There is no doubt that one of the obvious effects of globalization on languages is the redrawing of the world's language system: languages that were once powerful are becoming more powerful, and languages that were previously in a weak position have either died out or are on the verge of death in the wave of globalization. As Chinese humanities scholars, we may be more concerned about the status and future of our own language, the Chinese language. It is well-known that Chinese is the most widely spoken language in the world as the mother tongue, which is also benefited from globalization. According to Francis Fukuyama, a Japanese American theorist, China is the biggest winner of globalization (Yu, 2011), not only in terms of its economic rise and its emergence as a political power but also in terms of its language and culture. Indeed, the Chinese language and culture have also benefited from globalization. Chinese scholars of literature also pay particular attention to Anglo-American literature, especially English literature. The study of English literature in the Chinese context not only enables Chinese scholars to contribute to the study of international English literature but also strengthens the relationship between Chinese and English literature.

In the Chinese literary world, the late scholar Wang Zuoliang's (1916–1995) contribution to promoting English literature has been very phenomenal. He once commented on the status of English literature in world literature by highlighting the English language: the worldwide influence of English literature is first of all due to the expansion and popularization of English as a universal language. No literature in any language has had the global impact of English literature, above all because English is the most popular language in the world. No other language in the history of the world has achieved this level of coverage and utilization rate (Wang, 2016b, pp. 759–760). Indeed, since literature is the art of language and language is the carrier of literary expression, what is the status of English literature in the English-speaking world? According to Wang's investigation and analysis, although in the 20th century, American literature became more influential and its impact spread all over the world, yet English literature did not decline because of this. "English literature is far from being an insignificant regional literature, but still retains its worldwide influence" (Wang, 2016a, p. 760). The reasons are embodied in the following five aspects: first, "its strong and far-reaching historical influence still exists"; second, "English literature is still developing and full of creativity, which is manifested in the continuous activity of drama, the repetition of famous novels and the great masters in the age of poetry. The pragmatic spirit of literary theory and the concern for the overall cultural situation is manifested in this literature's continuous concern for the fate of mankind and the future of the world and its continuous exploration of art"; third, "Britain has a qualitative advantage in the cause of communication," that is, the British publishing industry is very developed, which undoubtedly plays an important role in the dissemination of English literature in the English-speaking world; fourth, "In former British colonies around the world, there is an important body of work by local writers in English, some of which has an impact far beyond the region. These writers were mainly influenced by English literature, and to a certain extent, their works have also influenced English literature"; fifth, the advantages of English as the world's common language (Wang, 2016a, pp. 760–765). These judgments were made before the formation of the concept of "global English" in the era of globalization, and certainly contributed to the discussion of cultural globalization, "global English" and world literature by Chinese scholars.

Wang Zuoliang also has his own unique views on how Chinese scholars should write the history of English literature, and it is these critical comments from all sides that greatly enrich the understanding of a literary work: "Although the works were written in one country, the interpretations come from all over the world, and here the cosmopolitan nature of literature is revealed" (Wang, 2016b, pp. 6–7). I should say that it is thanks to the combined efforts of scholars of English literature around the world that English literature today enjoys worldwide influence and prestige. It is obvious that the previous insightful ideas have important implications for China's scholars of comparative and world literature.

Take the discipline of comparative literature as another example. It is one of the most international disciplines in the humanities in China today, although it was imported to China from the West. If we accept the first phase of Chinese comparative literature studies as reception and influence studies, especially how Western literature affects Chinese literature, then we will enter the second phase, that is, we should pay more attention to the translation and critical reception of Chinese culture and literature in the world. In this way, it is more important to publish our research results in English and introduce the glorious heritage of Chinese culture and its excellent literary works to the world. Only by this will more and more Westerners be able to understand China and its culture without being misled by the writings of some scholars with hostile attitudes toward China, who, out of ignorance or prejudice, misunderstand or even misinterpret China. In this sense, the critique of cultural decolonization does not necessarily mean the elimination of the spread and improvement of English and its teaching, because Chinese culture has not been colonized. There is no contradiction between the popularization of English and the construction of Chinese literary critical discourse.

Publishing Internationally and Enabling Chinese Culture to Go Global

In the summer of 1983, Indian American literary critic and postcolonial theorist Gayatri Spivak delivered an important but controversial speech, which was later re-titled "Can the Subaltern Speak?", at the Institute on "Marxist Interpretations of Culture: Limits, Frontiers, Boundaries" (Spivak, 1985). In that eloquent and thought-provoking speech, Spivak wants to argue that those from the lower classes, especially from the so-called Third World countries, have long been unable to utter their voices at international forums. Sometimes, even if they do intend to speak, they cannot be "heard" or "acknowledged." What they could do is to find some agencies through which they could utter their voices in a round way. It is true that China has long been a Third World country although it is in recent years undergoing a sort of "deporvertizing" and "de-Third-Worldizing" experience (Wang, 2015a). So if we apply her speech to describing the state of international China studies at the time, it is particularly true, especially in the humanities. In this sense, we might well change the title of her speech to "Can the Chinese Speak on the International Forum?" in the Chinese and international context. In my opinion, Chinese scholars could certainly speak, even in the past, but they did not have the chance to speak. Or no one wanted to listen to them speaking even if they did have the chance to utter their voices, for they could not be heard or even overlooked. Let alone make any influence. What they could do is to speak to themselves or speak among themselves.

That has long been the state of China studies in the West. During those years, when we took up an English language journal of China studies, we could hardly find a Chinese name as the author. Even if we occasionally find a Chinese name, he or she was either from Hong Kong or Taiwan or was a Chinese diaspora living in a Western country. Domestic Chinese academics did indeed hardly have any chance to utter their voices at international forums, especially in the humanities and social sciences, although many of the Chinese scientists had already aimed at the most advanced scientific research in the world and started to publish in leading international journals.

In contrast, as we all know, modern China has always been famous for opening to the outside world. During the May Fourth period, there was even a famous slogan "nalaizhuyi" (grabbism) by Lu Xun, that is, grabbing everything useful to solve the problems in the then Chinese society. In the mid-1980s, China was actually in a most open state. During the time, almost all the cutting-edge Western academic works and literary writings had been translated into Chinese, mostly by green hands. I myself, as a young humanities intellectual and literary scholar then, joined in translating almost all the major Western cultural theories into Chinese. With our great effort made to introduce and translate Western theories and cultural trends, there even appeared a so-called "Nietzsche fad," "Sartre fad," and "Freud fad," with different versions of their works, no matter how poor the quality of translation might be, flooding into China's book market, strongly influencing China's humanities and social sciences as well as contemporary Chinese literature

(Wang, 1993). Among the Chinese intellectuals at the time, talking a lot about Nietzsche and Freud was an academic fashion.

As we know, 1976 witnessed the end of the Cultural Revolution in China, which had been launched by Mao Zedong (1893–1976) in 1966. It was actually after 1978, when Deng Xiaoping (1904–1997) became the paramount leader, that China started to practice economic reform and open up to the outside world. There appeared the second large-scale translation of Western literary and critical works. Modern and postmodern Western literary masters such as T.S. Eliot, William Faulkner, Marcel Proust, James Joyce, Ernest Hemingway, V.S. Naipaul, Gabriel García Márquez, and Milan Kundera were introduced to China. In the academic and intellectual circles, important Western philosophers and thinkers such as Schopenhauer, Bergson, Nietzsche, Freud, Heidegger and Sartre were translated.

At the beginning of the 1990s, globalization came to China, contributing to the development of its economy and culture. This issue is frequently reduced to a simplified claim: globalization is nothing but Westernization, and Westernization is simply Americanization, as the United States has been politically and economically most powerful and culturally most influential. Modern Chinese culture and literature are deeply influenced by Western culture and literature, but they are also attempting a dialogue with world culture and literature. Translation has indeed played a vital role in the former movement, but it appears rather feeble in the latter. Consequently, modern Chinese literature and culture are little known to the outside world.

Since we now live in an age of globalization, where literature has gone far beyond fixed national and linguistic boundaries, it is necessary to re-examine modern Chinese literature that has been under Western influence from a cross-cultural and global perspective from the beginning of the 20th century. We find that translation has played an increasingly important role. When modern Chinese literature is placed in a broader cross-cultural context of world literature it is indeed a process of moving toward the world and trying to identify with world literature as part of the process of cultural globalization. Here translation does not necessarily mean merely word-for-word rendition, but rather, a kind of cultural translation, through which global cultures are "relocated" (Wang, 2015b).

It is well-known that Chinese literature once had both a long tradition and grand cultural and literary heritage. But along with the swift development of European countries after the Renaissance, Chinese culture and literature were "marginalized" for a long period of time due in the main to the corruption and inefficient government of feudal and totalitarian regimes isolating the country from the outside world. Upon entering the twentieth century, Chinese literary scholars increasingly acknowledged the "marginalized" role of its literature in the broad context of world literature. To regain its former grandeur, it needed to move from the periphery to the center by identifying with a prior dominant force: Western cultural modernity or modern Western literature. That is why these scholars strongly supported the widespread translation of Western literary works along with cultural and academic reflections on this practice as the best way for China to emerge from its state of isolation. Of course, this effort to translate Western literature has also promoted the internationalization or globalization of modern Chinese literature, giving it a different turn of its own. Indeed, largely under Western influence, modern Chinese literature has formed a unique tradition that could form a dialogue with both classical Chinese and modern Western literature. Here, translation played a very inevitable yet pragmatic role in bringing modern Chinese literature closer to the world.

From the stated fact, we can easily find the imbalance in the process of Sino-Western cultural and academic exchange. Obviously, there are many reasons behind this which might well account for the striking contrast. Of course, China was at the time very poor economically. A poor country could not offer any good experience to the world. Another important reason is that Chinese scholars could not speak or write in good English, nor could they publish internationally. Many well-known humanities scholars in China are little known outside of the country, largely because they could not publish in English, nor have their works been translated into this hegemonic language. As a result, during the years, those who had a chance to go abroad, especially to an English-speaking country, should at least pass a very strict English proficiency test. No matter how poor their English might be as compared with the English native speakers, they could at least make themselves understood. So this cannot convince us at all.

During the "aphasia" of the domestic Chinese scholars on the international forums, international scholarship largely depended on the Sinologists who were supposed to speak for China and publish in international journals on China studies. Frankly speaking, most of the Sinologists are very friendly to China and Chinese scholars. They love China and publish their research results on the basis of their careful investigation and consideration. But due to the false descriptions about China as a result of Orientalism, some of these Sinologists appear very naughty, holding that it is they rather than domestic Chinese scholars who are qualified to speak or write about China. Domestic Chinese scholars could have their voices heard only through their agency. But ironically speaking, what they speak or write about China is mostly based on their incomplete knowledge or even misunderstanding of China and Chinese people. Of course, during those isolated years, they could more or less convince the outside world. But in essence, they can by no means represent entire China studies scholarship.

During the past decades since globalization came to China, tremendous changes have taken place in China's humanities and social sciences. China is now in a post-revolutionary state, with no intention to export its revolutionary ideas, while even more eager to have communication and dialogue with international scholarship, especially with international China studies scholarship. We are very delighted to see that in any research universities in the world, we can easily find some English academic journals on China studies. What makes me even more delighted to see is that in almost all these academic journals on China studies, we have no difficulty finding quite a few Chinese names as authors, some of whom are affiliated with mainland Chinese universities or research institutes. Almost all the editors of these journals, so far as I know, are very eager to know what domestic Chinese scholars are speaking and writing about. People may well ask the question: is the English of these Chinese scholars much better than those in the 1980s? I do not think so. I myself published my first long English article on the reception of Freudianism in modern Chinese literature in the Dutch journal *China Information* in 1991. I still remember how friendly the editor in inviting me to contribute to the journal and how patient she was in revising and editing my manuscript (Wang, 1991). It was through the publication of my article in an international China studies journal that I became familiar with the way of writing an academic article in English and the fixed format of an international English journal.

In any event, this is really a great advance in the age of globalization, from which China benefits most, not only economically but also politically and culturally. Together with the rapid development of the Chinese economy, China's international image as political and economic power is no longer in question. Indeed, globalization has provided us with a common ground where scholars from different countries can have equal dialogues, exchange views, and discuss issues of common interest. In this respect, scientists have taken a pioneering step by publishing internationally.

As a newly emergent power in science and technology, China's status has increasingly been recognized by the international community. But what about China's humanities and social sciences on an international scale? We should not be so optimistic, even though more and more domestic Chinese scholars have realized the importance of publishing internationally. Although domestically we have been talking a lot about globalization in the Chinese context, very few of them have been published in English language journals or with international prestigious presses. So far as I know that in many fields of the humanities and social sciences, only a few Chinese scholars have published in the leading academic journals. Apart from the linguistic hegemony in the English-speaking world, we Chinese scholars should also be more or less responsible. Take the humanities for example. Many of the Chinese scholars do not even read international journals. They are only satisfied with domestic publications without pointing to international scholarship. Therefore, in the mainstream journals of philosophy and social sciences, Chinese scholars can hardly utter their voices, nor are they able to discuss the fundamental theoretical issues with their international colleagues in an equal way. I think that apart from lack of professional English writing, they lack basic academic training in critical thinking and academic writing. That is, they do not have a common academic discourse in discussion with their international colleagues. But even so, the editors of some of the international journals, including China studies journals, are very sympathetic. They know that in discussing some fundamental theoretic issues, they should listen to all the scholars, be they from the West or from the East. Some of them even ask leading Chinese scholars to edit special issues by inviting distinguished Chinese scholars of the relevant fields to contribute to the journals. In this way, they could hear directly from Chinese scholars on the cutting-edge issues of common interest and concern. In this respect, I am most benefited from their kindness and openness.

But not all the Chinese scholars have enjoyed the international recognition and reputation as I have enjoyed, although some of them have been my teachers or at least inspired me in my early academic research. I here just take the example of Li Zehou, who had, in the 1980s and 1990s, made tremendous influence on China's emancipation of the mind as well as an entire generation of young scholars, including myself.

Undoubtedly, Li Zehou (1930–2021), one of China's best-known thinkers and theorists in the 1980s–1990s, should also be viewed as a world-class thinker and scholar in terms of his theoretical contributions and academic influence in the Chinese-speaking world although he became an American citizen later on. But for a long period of time, his major works have not received the due scholarly attention of the international academic community and have even been seriously underestimated. Although he has long been a naturalized American and has lived in the United States for decades, his major works have not been translated into English or other major Western languages and published by famous publishing houses in the United States for a long time, nor have they been recognized by the mainstream academic and theoretical circles in Britain and the United States. This is in sharp contrast to his position in the Chinese-speaking world.

Fortunately, there are still some impartial scholars in the academic world who have discovered the value of Li Zehou and his thought. For example, Vincent Leitch, general editor of the prestigious *Norton Anthology of Theory and Criticism* (second edition), is one of such mainstream theorists in the English-speaking world with an academic conscience. In compiling the second edition of this prestigious anthology, Leitch solicited a wide range of recommendations and finally decided to include Li Zehou's earlier essay "Four Essays on Aesthetics: Toward a Global View" (Meixue si jiang), which was originally four lectures on aesthetics, in the anthology (Li, 2010). This has undoubtedly made Chinese literary theory and aesthetics truly accessible to the world and recognized by the international academic community and laid the foundation for the large-scale translation of Li's other works into the West. However, regrettably, as an 80-year-old scholar at the time who died in 2021 at the age of 91, he got such recognition from Western and international academia so late. Actually, we all know, Li became famous in China as a young man and has a certain degree of international fame, at least among those Western Sinologists, so it is indeed too late for this day to come for him. It is true that as compared with those who were included in the anthology at the same time: Slavoj Žižek (1949–) and Homi Bhabha (1949–), who were almost 20 years his junior, and the younger gender theorist Judith Butler (1956–) and the Neo-Marxist theorist Michael Hardt (1960–), 30 years his junior. So it is no wonder that Li Zehou, in an interview a decade ago, was pessimistic about his view of Chinese philosophy and culture going global when he said, "I think it's going to be 100 years before the Western academia is interested in China, and 100 years after that for me personally I will be long gone, but it's not a long time in history" (Wang, 2010b). In fact, at that time, Li Zehou did not expect that Chinese culture would move so quickly to the world that in the past decade, several well-known literary theorists, especially Zhang Jiang, who is more than 20 years younger than him and was more or less influenced by him, has come forward and attracted the critical and scholarly attention of the international academic community, and his writings have been published in international authoritative academic journals.[2] That should give us some hope. But even so, we still have to make our subjective efforts and cannot passively wait to be "rediscovered" by our Western counterparts.

Recognizing the importance of writing and publishing internationally, since the mid-1990s, at the invitation of my international colleagues, I have edited and published over 20 special issues in a dozen prestigious international English language journals, from which we can see what international literary and cultural scholars are most interested in and what they want to know from domestic Chinese scholarship.

Although very few of these special issues have been published in the international journals of China studies, we can still find that almost all the special issues or clusters are closely concerned with China studies, or at least about Chinese-Western comparative studies of literature and culture. That is to say, we Chinese scholars should focus our international publications mainly on topics dealing with China studies, especially contemporary China studies, which can hardly be handled well outside China. But in inviting who will contribute to these special issues on China studies, I chiefly depend on those, whether Western Sinologists or domestic Chinese scholars, who have a good command of English and are able to write excellent articles of international standard, but I do not neglect those who have had careful studies of the relevant theoretic topics and even made some previous achievements. These scholars perhaps are not able to write in good English, nor are they familiar with the fixed format of the international journals, but I usually have their excellent articles translated into English and revise and even heavily edit them so that their voices can be heard on the international forums, and their research results will be shared by their international counterparts. Sometimes, I send the edited manuscript to an eminent Western scholar whose field is not China studies but who is very interested in China and ask him/her to write a comment on these articles so that a real dialogue between Chinese and Western scholarship is made possible and effective. In this way, international scholarship of humanities and social sciences will at least have a comprehensive picture of China studies scholarship. I am sure that in the years to come, the international journals of China studies will play a more and more important role in translating and publishing Chinese scholars' excellent works so that Chinese scholars will really be able to speak on international forums.

Notes

1 Ironically, Xin dongfang xuexiao (The New Oriental School), a non-governmental school based in Beijing, has made huge profits in recent decades by teaching young students how to achieve high scores on the TOEFL and GRE.
2 Cf. Zhang Jiang and J. Hillis Miller, "Exchange of Letters about Literary Theory between Zhang Jiang and J. Hillis Miller," *Comparative Literature Studies*, 53(3), 567–610. I was invited to write an introduction to their dialogue. Cf. Wang Ning, "Introduction: Toward a Substantial Chinese-Western Theoretical Dialogue," *Comparative Literature Studies*, 53(3), 562–567.

References

Bhabha, H., 1994, *The Location of Culture*, London and New York: Routledge, especially pp. 212–235.

Burchfield, R., 2002, *The English Language*, Oxford and New York: Oxford University Press, p. 169.

Kirkpatrick, A., 2007, *World Englishes: Implications for International Communication and English Language Teaching* (especially Part A: 3. "Models of World Englishes"), Cambridge: Cambridge University Press, pp. 27–37.

Li, Z., 2010, "Four Essays on Aesthetics: Toward a Global View," in Vincent B. Leitch ed., *The Norton Anthology of Theory and Criticism*, 2nd ed., New York: Norton, pp. 1748–1760.

Singh, M., P. Kell and A. Pandian, 2002, *Appropriating English: Innovation in the Global Business of English Language Teaching*, New York: Peter Lang.

Spivak, G., 1985, "Can the Subaltern Speak? Speculations on Widow-Sacrifice," *Wedge*, 7/8 (Winter/Spring), 120–130.

Spivak, G., 1999, *A Critique of Postcolonial Reason: Toward a History of the Vanishing Present*, Cambridge, MA & London: Harvard University Press, p. 64.

Wang, N., 1991, "The Reception of Freudianism in Modern Chinese Literature," Part 1: *China Information*, 5(4), 58–71; Part 2, *China Information*, 6(1), 45–54.

Wang, N., 1993, "Confronting Western Influence: Rethinking Chinese Literature of the New Period", *New Literary History*, 24(4), 905–926.

Wang, N., 2000, "The Popularisation of English and the 'Decolonisation' of Chinese Critical Discourse," *ARIEL*, 31(1–2), 411–424.

Wang, N., 2010, "Global English(es), and Global Chinese(s): Toward Rewriting a New Literary History in Chinese," *Journal of Contemporary China*, 19(63), 159–174.

Wang, N., 2014, "Cosmopolitanism and the Internationalization of Chinese Literature," in Angelica Duran and Yuhan Huang eds., *Mo Yan in Context: Nobel Laureate and Global Storyteller*, West Lafayette, IN: Purdue University Press, pp. 167–181.

Wang, N., 2015a, "Globalisation as Glocalisation in China: A New Perspective," *Third World Quarterly*, 36(11), 2059–2074.

Wang, N., 2015b, "Translation and the Relocation of Global Cultures: Mainly a Chinese Perspective," *Asia Pacific Translation and Intercultural Studies*, 2(1), 4–14.

Wang, Y. (王岳川), 2010b, "Cultural Weight and Overseas Prospects – An Academic Dialogue between Wang Yuechuan and Li Zehou in the United States (part I)" (文化重量与海外前景 – 王岳川与李泽厚在美国的学术对话（上）), 2010, *China Reading Weekly* (中华读书报), August 9, "International Culture Column"(国际文化版).

Wang, Z. (王佐良), 2016a, *A History of English Literature* (英国文学史), *Collected Works of Wang Zuoliang* (王佐良全集), Vol. 1, Beijing: Foreign Language Teaching and Research Press, pp. 759–765.

Wang, Z. (王佐良), 2016b, *A History of English Romanticist Poetry* (英国浪漫主义诗歌史), *Collected Works of Wang Zuoliang* (王佐良全集), Vol. 3, Beijing: Foreign Language Teaching and Research Press, pp. 6–7.

Yu, K. (俞可平), 2011, "Quanqiuhua, dangdai shijie he zhongguo moshi – Yu Keping yu Fushan de duihua" (Globalization, Contemporary World and the China Mode: Yu Keing in Conversation with Francis Fukuyama) （全球化, 当代世界和中国模式——俞可平与福山对话）, *Beijing Daily* (北京日报), March 28.

Index

Aboriginal language, incorporation 19
academic expression, thinking mode (links) 195
action, imitation 86
Acton, H. 95–96
Adorno, Theodore 162
aesthetic value 10, 15
African postcolonial literature 166
"Afternoon of a Gladiolus" 58
Against World Literature (Apter) 16–17, 52–53
allegory: Subject, breaking (interconnection) 43; usage 39
Allen, Joseph R. 62
Allen, Paul 91
allusions 103; abundance 179; cultural allusion 182; handling 100–101; usage 45
American English 202–205
analogue, usage 52
ancestry, forgetting 122
Ang, Li 115
Anglo-American writers, virtue 42
"Annual Writer" title 177
Anonymous (movie) 194
"The Answer" (Bei Dao) 40
anthologies, defining 135
anthologizing, representation sites 135–136
anthology: creative rewriting 68; etymology 67
Anthology of Contemporary Hong Kong Short Stories, An 144–145
Anthology of Modern Chinese Poetry (translated poetry collection) 73
Anthology of Singapore Chinese Literature, An (Moon/Wah) 114
anxiety, silence 113, 122
Anyi, Wang 47, 73, 76

aphasia 188–189, 206–207, 211
Apter, Emily 16, 17, 19, 34, 52–53
artistic organization 76
Assmann, Jan 192
Assmanns, study 191–192
audience, restriction 21–22
audiovisual translation (AVT) 97
August Sleepwalker, The 39
Autumn in Han Palace 93
avant-garde writings 72–73

baihua 134
Bakhtin, Mikhail M. 165, 169–170
Bandia, Paul 152, 153, 166
Banquet, The (movie) 191, 194
bāo fù (burden) 118
Barthes, Roland 35
Bermann, Sandra 195
Bhabha, Homi 170–171, 206, 213
Bibliography of Hong Kong Literature in Foreign Languages, A (Hsu) 139
"big translation": basis 195; cultural memory, relationship 188, 193–196; generation 196–198; sensory effect 196; temporal narration, supplementation 197
bilingual poets 145
bimo, vigil 56, 61
binaries, set 39
Birch, Cyril 96, 98–99, 101, 105, 108, 110
Bitter Harvest (translation anthology) 69
blackness, word (usage) 56
block language 180
Book and the Sword (Yong) 25
Book of Job, narrative of justice 92
Book of Odes 59
Boxer Rebellion of 1900 43
Bradbury, Steve 54, 57, 61–62
Brecht, Bertolt 92
Brontë, Emily 170

Buck, Pearl 22
Buddhist teaching, aim 88
Butler, Judith 213
By the River: Seven Contemporary Chinese Novellas: polyphonic space case study 76–78; translation anthology 4

Camus, Albert 86, 92
Canclini, Néstor García 170, 185
"can do spirit" 180
Cassin, Barbara 52
Catford, J.C. 153
cha canting, setting 178–179
Chang, Eileen 44, 47, 198
Chan, Mary Jean 167
characters, articulation 21
chaste woman, portrayal 85
Chen-Adndro, Chantal 20
Cheng, Ah 73
Cheng, Gu 62, 73
Chengzhi, Zhang 73
Chen-Ho, Wang 115
Chen, Juliette 139
Chen, Yi-Chiao 5, 113
China: foreignization, concept 189; globalization-212 210; translation, importance 18; translation studies 193; writers/works, quality 18
China Information 212
Chinese culture: colonization 175; enabling 209–214
Chinese drama, interest 91
Chinese fictional art 77
Chinese fiction, discrimination/evaluation 37
Chinese language: Europeanization/Westernization 204; grammatical inflection, near-absence 61–62; Shanghainese translation 47; usage 44
Chinese literature: definition 3; Hong Kong literature marginality, relationship 142–144; internationalization/marginalization 211; translation 2–3
Chinese Literature (magazine) 1
Chinese Literature Today 56
Chinese literature, translation 33
Chineseness, hegemonic call 142
Chinese opera, translation 95
Chinese People's Political Consultative Conference, nationalistic sentiments 205
Chinese poetry, English translation 52
Chinese syllables, proper names (cumbersomeness) 24

Chinese syntax, English syntax (contrast) 58
Chinese text, world literature (relationship) 7
Chinese Translators Journal 189
Chinese-Western cultural hybridity 156–157
Chung, Chan Koon 5–6, 169; introduction 176–177
Chungou, Yan 140
chun qing 107–108
chun (spring), *qing* (relationship) 109
chun se ("spring scenery") 110
Chun (spring), translation 109–110
Chunxiang, symbol 109
City Poetry 143
City Voices 139, 141; anthologizers, impact 144; essays 145
"clamour of voices" 4, 66; accommodation 74–76; expression 75
classics, canon (reassessment) 74
code-switching strategy 155
coinage, usage 179
Cold War, ideologically polarized colony 163
collaboration, aim 192
collections, impact 67
collective cultural memory: basis 192; "Big translation" generation 196–198
colonialism 152
the colonizer's language 165
Columbia Anthology of Modern Chinese Literature, The 46, 70–71
commentary, translation (comparison) 22
Common Strangeness, A (Edmund) 39
communal domestic activities, scene 78
communication, context 9
conceptual design 15
Confucian ethic, impact 84
contemporary Chinese literature, translation anthologies 66
contested readings, emphasis 39
controlling identities, countering 138
Conversi, Leonard W. 88, 89
Corneille, Pierre 86–87, 91
creative rewriting 68
creative space, interpretation (correlation) 9
"Cries from Death Row" 70
criteria, question/impacts 67–68
criticism, job 79
cross-cultural aesthetic taste, impact 8
cross-cultural experience 25–29
cross-cultural imagination, absence 12

cross-cultural incommensurability 25
cross-cultural intertextuality 22
Crouching Tiger, Hidden Dragon (Lee) 25
cultural allusion 182
cultural castration 27–28
cultural-centrism, influence (avoidance) 195
cultural consciousness, suppression 161
cultural diversity 4, 79, 201, 203
cultural globalization, process (acceleration) 205
cultural hybridity 179, 181
cultural identity, issue (complexity) 164
cultural-intellectual form, breakdown 43
Cultural Medallion, The 114
cultural memory: "Big translation," relationship 188, 193–196; continuity, attainment 192; intertextuality, relationship 193; segmentation/fragmentation 193; translation studies, relationship 191–193
cultural references 25, 181–182
Cultural Revolution 46, 204; cessation 210; misery, depiction 70; tradition, isolation/erasure 39
cultural traits 169
cultural untranslatability 23, 152
culture-bound poetry, translation 57
culture-loaded words, handling 100–101
cultures of hybridity and heterogeneity, translatability 153
cuncao xin (inch-long grass) 101
Curien, Annie 141

daft hilarity 42–44
Damrosch, David 34–35, 40–41, 45–47, 113
Dante, reading 40
Dao, Bei 39–41, 44, 73; affair, drawn-out nature 41; poems 40; poems, English readings 46–47; reading 40
Daoist diction 55
Dawa, Zhaxi 73
Death of Orfeo, The (Berlioz) 194
Death of Tragedy, The (Steiner) 87
Deer and the Cauldron, The (Yong) 25
"Deer Park" (translation) 54
defamiliarization, concept 158
Deleuze, Gilles 75
deporvertizing 209
de-Third-Worldizing 209
diachronic translation 193, 195
dialogized heteroglossia 165–166
Dictionnaire des intraduisibles (Dictionary of Untranslatables) (Cassin) 52

Di, Ming 54–55
Ding, Ersu 83
discursive sedimentations 43
disguised homophony 76
disjointed linguistic style, capture (impossibility) 45
distant past, fascination 77
domestication 23
double control factor 68, 71–72; manipulation 68
drama, importance 143–144
drama-producing cultures, examination 87–88
Dream of the Red Chamber, The 28
dual orientation 56
Duo, Duo 73
Durians Are Not the Only Fruit (Tiang) 114
Dutrait, Noël 20

Eagleton, Terry 89, 92
Earnshaw, Graham 25, 170
East Journal of Translation 188
East-West antagonisms 74
East-West Comparatism 62
Edmund, Jacob 40
Eliot, T.S. 160–161, 210
emotions, catharsis 86
"enchanted spring" 101
English: anthologies, Hong Kong literature translation 132; cultural communication, function 201, 205–208; hegemony, worry 206–207; internationalized varieties 202; international language 206; life-force 202–203; limitations 18; lingua franca 202; literary communication, function 201; literature, impact 20; popularization 202; rendering, linguistic differences 61–62; translation, case study 169
Enlightenment movement 87
Epigram Books 115
Epstein, Jason 66
equivalence, aim 61
Espenbaum (Celan) 116
Esperanto (artificial language) 203
Euripides 89, 91
European-language words, usage 155–156
Evolution and Ethics (Huxley), translation 15
explosive literature (Latin America) 206

Fang 76
Faulkner, William 210

fear, cathartic effect (enhancement) 86
Feeley, Jennifer 54, 59–60
Fenollosa, Ernest 14
fidelity, complexity 27
"Filial Woman of Donghai, The" 85–86
First Hong Kong Poetry Festival 143
Flood Dragon River Farm, transformation 42–43
Fogarty, Lionel 19
Foley, Todd 3, 33
Folkart, Barbara 10
foreign cultural context, restoration 22
foreignization 23; concept 189
foreign otherness, encounter 28–29
foreign texts, ingenious translations (Derrida) 16
Fortress Besieged (Zongshu) 26
Foucault, Michel 75
Found in Transition: Hong Kong Studies in the Age of China (Chu) 132
"Four Dreams in the Camellia Hall" 103
Fox Volant of the Snowy Mountain (Yong) 25
Fragrant Weeds (translation anthology) 69
France anthologies, Hong Kong literature translation 132
free agents 72
Freud fad 209
Frisch, Nick 24
From the Bluest Part of Harbour: Poems from Hong Kong 138
Fu, Yan 15

Garcia Marquez, Gabriel 210
Garlic Ballads, The (Yan) 19–20
gau wu 59
Gershwin, George 56
global allegory 40
global canon, Kinsella (exclusion) 19
"global concern" 195–196
global English, concept (formation) 208
global Englishes (formation), globalization (relationship) 201–205
global frameworks 173–174
globality, function 62
globalization 40; advent 202–203
glocalization 201–202
God's remembrance, accessibility (issue) 47
Goethe 36
Goldblatt, Howard 3, 7, 19–22, 42, 44–46, 70–71, 115, 206
Gong, Yam 166
Gong, Zhang 156, 165

gouwu 59
grand narratives, countering 136, 138
Guangqian, Zhu 91
Guangxi Wenyi (Guangxi Wenxue) 70
Gustafsson, Anna 20

Haishang Hua 198
Haishanghua Liezhuan 198
Haishang Hualuo 198
Halbwachs, Maurice 192
Hamlet (animal version) 191
Handover, anxieties 144
Hanqing, Guan 83, 86, 88, 93
Hao, Jiang 53–55, 62; poems, English translations 4
Hardt, Michael 213
Hawk of the Mind: Collected Poems (Mu) 54
Heavenly Principle, preservation 103
Heijns, Audrey 52
He, Jiang 73
Hemingway, Ernest 210
heterogenization, impact 153
heterogenous discourse 169
heteroglossia 74–75, 152–167; cultural untranslatability 2–3, 16, 23, 25, 152; dialogized heteroglossia 165–166; misconception 75–76, 86; reverse heteroglossia 155–156, 158
heteroglossic lierature, (un-)translatability 152
heteroglossic poems 152–153, 162–164
heteroglossic poetry: colonial period 166; review 165–166
"His Days Go by the Way Her Years" 57
historical flux, emphasis 39
historical memories, multiplicity 43
History of Modern Chinese Fiction, A (Hsia) 36, 38
history, repair 39
Holmwood, Anna 3, 23
Holocaust literature 122
Ho, Louise 139
homogenizing language, expression 153
homophony 76
Hong Kong: authors 137; bilingual artistic environment 146; colonial background 146; cultural identity, impurities 134; fictional works, anthology (definitiveness) 140; *Renditions* issue 137–138, 141, 145; self-invention 134
Hong Kong 20/20 144, 145
Hong Kong: approaches littéraires 139
Hong Kong Collage, introduction 140

Hong Kong literature: anthologizing/ translating, representation sites 135–136; controlling identities, countering 138; defining, debate 133–135; definition, clarity 141; definitions, avoidance 139–142; development 133–134; findings 138–146; grand narratives, countering 138; histories/authors, appearance 138; marginality, Chinese/Western literature (relationship) 142–144; marginalization 143; master images, countering 138; multiauthored translation anthologies 132–133; nationalist rhetoric, alignment 138–139; personal preferences 141; poet, education/professional lives (perspective) 139; production 141; representation, fragility 139–142; self-representations, voices from the outside (contrast) 138–139; silenced marginalization 133; study, sources 136–137; translation 132; translation, study 136

Hong Kong literature marginality: language 142–146; translation 144–146

Hong Kong poetry: colonial time 152; scene, representation 140

Hong Kong Stories: Old Themes New Voices 142

Hongtao, Liu 76

Horkheimer, Max 162

Howe, Sarah 167

Hsia, C.T. 36–38, 44–45

Hsieh, Wen Tung 14

Hsüan-t'ung, Ch'ien 37

Hsün, Lu 37

Hua, Gu (language) 18

huai chun (spring in heart) 109–110

Huiyi, Kong 198

human desire, elimination 103

human misery, depiction 84

Huxley, Thomas 15

hybrid: concept 169–171; postcolonial hybrid literature, definition 175–176

hybrid grammatical features 173

hybridity: analysis 177–179; characterization 172; concept 169–171; impact 171; optimal degree, achievement 184; presence 174–175; representation 171–173; study 175; text types, combination 173–174; translation, scenes-and-frames approach 183–185

hybridity-identifying procedure 172

hybridization 169

hybrid postcolonial literature, translation 176–179

hybrid texts, translation 169

hybrid translations 172

Ibsen, Henrik 92

ideas, structure 92

ideological influences 13

ideological/poetological currents 68

ideologies, impact 8

idiolects 179

in-between: cultural context 5–6; literary language 8, 10, 170, 181–182; space 174–175

inclusiveness, dispensation 110

indigenous translation theories 189

influence/technique, study 37

ingenious translations (Derrida) 16

Injustice Done to Tou Ngo, The 83

Injustice to Dou E, The (Hanqing) 4, 83–86, 89–93; exposition, application 92; repositioning, global generic context 83

Injustice to Tou O 83

intangible cultural quality 180

intellectualism 161

interactive criticism 52

interdisciplinary studies, diversity 195

international publishing, impact 209–214

interpretation, totality 183

interpretative acumen 14

inter-semiotic translation 197

intertextuality: cultural memory, relationship 193; loss, compensation 22

intertextual relation, significance 22

Iphigeneia at Aulis (Euripides) 89

iteration, process 170–171

I Wish I Were a Wolf (translation anthology) 71

James, Jean M. 26–27

Japanese aggression, coastal defense 159

Japanese invasion, trauma 5, 122–126; back translation 123–125; official translation 123–126; transliteration 123–125

Japanese Occupation Period 126

Japanese theatre, ferocity/death 87

Japan-worshipping 118–119

jargon, usage 179

Jesus Christ, sacrificial character 89–90

Jianghe, Ouyang 54

Jiankong, Chen 73

Jiao, Meng 101
Jia, Zhao 45
Jing Ke 120
Jingquan, Wang 70
Jingwei Tianhai 196
ji ri (death anniversary) 118
Johnson, Barbara 16
John the Baptist (mentorship) 90
Joyce, James 210
justice: dispensation 92; narrative 92
Juyi, Bai 194

Ka-Man, Poon 179
Kamdu cha canting (Chung): analysis 177–178 English translation 179–182; English translation, case study 169, 176–179; hybridity, analysis 177–179; hybridity, translation (scenes-and-frames approach) 183–185; textual analysis 179–182; translation studies, hybridity 171–176
Kelly, Jeanne 26
Ke, Mang 73
King, Evan 26
King of Qin 120
King's English, usage 202, 204, 207
Kinsella, John 19
Klein, Lucas 54; reader effect, concern 59
Kuafu Zhuiri 196
Kuang, Li 140
Kubin, Wolfgang 19
Kundera, Milan 210
kung-fu maneuver 24
kunqu musical drama 96
Kwang-chung, Yu 137
Kwok-pun, Laurence Wong 137, 145

language: block language 180; concepts system, presence 47; functions, linking 174; poetic function 12; usage 9; varieties 176, 179
laotaiye 45
late Ming literature, *Qing* (presence) 103–104
Lau, Carina 198
Laughlin, Charles A. 76–78
Lee, Ang 25
Lee, Hacken 181, 182, 184
Lee, Leo (critique) 11
Lee, Leo Ou-fan 73
Lefevere, André 11–13, 68, 133, 135
Legend of Mountains and Seas 197
Legends of the Condor Heroes I (Leung-yang) 23–24

Leung, Tony 198
Leung-yung, Louis Cha 23
Lian, Yang 73
Liberati, Patrizia 21
Li, Dechao 1, 5, 169
lingdaozhe (leader), term (usage) 43
Lingenfelter, Andrea 54, 57–58
lingual access, absence 14
linguistic consciousness, mixing 169
linguistic frames, retention 184
linguistic hybridity 181, 186
linguistic impurities 134
linguistic level, semantic level (interconnection) 43
linguistic objects, quality 9
linguistic skills 48
Linguistic Theory of Translation, A (Catford) 153
Liniang, Du 95, 98, 100, 103, 107
Lin, Sylvia Li-Chun 115
Lintao, Qi 71
Lion King, The (movie) 191, 194
li, resistance 103–104
Li, Sapore 22
literariness: linguistic objects, quality 9; ownership 8–9
literary anthology, perspective 140
literary criticism, hybrid/hybridity (concept) 169–171
literary expression 73, 77
literary features: transfer 8; transferability 11
literary histories, production 68
literary hybridity 179
literary language, source language (relationship) 18
literary reading 115–116
Literary Review, The 179
literary scientific method 38
literary status, maintenance 10
literary system, functions 13–14
literary text, translation 8, 26
literary themes, process (mixing) 169
literary translation: challenges 8; discussion, literariness (relationship) 8–9; projects, schemes 71; reading, experience 28–29; untranslatability, threat 27
literary world, course (charting) 66–67
literature: marginalized role 210–211; politics, relationship 68–72; repair 39; role 14
Li, Wenjing 4–5, 95
local knowledge, leavening 40–41

222 Index

Location of Culture, The 170
long-term cultural memory 191–192
Lord of the Rings (Tolkien) 25
Lost Garden, The (Ang) 115
Lucas, F.L. 91
Luen, Lo Wai 141–144
Luotuo xiangzi (Rickshaw Boy) 26
Luo, Xuanmin 6, 188
Lychee Fragrance: The Selected Works of Chen Qing Shan (Minliang/Minhua) 114

macro linguistic features 179
Mair, Denis 54–56
Majia, Jidi: observations 56; poetry 53, 55–56, 61; English translations 4
"Major Yokoda" 123–127
Making of Chinese-Sinophone Literatures as World Literature 34, 47–48
Mao, Nathan K. 26
maoqiang 45
MaoSpeak 43
Mao-ti (Maoist literary form) 43
marginal Chinese communities, literature 142
Marin-Lacarta, Maialen 5, 132
Mark, Lindy Li 96, 98
marriage, objection 85
Mar, Ronald 140
martial arts fiction 23–25
Mason, Richard 139
master images, countering 138
masters, canon (reassessment) 74
May, Francis Henry 159–160
McDougall, Bonnie 39–40
Mehrez, Samia 175
melodic character 76
Mengmei, Liu 95, 102, 107
metaphors, usage 179
métisses texts 177
micro textual features 179
Midnight's Children (Rushdie) 176
Midsummer Night's Dream, A (Shakespeare) 194
Miller, Arthur 92
Mimi, Ye 53, 57, 62; poems, English translations 4
Minford, John 25, 137
Minhua, Chen 114
Minliang, Chen 114
Min, Wang 197
Modern Chinese Literature and Culture (MCLC) 34
modernisms 62
Modern Tragedy (Williams) 92

Mok, Olivia 25
Moon, Wong Meng 114
Moor's Last Sigh, The (Rushdie) 175, 176
mosquitos, cultural allusion 182
mother tongue/culture, loss (anxiety) 116–121, 129
Mourning Becomes Electra (O'Neill) 89
movies, novels (links) 194
multi-semiotic translational activities 195–196
multi-voiced playwrights, examination 116
Mu, Yang 53; expressive line breaks 58; poems, English translations 4; poetry, translation 57–58

Naipaul, V.S. 210
"nalaizhuyi" (grabbism) 209
narration, improvisation 72
national images, construction/transmission 188
national literature, elliptical refraction 35
nation-states, self-colonization 203–204
native critics, partisan nature 38
Nazis, genocide 122
Neather, Robert 179
New Cathay, Contemporary Chinese Poetry (Hao) 54
New China, literary works 72
New Critical formalism, practice 38
New Criticism 9
New Culture Movement, influence 153–154
New Ghosts, Old Dream (translation anthology) 69
new language, creation 174–175
New Literary History of Modern China 75
new society, accomplishments (celebration) 46
New Testament 89–90
Ng, Florence 166
Nida, Eugene 27
Nietzsche fad 209
"Nineteen Ways of Looking at Wang Wei" (Weinberger) 54
Nobel Prize for Literature, translation (relationship) 19–22
Norman conquest (1066) 202–203
Norton Anthology of Theory and Criticism 213
Norton Anthology of World Literature 69
Not Written Words (Xi Xi) 60
Nuosu culture 55–57, 61
Nüwa Butian 196

Old Testament 91
O'Neill, Eugene 89
onomatopoeic sign 158
oppressive governments, life 42
Oriental art, violence/grief/disaster 87
Orientalist mindset 71
Orphan of Zhao, The 93
Outer Out 157, 158, 160, 166; scripts juxtaposition 157; writing, intention 158; Zhecun influence 158
Out of the Howling Storm (translated poetry collection) 73
"Over the Counter-Revolution" 59
Owen, Stephen 38–40, 45

Pai, Hsien-Yung 98
Pan, Da'an 12
Paper Republic (annual report) 66
paratextual information, impact 22
PEN Hong Kong, anthologies 137
Peony Pavilion, The (The Young Lovers Edition) 4–5, 95–111, 191; allusions, handling 100–101; culture-loaded words, handling 100–101; English script 95; English script, *Qing* concept representation 103–110; English script, translation strategies 96–103; historical context 95–96; layout, line-by-line translation 98–100; puns/wordplays, usage 102–103; purpose 96–97; *Qing*, concept 104–109; Surtitling (ST) adaptation 98; Surtitling (ST) translation, features 97; theater translation 96–97; translation strategies 96–103
People or Monsters and Other Stories and Reportage from China after Mao (translation anthology) 69, 70
People's Republic of China 1, 166, 204; national anthem 164
perception, prejudice 135
performability, focus 97
performance, importance 96–97
Peripetia (Aristotle) 91
personal suffering/heroism, representation 87
Philoctetes 91
photography, essays (links) 195
Ping-kwan, Leung 139, 145
pinyin, usage 145
pity, cathartic effect (enhancement) 86
plurality, unity 75–76
plurilingual source text 152
poems: English origin 145; translation 160

poetically competent translation 10–11
poetic intention 14
poetics 14; concept, investigation 13; domestication 10; importance 72–74; normative expectations 14
Poetics (Aristotle) 86
poetry: dance performance, links 195; translation, equivalence (aim) 61
Poetry Lives! 138
politics, literature (relationship) 68–72
polyphonic space, construction 76–78
polyphony 75–76, 170; archetype 76; misconception 75–76; voices 75
postcolonial bilingual subjects 175
postcolonial hybrid literature, definition 175–176
post-colonialism 152
"Postcolonial Literary Heteroglossia" 152
postcolonial studies: hybrid/hybridity, concept 169–171; perspective 175
postcolonial translation studies, hybridity (presence) 174–175
postnational condition, shift 40
Pound, Ezra 60–61
power holders 72
pre-modifiers, rephrasing 181–182
primal noun/verb, correspondence 47
Prince, The (Shakespeare) 191
proper names, cumbersomeness 24
Proust, Marcel 210
Puchner, Martin 69
puns, usage 45, 102–103, 179
Pym, Anthony 14

Qichao, Liang 204
Qing: Chun, relationship 109–110; concept 104–109; cult 95; late Ming literature presence 103–104; movement, cult 104; physical desire 107–109; representation 103–110; romantic sentiment 105–107
Queen's English, usage 202, 204, 207
qupai 97

Racine, Jean 86–87, 91
Raffles, Stamford 113
reader-related factors 172
readers, emotions (trigger) 128
reading, mode 35
Red Azalea, The (translated poetry collection) 73
Red Is Not the Only Color (translation anthology) 71
Red Sorghum (movie) 25

referential constitution, usage 9
Refsum, Christian 14
Reis, Michelle Monique 198
Renditions (issues) 137, 138, 141, 145
Republic of Singapore, independence 116–117
Republic of Wine, The (Yan) 21, 43, 45
reverse heteroglossia 155–156, 158, 160
rewriting, form 68
rewriting/manipulation 12–15
Rhapsody in Black (Mair) 56
Rhapsody in Blue (Gershwin) 56
rhythmic character 76
Rickshaw Boy (She) 26–27
river image, recurrence 78
Robinson, Douglas 23
romantic "love," focus 104
Rose Colored Dinner, The (translation anthology) 71
Rose, Rose I Love You (Chen-Ho) 115
Roses and Thorns (translation anthology) 69, 70
"Roundabout" 121
rou qing 106, 108
Running Wild: New Chinese Writers (Tai/Wang) 73
Rushdie, Salman 175, 176
Russian Formalism 9

Sæthre, Brith 20
Said, Maire/Edward 35–36
Sandalwood Death (Yan) 4, 21, 43, 45
Sartre fad 209
Scar Literature 122
scenes-and-frames approach 183–185
"School's Anniversary" 118
Scott, Clive 27
"Sealed Off" (Chang) 47
Seeds of Fire (translation anthology) 69
Selected Stories of Xi Ni Er 5, 123; back translation 118, 119–120, 121; English translation, anxiety/trauma (silence) 113; mother tongue/culture, loss (anxiety) 116–121; official translation 118, 120, 121; research implications 127–128; research methodology 115; results/discussion 115–128; transliteration 118, 119, 121
self-colonization 203–204
self-representations, voices from the outside (contrast) 138–139
Self, sense 135–136
self-sufficient aesthetic entity 46

semantic level, linguistic level (interconnection) 43
semantic nub, resistance ability 53
sentence structure, mapping 58
se qing 109
Serenity of Whiteness, The (translation anthology) 71
Sewall, Richard B. 88, 89
"sex dream" 106
Shakespeare in Love (movie) 194
Shakespeare, William 95, 191, 194
Shandong localisms 45
Shanhai Jing 196–197
Shaogong, Han 73, 76
shape-shifting lyricism 57–59
Shea, James 166
She, Lao (Lau Shaw), King translation 26
Shifu, You'll Do Anything for a Laugh (Yan) 115
Shi, Hu 198, 204
short-short stories, importance 143–144
short-term communicative memory 191–192
Shuk-han, Wong 140, 144
Shu-mei, Shih 132, 134
Shuying, Cao 54
sichanjuan renyue 103
sideways glance, notion 35
silence interstitiality 132
Singapore: geopolitical importance 122–123; modernization 113–114; national identity 128; Westernization 116
Singaporean Chinese literature (Xi Ni Er) 114–115
Sing-Song Girls of Shanghai, The 198
Sinophone sphere 3
Siren, Wang 103
"sleeping form" 108
Snow in Midsummer 83
socialist realism, examples (omission) 46
sociomoral form, breakdown 43
Song, Chris 152
Sontag, Susan 48
Sook Ching (operation) 123, 126
Sophocles 89
source language, raciness/earthiness 18
source-orientation 23
source text: Daoist aspects 54–55; incommensurability/untranslatability 17, 53; innovation 57; Nuosu culture 55–57; political significance 59; quality 54–62; shape-shifting lyricism 57–59; translation 28; wordplay 59–62

Sparks, Stephen 21–22
Speak Mandarin Campaign 117
Spivak, Gayatri Chakravorty 160, 170, 203–204, 209
Splintered Mirror, A (translated poetry collection) 73
Spring Bamboo: A Collection of Contemporary Chinese Short Stories 73
Stalling, Jonathan 76
Starr, Chloë 28
Steiner, George 89, 92–93
Stephen, Mary 143
Stern, Jennifer 54
Stewart, Frank 55
story, linguistic hybridity 180–181
Story of Pipa, The 93
Story of the Stone, The 28
Structurailsm 9
Stubborn Weeds (translation anthology) 69, 70
stylistic features, retention 9–10
stylistic prose, usage 45
Sun, Yifeng 1, 3, 7
Surtitling (ST) adaptation 98
Surtitling (ST) translation, features 97
Sweet Violence: The Idea of the Tragic (Eagleton) 89
"Sword Goes Rusted, The" 120
symbolic meaning, multiple layers 180
symptoms of difference 53
synchronic translation 195
syntactic hybridity 182
syntactic structures, defamiliarization 180–181
syntax 179
Syonan City Council 124, 126

Ta-Chao, Li 37
Tai, Jeanne 73
Tak, Chan Chi 143, 144
Tam, Alan 182
target culture 171
target text (TT) 182; block language, usage 180; meaning 127; special linguistic features, hybridity representation 171–173; unnatural linguistic features 172
Tempest, The (Shakespeare) 194
temporal narration, supplementation 197
"tender feelings" 106
text: absolute humility 54; anthologies/collections, impact 67; approach 35; canons 35; hybridity 178–179; multifunctionality 174; plurilingual source text 152; representation 10; translation, aesthetic quality 28; types, combination 173–174; typology, classifications 173–174
textual accountability, translator (nonexemption) 21
textual selection, bases 67–68
theoretical aphasia 188
Three Songs of Shakespeare (Quilt) 194
Tiang, Jeremy 114
Tianlai, Wu 154, 155
Tie, Li 76
T'ien Hisa Monthly (Acton translation publication) 95
Tiesheng, Shi 73
tone, importance 14
To Pierce the Material Screen (Hung) 141
Toury, Gideon 17, 19
traditional Chinese opera, translation 95
tragedy: Aristotle definition 86; conceptual basis, importance 87–88; death, fallacy (rebuttal) 92; endings 91,
transcultural poetics 2, 3, 11, 30; translational poetics, link 11
translatability 16, 17, 23, 34, 39, 40, 153; assumption 8, 10, 16, 29, 36, 37, 42, 193; degree 2, 4, 10, 15, 25, 97, 110, 143, 155, 172, 176, 184, 188, 213; optimism 16; question 2, 3, 8, 9, 16, 17, 19, 20, 22, 27, 34, 40, 43, 47, 54, 55, 67, 92, 139, 144, 153, 164, 165, 170, 203, 211, 212
translation: absence 18; commentary, relationship 22; defining 135; dialogue, equivalence 52, 60; difficulty 45; equivalence, aim 61; faithfulness 15, 60, 97, 190; fidelity 24–25; fidelity, absence 26; gains 35; hijacking 52–53; inaccuracy/inadequacy, fear 24; linguistically/culturally fettered activity 7; mediation 10; Nobel Prize for Literature, relationship 19–22; pleasure 190–191; presence 152; process 170–171; production 68; recipe 28; representation sites 135–136; rewriting, equivalence 12–15; studies, scientific/humanistic approach 190; theory, innovation 188
translational language 171, 172, 180
translational poetics 2, 3, 8–12, 30; transcultural poetics, link 11
translational reading 35
translation anthologies 4–5, 66–67, 69, 72, 74, 76, 78–79, 83, 132–133, 135–136,

146–147; prominence 13,; study 4–6, 13, 16, 37, 43, 52–53, 74, 92, 95, 104, 132–139, 147, 152, 169, 171, 173–176, 186, 191, 193–194, 197, 204–207
Translation Forum 188
Translation Horizons 188
Translation in Anthologies and Collections 135
Translation, Rewriting and the Manipulation of Literary Fame (Lefevere) 12, 68
translation studies: blind spots, elimination 195; cultural memory, relationship 191–193; dilemma 188–191; hybridity, presence 171–173
Translation World 188
translator: demand 18; ego, dissolution 54; individual approach 52, 53, 54; literal meaning, image/enjambment sequence (contrast) 58; numbers/shortage 18; primary task 16
transliteration strategy 155
trauma, silence123, 126–127
Trees on the Mountain (translated poetry collection) 73
Trilling, Lionel 68–69
trochaic pattern 155
Tse, Dorothy 166
Tuo, Li 73
"turbulent heart" 108
Twelfth Night (Shakespeare) 194
Tzu, Lao 24

universal humanity, expressions 38
universal language 93, 207
universal literary values 40
universal, presumption 34
unnatural linguistic features 172
untranslatability 1–3, 5, 10, 15–17, 19, 23–27, 29, 30, 34, 52–53, 152–153, 155–156, 165–166; 2, 4, degree 10, 15, 25, 97, 110, 143, 155, 172, 176, 184, 188, 213; engagement 26, 35, 41, 47, 58, 71; problem 9–12, 24–25, 29, 34–36, 41, 43, 53, 55, 191, 201
untranslatable, globality (function) 62
untranslatables, symptom description 53
Upper Cross Street, familiarity/strangeness123, 126

Venuti, Lawrence 52–53
verbal felicity 14

Wah, Wong Yoon 114
Waitong, Liu 4, 53–54, 59, 62; poems, English translations 4
Wang-chi, Wong 134
Wang, David Der-wei 67, 73, 75, 79
Wang, Ning 6, 201
Wang, Rongpei 96
Wang, Xiulu 4, 66
Wanlong, Zheng 73
"WAR!" translation 158
Water Margin (Naian) 22
Wedding March (Mendelssohn) 194
Weinberger, Eliot 54
wenyan 134, 164
West-centrism, Link charge 42
Western literature, Hong Kong literature marginality (relationship) 142–144
Western tragedy, life celebration 88
What Is World Literature (Damrosch) 34
Wild Board in Victoria Harbor 166–167
Wild Lilies, Poisonous Weeds (translation anthology) 69
Williams, Raymond 92
Woerner, Austin 54
Women of Trachis, The (Sophocles) 89
Wong, Jennifer 167
Wordplay54, 59, 60, 61, 118, 122usage 61, 169, 171
work: contextual understanding 40; multilanguagedness 165
world literature: Chinese poets/writers, incorporation 48; Chinese text, relationship 7; genre, consideration 33; locus 19, 23; new life 41; problem 36; threefold definition 35; translation 16–19
world, national literature 113–114
World of Suzie Wong, The (Mason) 139
World War II sufferings, indignation 128
Wounded, The (translation anthology) 69
Wulingyuan 101
Wuthering Heights (Brontë) 169,

Xia, Liu 54
Xiandai (Les Contemporaines) 154
Xianyi, Yang (translation style) 11
Xianzu, Tang 95, 103, 104, 191; translation 4–5
Xiaoping, Deng 210
Xichang, Cai 197
xin, da, and *ya* dictum, formulation 15
Xingjian, Gao (Nobel Prize in Literature) 41, 197

Xi Ni Er (Singaporean Chinese literature) 114–115; post-war Japanese government, action (controversy) 126
Xinzhang, Luo 189
Xi, Xi 4, 53, 54, 59, 60, 61, 62, 137, 140; *Not Written Words* 60; poems, English translations 4; translation 54
Xi, Xu 139, 141, 145
Xue, Can 47
xu ji (rising sun) 118
Xun, Lu 36–38, 189, 198, 204, 209

Yang, Evan 140
Yang, Gladys 18
Yanhua, Jin 70
Yan, Mo 4, 7, 19–21, 41–45, 73, 206; daft hilarity 42–43, 44; detractors, impact 42; incongruous style, translation (difficulty) 45; international reception 19; language, characteristics 43; limits, challenges 41; literary works, controversy 3–4; Nobel Prize for Literature 7, 19,; puns, usage 45; "shimmering poetry" 45, 46; Western scorn 42; world literature, comparison 44
Yichang, Liu 140
yingyan dui 100

"yingyi" 189
Yip, Wai-lim 162
yiqing kang li 104
Yong, Jin 23
Yoshida, Tomio 20
Young Lovers' Edition, The (YLE) 95, 96, 104; difference 105; English translation 103; *qing,* rendering 109; source text 98
yu (desire) 107
Yuan Dynasaty, plays (writing) 91
Yuechuan, Wang 213
yue (adverb), structure 57
yueyu 134
Yun, Jiang 76
Yun, Xi 166

zapitalism 62
Zedong, Mao 41, 46, 210
Zehou, Li 213
Zhaohua, Lin 297
Zhecun, Shi 154–155; influence 158
Zhiqin, Jiang 71
Zhonghsu, Qian 26
Zijian, Chi 76
Zizek, Slavoj 213
Zuiliang, Chen 109
Zuoliang, Wang 207, 208

Taylor & Francis eBooks

www.taylorfrancis.com

A single destination for eBooks from Taylor & Francis with increased functionality and an improved user experience to meet the needs of our customers.

90,000+ eBooks of award-winning academic content in Humanities, Social Science, Science, Technology, Engineering, and Medical written by a global network of editors and authors.

TAYLOR & FRANCIS EBOOKS OFFERS:

A streamlined experience for our library customers

A single point of discovery for all of our eBook content

Improved search and discovery of content at both book and chapter level

REQUEST A FREE TRIAL
support@taylorfrancis.com

For Product Safety Concerns and Information please contact our EU representative GPSR@taylorandfrancis.com
Taylor & Francis Verlag GmbH, Kaufingerstraße 24, 80331 München, Germany

www.ingramcontent.com/pod-product-compliance
Lightning Source LLC
Chambersburg PA
CBHW050533300426
44113CB00012B/2072